Network Controllability Robustness

Analysis, Evaluation and Optimization

AI, Memristors and Nonlinear Dynamics

Series Editor: Guanrong Chen *(City University of Hong Kong, China)*
Advisory Editor: Leon O Chua *(University of California at Berkeley)*

Published

Vol. 2 *Network Controllability Robustness: Analysis, Evaluation and Optimization*
by Yang Lou, Lin Wang and Guanrong Chen

Forthcoming

Vol. 1 *Artificial Intelligence and Quantum Dynamics for Memristor-System Computing*
edited by Ivan Zelinka, Felix Yang Lou and Guanrong Chen

AI, Memristors and Nonlinear Dynamics – **Volume 2**

Network Controllability Robustness

Analysis, Evaluation and Optimization

Yang Lou
Hiroshima University, Japan
Lin Wang
Shanghai Jiao Tong University, China
Guanrong Chen
City University of Hong Kong, China

World Scientific

NEW JERSEY • LONDON • SINGAPORE • BEIJING • SHANGHAI • HONG KONG • TAIPEI • CHENNAI • TOKYO

Published by

World Scientific Publishing Co. Pte. Ltd.
5 Toh Tuck Link, Singapore 596224
USA office: 27 Warren Street, Suite 401-402, Hackensack, NJ 07601
UK office: 57 Shelton Street, Covent Garden, London WC2H 9HE

British Library Cataloguing-in-Publication Data
A catalogue record for this book is available from the British Library.

AI, Memristors and Nonlinear Dynamics — Vol. 2
NETWORK CONTROLLABILITY ROBUSTNESS
Analysis, Evaluation and Optimization

ISBN 978-981-98-3358-0 (hardcover)
ISBN 978-981-98-3359-7 (ebook for institutions)
ISBN 978-981-98-3360-3 (ebook for individuals)

For any available supplementary material, please visit
https://www.worldscientific.com/worldscibooks/10.1142/14891#t=suppl

Desk Editor: Muhammad Ihsan Putra

Typeset by Stallion Press
Email: enquiries@stallionpress.com

Dedicated to our families, whose constant support and encouragement made this work possible and enjoyable

Preface

Complex networks as a specific notion of network science has become a self-contained discipline after a near three-decade research development with persistent efforts from various scientific and engineering communities across diverse fields of applied mathematics, statistical physics, big data computing, multi-agent systems, brain science, structural biology and social studies.

The interdisciplinary field of complex networks, especially along the research direction merging with control systems theory, has developed very rapidly in recent years. On one hand, complex networks has become a stand-alone scientific paradigm associated with the classical graph theory developed since Euler in the 18th century and the Erdős–Rényi random graph theory, followed by the Watts–Strogatz and Neuman–Watts small-world network frameworks as well as the Price–Barabási–Albert scale-free network model. On the other hand, control theory has become indispensable not only for classical systems but also for networked systems, particularly multi-agent systems, paving the way to investigating a broad range of real-world applications of complex dynamical networks.

The current fast-evolving research direction in network control has created many promising opportunities as well as great challenges to network scientists, control theorists and system engineers. A complex dynamical network typically has many nodes and edges, where the nodes are higher-dimensional dynamical systems interconnected through a complicated topology possessing random, small-world or scale-free characteristics, usually with multi-stabilities. For such complex dynamical networks, to achieve some optimal objectives in applications, one practically can only control a small portion of their nodes and edges by adding external control inputs. This observation had motivated the continued development of the innovative "pinning control" theory and methodology, as an effective practical control strategy, to answer the fundamental question of *how many and which nodes to control* (to pin) in order to accomplish the preset objective for a complex dynamical network.

The pinning control question actually asks whether or not a network is controllable and, if not, how to make it become so. This refers to as a *network controllability* problem. Conceptually, for a complex network of linear or linearized dynamical systems, the network controllability is the ability of the network to be driven by the system internal control input from any initial state to any target state in finite time. If such a network is not controllable, then external control inputs are needed to be pinned at some nodes, called *driver nodes*, to make the network controllable. Therefore, the network controllability can be measured by counting the number of driver nodes needed. With normalization, the ratio of the minimum number of driver nodes over the total number of nodes in the network can be used as the effective measure to quantify the network controllability. Under this measure, the smaller the ratio, the better the network controllability, implying the lower the external control energy and cost.

Furthermore, in engineering applications it is a basic requirement for various networks of dynamical systems to be controllable and meanwhile be strong against malicious attacks or random failures, which typically emerge in the form of node- or edge-removals. Today, more and more severe attacks and frequent failures occur everywhere in the networking world, hence a controllable network has to be robust against such attacks and failures, leading to the concept of *controllability robustness* for complex networks of dynamical systems. This particular characteristic measures the ability of a network to retain or regain its controllability after being destructively damaged.

This book studies the important notion of controllability robustness for complex dynamical networks in the linear or linearized settings. Chapter 1 provides an overview of network controllability and controllability robustness, as well as some preliminaries and research problems. Chapter 2 introduces the basic concept and knowledge of network controllability, covering definitions, computational methods, and evaluation metrics. It explores key topological features of the controllability robustness. Chapter 3 analyzes the controllability robustness in complex networks, introducing key metrics, attack strategies, hierarchical attack methods, simulation criteria, and analytical models. Chapter 4 explores techniques for enhancing the controllability robustness, introducing robustness-oriented models, metaheuristic-based optimization, and an empirical necessary condition verified through extensive experiments. Chapter 5 examines data-driven approaches for evaluating the controllability robustness, focusing on input representation, model architecture, and output interpretation, from a machine learning-based approach. Chapter 6 introduces a framework for assessing and visualizing the controllability robustness enhancement potential, leveraging data-driven methods to deliver accurate predictions and interpretability at low computational cost. Finally, Chapter 7 reviews recent advancements, identifies key challenges, and outlines future directions in network controllability robustness studies.

The book is designed for self-study and as a handy reference for researchers and professionals working on network science projects and network-related engineering and technological problems, as well as for graduate students studying complex networks and related subjects. It requires a minimal level of knowledge in control systems and graph theory, suitable for both experienced researchers and new comers in diverse fields of applied mathematics, statistical physics, big data computing, multi-agent systems, brain science, structural biology and social studies.

The Authors

Acknowledgments

The authors would like to express their sincere gratitude to several collaborators, colleagues and friends, especially those who provided support and assistance in the extensive experimental studies, such as implementation of attack simulations, data-driven approaches, and optimization techniques, including Professor Xiao Fan Wang, Dr. Chengpei Wu, Dr. Wenli Huang and Dr. Liang Chen.

The Authors

Contents

Chapter 1

Introduction

This chapter provides an overview of network controllability and controllability robustness, presenting the development from classical control theory to modern network science. It reviews some foundational concepts, including structural and exact controllability, highlights recent advances addressing conventional, temporal and multilayer networks, and discusses energy-efficient and targeted control strategies. It examines the growing importance of robustness against random failures and hostile attacks, and formulates key research questions on maintaining functionality and optimizing robustness. It outlines the emerging machine learning techniques for analyzing dynamics, evaluating robustness, and optimizing structures. The chapter concludes with the motivation and organization of the book, positioning controllability robustness as a critical challenge for secure and resilient networked systems in dynamic and adversarial environments.

The chapter is organized as follows. Section 1.1 presents a brief overview of network controllability and controllability robustness. Section 1.2 discusses practical applications of the subjects across diverse domains. Section 1.3 examines various risks posed by adversarial attacks and their implications for network controllability robustness. Section 1.4 provides the motivation and outlines the structure of the book.

1.1 Overview of Network Controllability and Controllability Robustness

Controllability is a fundamental concept in control theory and network science, indicating the ability to steer a networked system from an initial state to a target state by a limited external input, called control, in finite time.

In this book, only networks of linear or linearized dynamical systems are studied. Recently, research on such linear network controllability has attracted substantial attention because of the significance and applicability of this concept across diverse domains, including biological networks such as gene regulatory and metabolic pathways, neural networks underlying cognitive processes, epidemiological networks modeling disease transmission, social networks governing information diffusion and influence propagation, engineered infrastructures such as power grids and transportation systems, logistical networks ensuring supply chain robustness, financial networks managing systemic risks, and communication networks supporting large-scale data transmission and distributed computing [1–5].

Verifying the controllability of a linear or linearized dynamical network is vital in engineering and technology, which ensures that a system in concern can meet theoretical and practical requirements for designated control tasks as well as reliability under varying conditions. Common methods include the Kalman rank condition [1, 6–8], the Popov-Belevitch-Hautus (PBH) rank condition [9], and the graph-theoretic criterion for structural controllability [10]. Simulation-based and energy-based approaches [11] are also useful for evaluating network controllability under realistic constraints, considering essential issues such as network structures, control nodes, and component dynamics.

The origins of network controllability can be traced back to the classical control theory on linear dynamical systems, particularly the foundational work of Kalman in the 1960s [1, 6, 8]. Kalman introduced the concept of controllability and established a criterion based on a system matrix, called the controllability matrix, which provides a rigorous mathematical framework for determining whether a linear system can be fully controlled by bounded external inputs in finite time. This principle was later extended to interconnected linear dynamical systems, forming a basis for the network control theory applicable to complex dynamical networks.

The classical notion of controllability in control theory primarily addresses the intrinsic dynamics of a single higher-dimensional linear system. With the emergence of network science in the early 2000s, one research focus was the extension of the system controllability toward the controllability of large-scale complex networks [12–14]. In such networks, nodes represent dynamical subsystems and edges capture the interactions among them, encompassing scientific, engineering and technological domains such as the Internet, power grids, transportation systems, neural networks, social networks and financial networks [4].

In the era of pervasive connectivity, Liu, Slotine, and Barabási advanced the classical concept of structural controllability [10], establishing a fundamental link between directed network topology and system controllability by introducing a driver node algorithm based on the maximum matching principle from graph theory, which identify the minimal set of nodes required to achieve full control of the network.

Building on this notion, the framework of exact controllability emerged as a complementary approach to refine the understanding of network controllability [9]. It determines the network controllability by considering both network topology and precise numerical values of system parameters. Diferring from the structural controllability, which depends solely on the zero or nonzero structure of the network controllability matrix and holds for almost all parameter choices, exact controllability provides a parameter-specific analysis. The minimal number of driver nodes required for full control of the network is equal to the maximum geometric multiplicity of the eigenvalues of the system controllability matrix, or the maximum algebraic multiplicity for diagonalizable undirected networks. Driver node locations are identified using the PBH rank condition with appropriate elementary matrix transformations. This approach applies to networks with arbitrary structures and edge weights and provides a universal tool for assessing controllability of directed or undirected complex networks.

Recent advances in network controllability extend beyond foundational state and structural controllability, addressing increasingly complex challenges. Key research directions include nonlinear networks [15], where progress in Lyapunov methods and basin-of-attraction analyses has enhanced stability control and feasibility for complex systems such as gene regulatory and ecological networks. Temporal and time-varying networks, with evolving connections in transportation and communication systems, require time-varying dynamic frameworks [16] and higher-order models to capture the impact of time-dependent interactions on the network controllability [17]. Energy-efficient control, critical for large-scale or resource-constrained networks [18], focuses on optimizing the number and location of driver nodes, reducing control energy, and ensuring robustness using fault-tolerant strategies for infrastructures such as power grids and cyber-physical networks. In addition, new directions include targeted control of specific nodes [19] and control of multi-relational and multilayer networks [20], all emphasizing practical applications and experimental verification to ensure scalability and real-world relevance.

Among the above key topics, a particular important and fundamental issue in network controllability is *robustness*, which raises two central research questions to be addressed by this book:

- *How can complex networks maintain intended functionality under structural failures and attacks?*
- *How can this capability be evaluated, analyzed and optimized?*

Structural disruptions can result from random failures such as natural disaster events, aging components, and unforeseen breakdowns, as well as from deliberate malicious attacks including cyber destruction and sabotage, often targeting critical nodes or edges to maximize the effect and impact. Ensuring robustness is thus essential for reliable operations of critical systems such as power grids, communication networks, and transportation infrastructure under uncertain and adversarial conditions.

Recently, on the other hand, machine learning has become a powerful tool for advancing research on network controllability and robustness. Leveraging machine learning algorithms enables efficient analysis of complex system dynamics, identification of critical nodes, and optimization of control strategies. Machine learning supports behavior modeling, pattern discovery, adaptive control, and higher-dimensional network analysis, accelerating solutions and improving controllability across diverse applications. Furthermore, both attack strategies and protective measures have evolved significantly through integration of network science theory and machine learning techniques [21–26]. Addressing these challenges is crucial for designing resilient and secure systems capable of maintaining functionality in dynamic and hostile environments.

1.2 Practical Applications of Controllability and Controllability Robustness

Network controllability has wide-ranging applications. In neuroscience, controllability aids in understanding brain activities and influencing regions for therapy [27]. In power systems, controllability supports the design of resilient grids for stability and fault recovery [28]. In transportation networks, controllability optimizes routes, traffic flow, and resource allocation for efficient operations [29]. Without controllability, a system may fail to respond effectively to control inputs, leading to degraded performance or instability.

Recent research has advanced network controllability across diverse topological types and configurations [4, 5]. In multiplex and multilayer networks, controllability is influenced by interlayer coupling and timescale differences. Control is more efficient when applied to the faster layer, and a critical timescale threshold determines whether control is dominated by one layer or shared between layers [30]. In evolving networks, a general rule predicts changes in the number of driver nodes during network growth, helping maintain controllability as new nodes and edges are added [31]. Regarding input-output configurations, comparative studies show that MIMO (multiple input multiple output) systems significantly outperform SISO (single input single output), SIMO (single input multiple output), and MISO (multiple input single output) systems in terms of channel capacity and reliability, making them ideal for high-performance communication and control systems [14,32,33]. While these improvements enhance control efficiency of a network, the structural controllability remains primarily determined by its topology.

Investigating network controllability focuses on analyzing the ability of a networked system, for those both already exist in the real world or are intended for future deployment, to be effectively fully controlled, while investigating controllability robustness extends this analysis by assessing the ability of such controllability under non-ideal conditions and in adversarial environments, ensuring its sustainability and maintenance.

Controllability robustness is essential for guaranteeing stable and continuous functionality, enabling fault recovery, and enhancing resilience, as it characterizes the capacity of a system to preserve the controllability under structural modifications or adverse conditions. Evaluating the controllability robustness of a system before real-world deployment is essential. Under stress tests conducted in intentionally designed non-ideal environments, where failures and attacks occur sequentially, system performance is measured in terms of the remaining controllability. It is then aggregated into an overall metric of controllability robustness, typically by averaging, although alternative computation methods are possible.

1.3 Adversarial Attacks and Controllability Robustness

Malicious attacks on complex networks have become increasingly critical in modern interconnected systems. Typical examples include Internet viruses, cyber intrusions, distributed denial of service (DDoS) attacks, and ransomware targeting critical infrastructure [34]. In addition, real-world systems encounter targeted disruptions on power grids and transportation networks, coordinated attacks on sensor networks, adversarial manipulation on social and communication platforms, and structural degradation in biological or ecological environments. Such disruptions can propagate across interconnected infrastructures, amplifying systemic vulnerability.

Other attack forms include data corruption, which undermines the integrity of information processed by nodes [35]; communication interference, such as jamming in wireless networks [36]; overload attacks, where specific nodes or edges are intentionally stressed to induce systemic failures [37], and cascading failures, where an initial disruption propagates through the network, triggering a chain reaction of malfunctions [38]. Cyber attacks on power grids exemplify these risks, demonstrating the potential to cause large-scale blackouts and cascading crashes across interconnected facilities [39, 40]. The accelerating digitalization of power systems further enlarges the attack surface, heightening exposure to advanced persistent threats and coordinated intrusions [41]. Addressing these challenges from a general topological perspective is essential, while domain-specific expertise remains indispensable for safeguarding individual systems.

When real-world infrastructures are modeled as complex networks, their entities, such as power stations in power grids, routers and switches in communication systems, intersections and stations in transportation networks, or individuals in social networks, are represented as nodes (also called vertices), and their relationships, such as transmission lines, data links, traffic routes, or social interactions and acquaintanceship, are represented as edges (or links).

Malicious attacks, random failures, traffic congestion, dissolution of social relationships, and other environmental disturbances that alter network structures are commonly modeled by node removal or edge removal. In these scenarios, the focus extends beyond the physical nature of the damage to emphasize its structural and functional implications for the network.

Attacks on complex networks can be categorized along several dimensions. First, based on the target, they can be classified as node attacks, which aim to disable specific entities, and edge attacks, which seek to disrupt the connections among the entities. Second, according to the selection strategies, attacks may be random where nodes or edges are removed without preference, or targeted where the deemed most critical components are deliberately chosen to maximize the disruption. Third, depending on whether the importance of nodes or edges is updated during the attack process, attacks may be metric-reevaluated where the importance is recalculated after each removal, or metric-non-reevaluated where the initial ranking remains fixed. Finally, based on the methods used to assess importance, attacks may be categorized as statistics-based which rely on metrics such as degree or betweenness, computational intelligence-based which employ heuristic algorithms such as evolutionary computation or swarm intelligence, and machine learning-based which leverage models such as graph neural networks and deep learning to identify key components automatically [42].

From an adversarial perspective, the advancement of computational intelligence and machine learning techniques has rendered both attack design and identification of critical components in complex networks increasingly adaptive and sophisticated. These developments enable adversaries to formulate precise and effective strategies, while simultaneously providing defenders with advanced tools for vulnerability detection and for implementing protective measures with greater accuracy and efficiency. Similarly, from the perspective of safeguarding networked systems, these advancements can be leveraged to strengthen the robustness and resilience, improve fault recoveries, and ensure reliable operations subject to evolving threats.

1.4 Motivation and Outline of the Book

Nowadays, as real-world environments become increasingly complex and life-threatening, robustness in network controllability has emerged as an important research focal issue. Progressively, robustness studies encompassing theoretical, computational and data-driven tasks have reached out to cover many other network functionalities such as connectivity and communication, which have contributed to the development of network science and technology.

This book addresses the fundamental challenge of assessing and enhancing network controllability robustness and provides insights into related topics, including robustness of additional network functionalities, graph learning with emphasis on performance evaluation, attack and defense strategies targeting network functionalities, and modeling random processes of malicious attacks on networks, among others.

1.4.1 *Motivation*

The rapid expansion of interconnected systems across natural, engineering, social, and biological domains has profoundly transformed their complexity to be perceived and managed in real-world applications. These networks deliver significant benefits to societies in terms of efficiency and connectivity.

Among their many functionalities and advantages, controllability is particularly important, meanwhile these systems also introduce substantial vulnerabilities. Malicious attacks, cascading failures, and unpredictable disruptions underscore the urgent need for resilient and intelligent control strategies of complex networks.

At the same time, breakthroughs in computational intelligence, particularly in graph learning, a specialized branch of machine learning that processes data represented as graph structures, and data-driven modeling, have created unprecedented opportunities to analyze, understand and optimize complex networks. These technologies provide effective tools for network analysis and computation, enabling discovery of hidden structures, evaluation of dynamic performance and behaviors, and development of adaptive solutions that respond effectively to evolving conditions.

This book is motivated by the need to bridge theoretical insights in network controllability with simulation-based studies and practical applications across diverse domains, by incorporating advances in graph learning approaches and using tools from data-driven methodologies. A unified framework for controllability robustness analysis is introduced, integrating analytical, simulation-based, and data-driven approaches for measurement and analysis, together with optimization using computational intelligence techniques. This self-contained framework provides an efficient in-depth exploration of controllability, robustness, resilience, and adaptability in complex networks.

By integrating graph theory, optimization techniques, and machine learning algorithms, this book equips readers with useful tools to address real-world challenges in network functionality robustness. The content begins with foundational concepts and progresses through theoretical analysis, practical strategies for robustness evaluation and enhancement, applications of machine learning, and future research directions. This book is intended for researchers, practitioners and students in network science, control theory, optimization, AI-assisted systems engineering, and related fields. The goal is to provide readers with a comprehensive understanding of the structural and functional properties of complex networks and to enable the design, analysis and control of these systems in an increasingly interconnected and dynamic environment, with emphasis on network controllability and its robustness.

1.4.2 *Outline of the Book*

This book is structured into seven chapters, each focusing on a specific aspect of network controllability and its robustness. The remainder of the monograph is organized as follows:

- Chapter 2 introduces the basic concept and knowledge of network controllability, covering definitions, computational methods, and evaluation metrics. The chapter analyzes controllability across synthetic and real-world networks, explores key topological features, and distinguishes the controllability robustness from the connectivity robustness.
- Chapter 3 analyzes the controllability robustness in complex networks, introducing key metrics, attack strategies, hierarchical attack methods, simulation criteria, and analytical models. Comparative studies on synthetic and real-world networks will be performed to reveal how topology and heterogeneity influence resilience of complex networks.
- Chapter 4 explores techniques for enhancing the controllability robustness, introducing robustness-oriented models, metaheuristic-based optimization, and an empirical necessary condition verified through extensive experiments. The chapter demonstrates that edge rectification transforms networks toward highly homogeneous structures, providing a practical pathway for improved network robustness in design and applications.
- Chapter 5 examines data-driven approaches for evaluating the controllability robustness, focusing on input representation, model architecture, and output interpretation. Experiments are performed to show that structure-preserving representations and advanced graph neural network (GNN) models deliver the most accurate and reliable performances compared to other approaches.
- Chapter 6 introduces a framework for assessing and visualizing the controllability robustness enhancement potential, leveraging data-driven methods to deliver accurate predictions and the interpretability at significantly lower computational cost, compared to state-of-the-art approaches.
- Chapter 7 reviews recent advancements, identifies key challenges, and outlines future directions in network controllability robustness studies, emphasizing analytical foundations, simulation frameworks, and enhancement strategies.

Chapter 2

Preliminaries

This chapter introduces the notion of network controllability as preparatory knowledge for the investigation of *controllability robustness* in subsequent chapters. Definitions and computational methods for both state controllability and structural controllability are presented, practical approaches for evaluating controllability are outlined, and normalized metrics for cross network comparison are established. In particular, the concept of *driver node* and its role in determining full controllability of a complex network is introduced. Furthermore, controllability characteristics of eight representative synthetic models, namely the Erdős–Rényi (ER), Barabási–Albert (BA), Watts–Strogatz (WS), Newman–Watts (NW), extremely homogeneous (EH), generic scale-free (SF), q-snapback (QS), and Henneberg growth models, together with some real-world network datasets, are described and analyzed, to reveal how topology and edge density influence the number of driver nodes required for full controllability of a network model. Key topological features such as degree distribution, internal loop, connectivity, sparsity, and assortativity are discussed, along with the role of the backbone structure in enabling near-optimal controllability. The chapter concludes by distinguishing controllability robustness from connectivity robustness, emphasizing their different underlying mechanisms and their need for dedicated analytical approaches. At the end, basic notation, symbols, acronyms, and abbreviations to be used throughout the book are systematically listed for convenient reference.

This chapter is organized as follows. Section 2.1 reviews basic definitions and computational methods for network controllability. Section 2.2 examines the controllability of some synthetic and real-world networks. Section 2.3 summarizes the chapter.

2.1 Definitions and Computation of Network Controllability

Network controllability characterizes the ability to steer a network of dynamical systems (nodes) from any initial state to any desired final state within a finite time interval by a control input, referred to as a controller [43, 44]. In case this task is infeasible, additional controllers are needed to be added to ("pinned" at) some network nodes. Obviously, the more external controllers are used, namely the more nodes are pinned, the easier the task can be accomplished. When the number of external controllers is large enough, the network will be under full control, that is, has full controllability.

However, when such a state transition is infeasible under given conditions and existing constraints, a fundamental question arises:

How many additional controllers are needed to enable the desired system state transition?

The network controllability theory has supported a wide range of applications across diverse domains, including systems engineering, chemical process control, power systems operation, aerospace engineering, and some emerging fields such as quantum control and nanoscale technologies.

The study of network controllability examines how the topology, local dynamics, external inputs, and system parameters of a complex dynamical network influence its controllability. This important subject emerged from the interdisciplinary field that integrates control theory, network science, and applied mathematics. This chapter reviews the theoretical bases of controllability in networked linear dynamical systems, covering key concepts for state controllability and structural controllability, and establishes a foundation for further analyzing the network controllability robustness under malicious attacks in subsequent chapters.

2.1.1 *State Controllability*

State controllability is a fundamental concept in control theory, which provides a rigorous framework for determining whether a system can be driven from any initial state to any target state in finite time through admissible control input. This property guarantees full maneuverability of the system and serves as a criterion for the system to be able to achieve desired dynamic behavior. State controllability enables systematic controller synthesis, ensures desired system behavior can be realized, and also facilitates system performance optimization. It is noted that some systems might be confined to limited regions of its state space where it is controllable, referred to as partial controllability, which will not be studied in this book; in other words, the state and structural controllability discussed throughout are both "full" or "complete" controllability in the system state space.

The mathematical foundation of state controllability is well established for linear time-invariant systems, where conditions such as the Kalman rank criterion provide a precise measure for defining and evaluating the system state controllability [1, 6, 8]. The concept extends beyond linear systems to linear time-varying, nonlinear, and hybrid systems, where advanced mathematical tools, including Lie algebra and differential geometry, are employed for analysis [45], which however are beyond the scope of this book.

State controllability is not merely a theoretical interest but a practical principle that underpins the design and operation of dynamic systems across diverse domains. By ensuring that a system can reach any desired state within its state space, controllability provides the foundation for full functionality, reliability, and adaptability in applications. This property is indispensable for a system to be useful in practice, therefore is of ultimate importance.

2.1.1.1 *Definition*

Consider a linear time-invariant (LTI) system, represented by the following state-space equations:

$$\dot{x}(t) = \mathbf{A}\mathbf{x}(t) + \mathbf{B}\mathbf{u}(t), \tag{2.1}$$

where $\mathbf{x}(t) \in \mathbb{R}^n$ is the state vector, $\mathbf{u}(t) \in \mathbb{R}^m$ is a control input, called the *controller*, $\mathbf{A} \in \mathbb{R}^{n\times n}$ is the system matrix, and $\mathbf{B} \in \mathbb{R}^{n\times m}$ is the input matrix. The controller is said to be *admissible* if it is physically realizable such as bounded or of finite-energy.

The system is said to be (completely) *state controllable* if and only if, for any initial state $\mathbf{x}_0 \in \mathbb{R}^n$ and any target state $\mathbf{x}_f \in \mathbb{R}^n$, there exists an admissible controller $\mathbf{u}(t)$ that drives the system state from $\mathbf{x}_0$ to $\mathbf{x}_f$ within a finite interval.

This definition of system controllability highlights two essential characteristics: (1) the ability to reach any point in the state space; (2) the existence of an admissible controller that can achieve this state transition in finite time. Note that this controllability concept requires only the existence of an admissible controller, regardless of how to find the controller, which belongs to the design problem to be considered in the next step and is not in the concern of the present study.

2.1.1.2 *Controllability Matrix*

The controllability of an LTI system can be evaluated using the controllability matrix

$$\mathbf{C} = [\mathbf{B}\ \mathbf{AB}\ \mathbf{A}^2\mathbf{B}\ \ldots\ \mathbf{A}^{n-1}\mathbf{B}]. \tag{2.2}$$

The system is said to be *state controllable* if and only if the matrix $\mathbf{C}$ has a full rank, i.e., $\text{rank}(\mathbf{C}) = n$. This condition, established by Kalman [43, 44] and so is referred to as the *Kalman rank criterion*, provides a rigorous and convenient criterion for assessing the system controllability.

2.1.1.3 *Discrimination and Calculation of State Controllability*

To determine whether an LTI system is state controllable, one can proceed as follows:

(1) Construct the controllability matrix $\mathbf{C}$ by iteratively multiplying the system matrix $\mathbf{A}$ with the input matrix $\mathbf{B}$, as defined in Equation (2.2).
(2) Compute the rank of $\mathbf{C}$ using numerical algebraic techniques such as singular value decomposition (SVD) or row-reduction.
(3) If $\text{rank}(\mathbf{C}) = n$, the system is *state controllable*; otherwise, it is *not* state controllable.

Clearly, the controllability of an LTI system is fundamentally a binary property: either yes or no.

For a network of LTI systems, a more practical non-binary question concerns achieving the network controllability: in case the given network is not controllable but we want to make it controllable, how many external controllers should be installed, which nodes should these controllers be placed at, referred to as *driver nodes*, and how much control energy such a controller needs, etc. Thus, the controllability depends on both the number and the placement of external controllers. The methodology to address these two issues is called *pinning control*.

In practical, *rather than merely asking whether a network of LTI systems is controllable, it is essential to quantify the control effort required, typically measured by the minimum number of external controllers needed to achieve the network controllability.*

If a network of systems, also called a networked system, is not controllable by using a single controller, i.e. a single input signal, the minimum number of driver nodes required to achieve controllability of the network can also be determined by applying the Popov–Belevitch–Hautus (PBH) rank condition [9,46]. According to this condition, a system is controllable if and only if the matrix $[\lambda\mathbf{I} - \mathbf{A}, \mathbf{B}]$ has a full rank n for every eigenvalue λ of the system matrix $\mathbf{A}$. In practice, this implies that the number of driver nodes needed corresponds to the maximum geometric multiplicity of the eigenvalues of matrix $\mathbf{A}$. For systems where $\mathbf{A}$ is diagonalizable, such as undirected networks, this simplifies to the maximum algebraic multiplicity.

To further streamline computation, the Exact Controllability Theorem established in [9] provides a direct and efficient formula applicable to networks of arbitrary structure, including directed, undirected, weighted, and unweighted networks. Specifically, the number n_D of driver nodes required for achieving network controllability is given by

$$n_D = \max\{1, n - \text{rank}(\mathbf{A})\}, \tag{2.3}$$

where n denotes the number of nodes in the network, and rank($\mathbf{A}$) represents the rank of the network adjacency matrix.

2.1.2 *Structural Controllability*

Structural controllability generalizes the concept of state controllability to systems in which the exact numerical values of parameters in $\mathbf{A}$ and $\mathbf{B}$ are unknown, but the pattern of zero and nonzero entries in these system matrices is known, which represent the system structure [47]. In this framework, parameters are treated either as independent free variables or fixed zeros, indicating the presence or absence of components or interactions, namely, a zero entry means that the corresponding system component or connection does not exist and a large nonzero value means that the corresponding component has a heavy weight or strong connection strength.

The controllability concept related to the system structure captures is particularly valuable in scenarios where system parameters are difficult to measure or subject to uncertainty. For example, in biological systems such as gene regulatory networks, interaction strengths may be unknown, yet usually the network topology can be inferred. Similarly, in large-scale communication or power networks, control strategies can be designed based solely on connectivity information rather than exact system parameter values. Structural controllability, thus, provides a robust foundation for analyzing and designing control strategies for complex dynamical systems where complete parameter knowledge is inaccurate or even unavailable.

2.1.2.1 *Definition*

Consider a parameterized LTI system represented by Equation (2.1), where the system matrices **A** and **B** contain some unknown or variable non-zero parameters. The system is *structurally controllable* if and only if it is state controllable for at least one set of parameter values that preserves the full-rank property of the system controllability matrix **C** [47]. In other words, the state controllability can be achieved by appropriately selecting some free parameters without altering the structural pattern of zeros and non-zeros of the controllability matrix.

This definition emphasizes that structural controllability is a property of the system topology rather than a specific set of numerical parameter values, making it particularly useful for large-scale or uncertain systems where exact parameters are unknown. The definition also shows that structural controllability is state controllability, but for systems with parameterized topologies; when the parameters are chosen and fixed, it reduces to the state controllability.

2.1.2.2 *Discrimination and Calculation of Structural Controllability*

Structural controllability of networked dynamical systems can be analyzed using graph-theoretic methods, for networked systems represented by directed graphs. In this representation, nodes correspond to dynamical systems, or state variables, and directed edges represent the flow of information or control signals within the network, indicating the source system or variable and the destination system or variable.

In this part of the book, in any network under consideration, a node system can be of higher-dimension but its input and output are both one-dimensional, referred to as single-input single-output (SISO) systems. Thus, the connection between any two nodes in such a network is one-dimensional, therefore this kind of network is also called SISO networks for convenience of description. A useful tool from graph theory for analyzing SISO networks is *matching* in directed graphs. In a directed graph, a matching is a set of edges such that no two edges share the same head node or the same end node. A node is *matched* if it is the head node of a directed edge in the matching; otherwise, it is *unmatched.* A *maximum matching* is a matching that contains the largest possible number of edges and cannot be further extended.

A networked system is structurally controllable if and only if the corresponding graph satisfies the following two conditions:

(1) Every node is *reachable* from at least one input node via a directed path (*accessibility*).
(2) There exists a *matching* that covers all nodes, thus every node is connected either by an input node or to another node through a directed edge (*matchedness*).

If both accessibility and matchedness conditions are satisfied, the networked system is structurally controllable with respect to a single input to the network. Here, the node to which the input is applied is called a *deriver node*.

If a single input node is not enough to ensure the network to satisfy the above conditions, additional input(s) must be introduced, namely, additional driver node(s) are needed. The minimum number of driver nodes n_D required for structural controllability can be computed using the minimum inputs theorem (MIT) [10], which is based on maximum matching, as follows:

$$n_D = \max\{1, n - |\mathcal{E}^*|\} , \tag{2.4}$$

where n is the number of nodes in the network and $|\mathcal{E}^*|$ is the number of edges in the maximum matching $\mathcal{E}^*$.

2.1.3 *Normalized Metric for Network Controllability*

Using Equation (2.3) or Equation (2.4), one can calculate the number of required driver nodes for achieving or retaining the controllability of networked systems. However, when comparing networked systems of different scales, it is necessary to introduce a normalization term based on the total number of nodes to ensure uniformity and fairness.

To effectively assess the robustness of network controllability under malicious attacks, the main topic to be investigated throughout this book, the following metric is defined as the proportion of driver nodes required to maintain the controllability of the networked system, namely to achieve full control of the network:

$$c_D = \frac{n_D}{n} , \tag{2.5}$$

where n_D denotes the number of driver nodes required for controllability, and n is the total number of nodes in the network. Thus, the metric c_D represents the fraction of driver nodes needed for controllability in the network. A lower value of c_D indicates a better controllability, as fewer driver nodes are required to maintain full control of the network, and obviously more economical. In contrast, a higher value of c_D reflects a lower controllability robustness, since more driver nodes are needed to maintain full control of the network under adverse conditions.

2.2 Controllability of Synthetic and Real-world Networks

The investigation of controllability in networks extends beyond theoretical analysis to deal with both synthetic models and real-world systems. The ultimate goal of the study is to design or refine system topologies to ensure strong controllability and its robustness against uncertain or hostile environments that introduce structural disturbances. Achieving this goal requires understanding how controllability behaves prior to such disturbances occur across different classes of networks. The insights are crucial for guiding the design and optimization of networked control systems, including technological, engineering, and social networks, where the controllability robustness is a basic requirement [48].

2.2.1 *Typical Synthetic Networks*

For theoretical design and analysis, numerical simulations based on synthetic network models are essential.

Synthetic networks are artificially constructed models designed to simulate real-world phenomena and analyze network properties under controlled conditions. They are widely used for preprocessing tasks such as evaluating system performance under adversarial attacks, conducting stress tests under extreme conditions, and generating representative training data to mimic real-world scenarios in model development. Some typical types of synthetic network models are discussed in detail below, which will be used frequently throughout this book for simulation and evaluation.

2.2.1.1 *Erdős–Rényi Networks*

Erdős–Rényi (ER) networks, one of the simplest and most widely studied models in network science [49], are generated by randomly adding edges between nodes with a predefined probability.

An ER random network, denoted as $\mathcal{G}(n, p)$, is constructed as follows: starting with n isolated nodes, edges are added non-repeatedly and independently between every pair of nodes with a predesigned and fixed probability p.

In the undirected ER model, each unordered pair of nodes is considered once, and an edge is added with probability p, resulting in a binomial degree distribution. For large n, when p is small and np remains fixed, the degree distribution approximates a Poisson distribution. As p increases, the network undergoes a phase transition near $p_c \approx \frac{\log n}{n}$, evolving from a collection of separated clusters of nodes to a fully connected graph.

In the directed ER model, each ordered pair of nodes is considered separately, and a directed edge from one node to another is added with probability p. This leads to independent binomial distributions for in-degree and out-degree, respectively. When n is large and p is small with np fixed, both distributions approximate Poisson distributions. As p increases, the network transitions from separated clusters of nodes to a strongly connected graph.

Alternatively, an ER network can be defined as $\mathcal{G}(n, m)$, where n is the number of nodes and m ($n < m \leq \frac{n(n-1)}{2}$) is the total number of edges, selected uniformly at random from the set of all possible edges. In this model, exactly m edges are placed uniformly at random among all possible node pairs, ensuring a fixed edge count rather than a fixed probability of connection.

As will be seen below, generally ER networks tend to exhibit strong controllability when the edge density is sufficiently high. However, at low edge densities, their controllability deteriorates due to the absence of large components, namely connected clusters, which are essential for effective network control [10].

2.2.1.2 *Extremely Homogeneous Networks*

Extremely homogeneous (EH) networks are constructed based on the empirical necessary condition (ENC) for achieving optimal controllability robustness [50]. This condition states that, for a directed network with n nodes and m edges to exhibit maximal robustness against exhaustive attack sequences (i.e., all possible permutations of node removals), the in-degree and out-degree of each node must satisfy the following condition:

$$\left\lfloor \frac{m}{n} \right\rfloor \leq k_i^{\text{in}},\, k_i^{\text{out}} \leq \left\lceil \frac{m}{n} \right\rceil, \quad i = 1, 2, \ldots, n\,, \tag{2.6}$$

where k_i^{in} denotes the in-degree and k_i^{out} and out-degree of node i, meaning that for each of them the above condition should be satisfied; the floor function $\lfloor \cdot \rfloor$ returns the greatest integer less than or equal to a given value, while the ceiling function $\lceil \cdot \rceil$ returns the least integer greater than or equal to that value.

The above condition can be naturally extended to undirected networks by applying the same constraint to total degrees:

$$\left\lfloor \frac{m}{n} \right\rfloor \leq k_i \leq \left\lceil \frac{m}{n} \right\rceil, \quad i = 1, 2, \ldots, n, \tag{2.7}$$

where k_i denotes the degree of node i in an undirected network.

Although any network, directed or undirected, can in principle be rectified through appropriate rewiring strategies to satisfy the ENC shown in Equation (2.6), EH networks in this study are specifically generated by applying random edge rectifications (detailed in Section 4.4.2) to ER networks of either type. The objective is to reshape the approximately Poisson degree distribution of an ER network to be one that exhibits extreme homogeneity.

2.2.1.3 *Generic Scale-free Networks*

Scale-free (SF) networks, commonly observed in real-world systems such as social, technological, and communication networks, are characterized by a power-law degree distribution [51–54]. Unlike ER networks with relatively homogeneous degree distributions, SF networks exhibit pronounced *heterogeneity*: a few nodes (hubs) have very high degrees, while most nodes have low degrees. This skewed structure generally limits controllability, as low-degree nodes often require to be pinned with controllers, namely become deriver nodes. Typically, the number of driver nodes needed for maintaining the controllability of a scale-free network is larger than that for a random network with a similar average degree.

SF networks can be generated using a static model [53], where each node i is assigned a weight $w_i = (i + \theta)^{-\sigma}$, with $i = 1, 2, \ldots, n$, $\sigma \in (0, 1)$, and $\theta \ll n$. Two nodes i and j are randomly selected with probabilities proportional to w_i and w_j, respectively, and a directed edge is added from node i to node j. The parameter σ controls the degree exponent $\gamma = 1 + 1/\sigma$, ensuring a power-law degree distribution.

For undirected SF networks, the same weight-based selection process is applied, but each selected pair of nodes i and j is connected by an undirected edge. The probability of selecting each node remains proportional to its weight, w_i, ensuring that the resulting network maintains the scale-free property while being symmetric in connectivity.

2.2.1.4 *Barabási–Albert (BA) Networks*

The Barabási–Albert (BA) model [51], a representative scale-free network model, is distinguished by its *preferential attachment* mechanism, which sets it apart from the generic SF model described above.

The generation process of a BA network begins with a small-sized connected nodes, and new nodes are added sequentially. In the undirected version of the BA network, each new node connects to existing nodes with a probability proportional to their degrees, forming undirected edges. In the directed version, each new node connects to existing nodes with a probability proportional to their current in-degree, forming directed edges. This growth and preferential attachment process produces a network whose degree distribution follows a power law, typically expressed as $p(k) \sim k^{-\gamma}$, where the BA model yields $\gamma \approx 3$, while most real-world networks exhibit $2 < \gamma < 3$.

2.2.1.5 *Small-world Networks*

Small-world (SW) networks are characterized by a high clustering coefficient and a short average path length. These two features are commonly observed from real-world networks, including natural, social and technological systems [55, 56]. By introducing random shortcuts into a highly clustered structure, or high clusters into a closely connected structure, small-world networks are generated, which can serve as an intermediate form between regular lattices and random networks. Typically, a small-world network can be constructed using generating algorithms of the Watts–Strogatz (WS) [55] model, the Newman–Watts (NW) [56] model, or other variants.

The undirected WS model begins with a regular ring-shaped lattice, where each node is connected to its $n_{\mathcal{N}}$ nearest neighbors. Then, with a rewiring probability p, edges are randomly redirected to other nodes, introducing shortcuts that significantly reduce the average path length while maintaining high clustering. When $p = 0$, the network remains a regular lattice; when $p = 1$, it becomes highly randomized and ER-like. In contrast, the NW model does not involve rewiring; instead, it randomly adds shortcut edges to the initial ring-shaped lattice.

For directed WS networks, edges are initially generated with a uniform direction, forming a directed ring-structured backbone. This design, while not part of the original WS model [55, 57], is highly beneficial for studying controllability and controllability robustness. The subsequent rewiring or edge-adding operations follow the same procedures as in undirected WS or NW model. In the directed NW model, because shortcuts are added without breaking the backbone structure, controllability can be exceptionally high under structural controllability theory: if the backbone remains strongly connected, only one driver node is required to guarantee the network controllability.

Small-world networks generally exhibit higher controllability than regular lattices because shortcuts reduce path lengths and enhance the overall connectivity. In WS and NW models, the initial ring-shaped backbone substantially improves the controllability. For instance, in the NW model, this structure remains intact, enabling full control by a single driver node through the connected network structure. For generic WS networks without a guaranteed backbone, controllability depends on the rewiring probability p. At intermediate p, the network maintains high clustering and short path length, offering better connectivity than a regular lattice but not exceeding the controllability of highly random networks. As $p \to 1$, the network becomes ER-like, requiring fewer driver nodes in general.

2.2.1.6 *q-Snapback Networks*

The q-snapback (QS) model, inspired by industrial assembly-line automation, is constructed on a backbone chain with additional snapback edges introduced probabilistically according to a tunable parameter $q_{QS} \in (0,1)$, which generally can be taken as a probability. Snapback edges function as feedback-like connections that emulate feedback control mechanisms in automated systems and production processes, enhancing structural diversity and dynamical potential of the network [58, 59].

A directed QS network comprises multiple layers indexed by $r_{QS} = 1, 2, \ldots, \ell$, where $\ell \leq n$. Each layer r_{QS} forms a directed chain, where nodes $i = r_{QS}+1, r_{QS}+2, \ldots, n$ connect backward to all preceding nodes $i-1, i-2, \ldots, 1$ with a uniform probability q_{QS}. Stacking all ℓ layers produces the final QS network. Removing edge directions yields an undirected QS network.

The backbone chain ensures strong controllability in a QS network. Additional details on QS construction and properties will be provided in Subsection 4.2.2.

2.2.1.7 *Henneberg Networks*

Henneberg networks are generated through an iterative procedure known as *Henneberg construction* or *Henneberg growth*, widely applied in graph theory to analyze network rigidity and structural properties [60–62]. The procedure produces random k-polygon networks. Henneberg growth is a dynamic process in which new nodes form polygons such as triangles, rectangles, or hexagons, by connecting one by one to adjacent nodes. It preserves connectivity and regulates the total number of edges by adding or removing edges when necessary.

An undirected random k-polygon network is constructed by repeatedly attaching k-polygon rings to existing parts of the network. The process begins with a simple k-node polygon and expands by randomly connecting new k-node polygons, namely sequentially adding rings of size k. The result is a modular network built through structured, undirected polygonal expansions. In the directed case, specific orientations, typically cyclic, are favored during polygon formation.

When the generated random k-polygons are triangles, rectangles, or hexagons, the resulting networks are referred to as random triangle (RT), random rectangle (RR), or random hexagon (RH) networks, respectively. These networks exhibit Poisson degree distributions with homogeneous structures, resembling ER networks but differing from highly heterogeneous SF networks [62].

Figure 2.1 illustrates the controllability characteristics of the eight synthetic network models with various edge densities, based on a fixed and small number of nodes ($n = 12$) for ease of observation and comparison. Red nodes indicate the driver nodes required for controllability of the network, while green flash icons represent the corresponding control inputs (controllers).

In Figure 2.1(a), the networks are sparse with an average degree $\langle k \rangle = 3.3$, exhibiting low controllability as reflected by the relatively large number of required driver nodes. As network density increases, as shown in Figure 2.1(b), where the average degree rises to $\langle k \rangle = 5.0$, the number of driver nodes decreases significantly. When the networks become even denser, as illustrated in Figure 2.1(c), with an average degree of $\langle k \rangle = 8.3$, all eight synthetic network models require only one driver node to guarantee controllability.

In general, dense and homogeneous networks exhibit higher controllability because, from a physical perspective, uniform connectivity and balanced degree distribution enable control signals to propagate efficiently throughout the system. These networks typically require fewer driver nodes, as each controller can influence a large portion of the network. Conversely, sparse or heterogeneous networks, particularly those with irregular topolo-

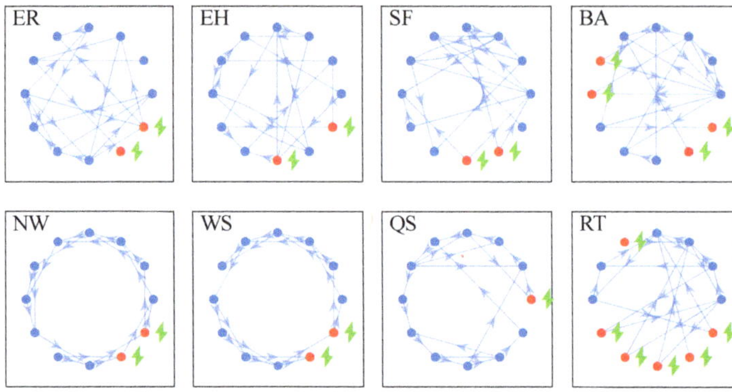

(a) $n = 12$, $m = 20$

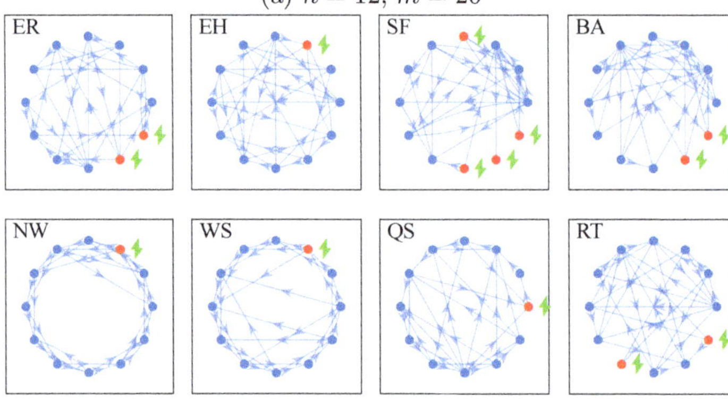

(b) $n = 12$, $m = 30$

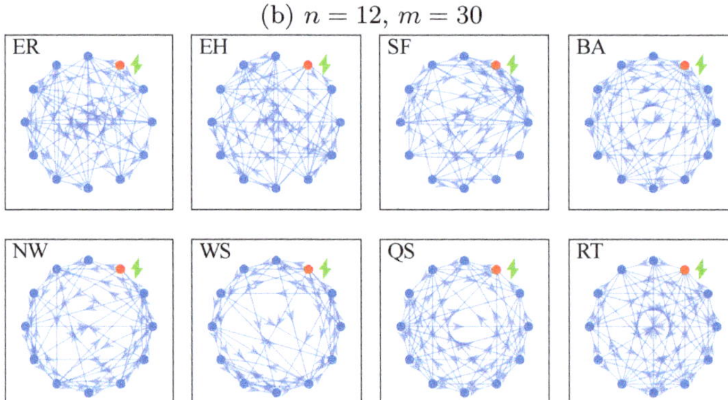

(c) $n = 12$, $m = 50$

Fig. 2.1: Exemplary instances of the eight synthetic network models, illustrating controllability under different configurations: (a) $n = 12, m = 20$; (b) $n = 12, m = 30$; (c) $n = 12, m = 50$. Red nodes denote driver nodes, and green flashes indicate control inputs (controllers).

gies or hierarchical structures, tend to display lower controllability. In such cases, controllers must be strategically positioned to overcome structural bottlenecks and ensure effectiveness. Moreover, backbone structures such as multiple rings and chains, or global configurations like a single chain or ring connecting most or all nodes, significantly enhance the network controllability.

2.2.2 *Controllability of Real-world Networks*

Real-world networks span a diverse range of complex systems. Here, the following representative datasets are utilized: Github Stargazers (GIT) [63], Deezer ego nets (DEE) [63], Protein (PRO) [64], Dobson & Doig (DD) [65], Scientific Collaboration (COL) [66], and Reddit (RED) [66]. Although the original datasets differ in size, 500 instances are randomly selected from each of them to ensure consistency and comparability across experiments.

Table 2.1: Summary of real-world network statistics: range of node counts $[n_{\min}, n_{\max}]$; average number of nodes $\langle n\rangle$; average number of edges $\langle m\rangle$; average degree $\langle k\rangle$; average number of required driver nodes $\langle n_D\rangle$; ratio of required driver nodes to total nodes $\langle n_D\rangle/\langle n\rangle$.

	$[n_{\min}, n_{\max}]$	$\langle n\rangle$	$\langle m\rangle$	$\langle k\rangle$	$\langle n_D\rangle$	$\langle n_D\rangle/\langle n\rangle$
GIT [63]	[100, 300]	171.2	676.11	7.73	82.7	4.8×10^{-1}
DEE [63]	[50, 250]	77.5	728.42	17.63	15.1	1.9×10^{-1}
PRO [64]	[20, 100]	41.8	159.72	7.64	1.7	4.1×10^{-2}
DD [65]	[100, 300]	196.6	979.21	9.91	1.0	5.1×10^{-3}
COL [66]	[100, 300]	153.8	25322.17	258.31	1.2	7.8×10^{-3}
RED [66]	[300, 600]	409.1	1879.66	9.20	198.9	4.9×10^{-1}

Table 2.1 summarizes the statistical characteristics of the aforementioned real-world network datasets. The primary objective is to illustrate recent advances in analytical and computational methods for network controllability robustness rather than to conduct an exhaustive evaluation of full-scale real-world datasets. To ensure consistency and comparability across experiments, 500 network instances are randomly sampled from each original dataset, which varies in size and structural complexity.

The last two columns of Table 2.1 report the number and proportion of driver nodes required for ensuring the network controllability. The results indicate that real-world networks exhibit highly diverse controllability properties, with the ratio of required driver nodes ranging from approximately 10^{-3} to 10^{-1}. This wide variation highlights the significant potential for structural optimization in real-world networks, particularly in the contexts where improving controllability robustness is critical.

2.2.3 *Controllability-related Topological Features*

The controllability of both synthetic and real-world networks is essentially determined by their underlying graphical structure and, for weighted networks, also by the distribution of connection strengths. In this book, particular emphasis is placed on the network topology, as structural features are dominant properties. Various topological characteristics influence not only network controllability but also its robustness under structural perturbations, a central topic of the present book. In this subsection, key network properties are examined, including degree distribution, internal loops, connectivity, sparsity, and assortativity, all of which critically affect controllability and its resilience.

2.2.3.1 *Degree Distribution*

Network controllability is closely associated with the degree distribution, particularly the prevalence of nodes with low in-degrees and out-degrees, which strongly influence the minimum number of driver nodes required for determining the controllability [67]. Networks with homogeneous degree distributions, such as random graphs, typically require fewer driver nodes. In contrast, scale-free networks, characterized by highly heterogeneous degree distributions with a few hubs and many low-degree nodes, usually demand a larger fraction of driver nodes due to the dominance of low-degree nodes in such networks [10]. Nonetheless, high-degree hubs can significantly enhance the control efficiency when strategically selected as driver nodes in pinning control applications.

Although a statistical tendency shows that heterogeneity correlates with controllability, exceptions exist. For example, in [68], a power-law distributed network with a backbone global chain is demonstrated to achieve perfect controllability, requiring only one driver node for such a network.

Therefore, while degree distribution exhibits some correlation with controllability, it is not sufficient to serve as a reliable stand-alone indicator. Additional structural factors must be considered to accurately assess controllability.

2.2.3.2 *Internal Loops*

Internal loops, or feedback loops, particularly when combined with a backbone chain in a network, enhance the controllability by introducing redundant pathways and alternative control routes, thereby increasing flexibility in steering the network dynamics. However, while loops improve controllability, they may also increase the risk of instability in networked dynamic systems. This trade-off between controllability and stability is especially evident in biological networks [69].

2.2.3.3 *Connectivity*

Overall connectivity, quantified by metrics such as average path length and clustering coefficient, influences the controllability by determining how efficiently control signals propagate through the network. Short average path lengths enable faster and more effective signal transmission, whereas high clustering can create local dependencies that may either facilitate or hinder controllability depending on the network structure [70].

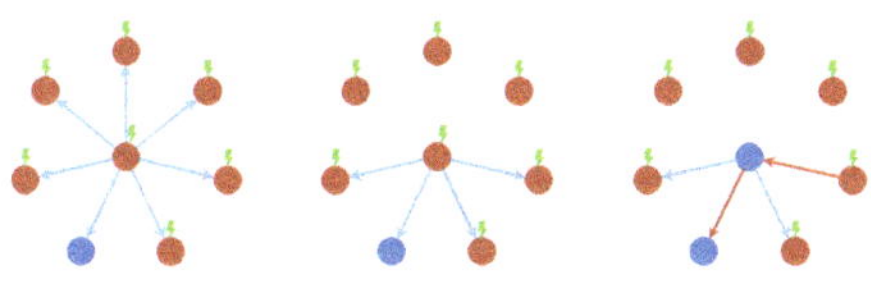

(a) (b) (c)

Fig. 2.2: An illustration of the relationship between connectivity and controllability. Red nodes indicate driver nodes, and green flash symbols represent control inputs. (a) A star-shaped directed network exhibits high connectivity but poor controllability. (b) After removing several edges, controllability remains unchanged while connectivity is significantly degraded. (c) Reversing the direction of a single edge partially improves controllability without affecting connectivity.

As illustrated in Figure 2.2, network (a) demonstrates higher connectivity than network (b), yet both exhibit the same level of controllability. Networks (b) and (c) share identical connectivity, but network (c) achieves better controllability through the direction reversal of a single edge (highlighted in red). In this context, *connectivity* is measured by the relative size of the largest connected component [71, 72]. Overall, while connectivity can enhance controllability in some scenarios, there is no consistent or direct correlation between these two properties, underscoring the need for topology-aware controllability analysis.

2.2.3.4 *Sparsity*

Network sparsity, defined as the ratio of existing edges to the total possible number of edges, is an important factor influencing controllability. Sparse networks generally require a higher proportion of driver nodes to achieve full controllability because of the limited pathways available for signal propagation. However, low sparsity alone does not guarantee strong controllability, as simply increasing the number of edges without proper structural organization may not improve their effect on the controllability. For a network to exhibit high controllability, it must be sufficiently dense and possess well-structured connectivity that facilitates efficient transmission of control signals [50].

An exception arises when the network contains a backbone chain or a ring that connects all nodes together. In such special cases, even a sparse network can achieve perfect controllability, requiring only a single driver node.

2.2.3.5 *Assortativity*

Assortativity reflects the tendency of nodes to connect with others sharing similar properties, specifically node degrees. In positively assortative networks, high-degree nodes tend to connect with other high-degree nodes, whereas disassortative networks feature connections between high-degree and low-degree nodes.

Positively assortative networks often form localized clusters of highly connected nodes, which can restrict the spread of control signals across the network. As a result, such networks typically exhibit reduced global controllability, since control inputs are less likely to propagate efficiently. In contrast, disassortative networks promote global controllability by enabling long-range signal transmission. This structure allows high-degree nodes to effectively influence low-degree nodes, resulting in broader control coverage. Consequently, disassortative networks generally demonstrate superior controllability compared to assortative ones [73, 74].

It is also worth noting that assortative networks are widely recognized for their robustness in maintaining connectivity under malicious destructive attacks. Since connectivity robustness is partially related to controllability robustness, assortativity may still contribute to controllability resilience in certain scenarios [75]. However, this relationship is indirect and context-dependent.

The above observation underscores that methodologies developed for analyzing connectivity robustness are not directly applicable to controllability robustness, even under the same threats such as targeted attacks. Although these concepts share superficial similarities, they are governed by fundamentally different mechanisms. Therefore, approaches designed for connectivity analysis should *not* be applied to control-related problems without careful adjustment and adaptation.

2.3 Summary

In summary, controllability of synthetic and real-world networks is fundamentally shaped by the network structural features that govern propagation of control signals and determine the number of driver nodes required for full controllability. Dense and homogeneous networks tend to exhibit superior controllability, whereas sparse or highly heterogeneous networks demand more strategic placement of control inputs to driver nodes. Real-world networks display substantial variability in controllability, underscoring potential for structural optimization. Topological properties such as degree distribution, internal loops, connectivity, and sparsity play critical roles in determining network controllability. Backbone configurations, particularly chain-like and ring-like structures, are especially effective as they facilitate smooth signal transmission and broad influence across the network [50, 76]. Although connectivity robustness and controllability robustness may appear related, these concepts arise from fundamentally different mechanisms and therefore require distinct analytical frameworks.

Chapter 3

Controllability Robustness

This chapter provides a thorough examination of the controllability robustness in complex networks. The discussion begins with some widely adopted metrics, including percolation-theory-based metrics, control-centrality-based metrics, and reachability-based metrics.

Attack strategies are classified into structural feature-based, damage based, computational intelligence-based, and data-driven approaches, with emphasis on their effectiveness and computational costs. A hierarchical attack strategy that is highly effective yet computation-intensive is first introduced, which targets critical nodes or edges to degrade the network controllability. Practical stopping criteria for attack-simulation-based evaluation are then proposed to better approximate practical conditions. Further, analytical modeling of controllability degradation is addressed through statistical approximations of attacks and degeneration processes. Finally, controllability robustness of eight synthetic network models and six real-world datasets under node- and edge-based attacks are compared, revealing how network density and heterogeneity affect the resilience. The findings offer theoretical insights and practical guidelines for analyzing and improving controllability robustness in diverse networked systems.

The chapter is organized as follows. Section 3.1 introduces widely-used metrics for measuring controllability robustness. Section 3.2 presents attack strategies in four categories. Section 3.3 describes the hierarchical attack strategy. Section 3.4 presents attack simulation and discusses practical stopping criteria. Section 3.5 explains analytical modeling of controllability degradation. Section 3.6 compares controllability robustness across eight synthetic network models and six real-world networks. Finally, Section 3.7 briefly summarize the study.

3.1 Metrics for Controllability Robustness

Robustness in this book refers to the ability of a network to maintain its structural integrity and preserve its functionality under adverse conditions such as failures, removals, or targeted attacks. Controllability robustness, in particular, concerns maintaining the network controllability in resistance to degradation and retaining the network ability to withstand disruptions without significant loss of control capability.

Furthermore, the network *resilience* emphasizes recovery after damage has occurred, prioritizing restoration and adaptation in addition to resistance. While robustness measures how well a system endures stress, resilience measures how effectively it rebounds from stress. These two concepts may overlap in certain context, but this book only focuses on the issue of robustness.

Other related terms, such as *reliability* and *fault tolerance*, address specific aspects of the network dependability, which do not fully capture the structural and dynamical dimensions inherent in robustness or resilience. Although some overlap exists, these terms are not equivalent. Understanding these distinctions is essential for designing networks that resist disruptions and adapt efficiently to dynamic environments, which is particularly critical when analyzing the controllability robustness in complex networked dynamical systems.

3.1.1 *Structural Robustness*

Structural robustness of networks refers to the ability of a network to maintain structural integrity, with or without preserving specific functionalities, under structural disruptions such as removals or malfunctions of nodes, edges, or both. Although structural robustness is a broad concept, its interpretation depends on the functionality of interest. For example, when the focus is controllability, connectivity, or pairwise communication, the corresponding robustness measures are controllability robustness, connectivity robustness, and communicability robustness, respectively. Evaluating network robustness is essential for understanding and improving reliability, resilience, and performance of networked dynamical systems.

Metrics related to structural robustness are generally classified into *a priori* and *a posteriori* categories [42]. *A priori* metrics assess robustness based on inherent network characteristics, typically derived from topological structure [55] or spectral properties of Laplacian or adjacency matrices [77]. These metrics rely on theoretical insights, well-founded assumptions, or empirical observations that indicate strong correlations between specific structural features and specific network functionality. When such correlations are theoretically justified or empirically validated, *a priori* metrics can be applied efficiently with confidence. However, the relationship between topological features and controllability, or other robustness-related functionalities, remains insufficiently established. Furthermore, theoretical analysis of robustness becomes increasingly complex due to the diversity of potential attack strategies and the nonlinear interactions between structural properties and dynamic performance.

In contrast, *a posteriori* metrics are obtained through posterior evaluations based on attack simulations, where network functionality is measured iteratively after the removal of some nodes or edges. The recorded trajectory of functionality degradation constitutes an *a posteriori* metric. These metrics are descriptive and adaptable but typically require substantial computational resources, because they involve repeated evaluations of network performances under progressive structural disruptions [42,78]. Unlike *a priori* metrics, *a posteriori* approaches do not rely on assumptions but are purely observational. Nevertheless, these metrics present several challenges: (1) they demand significant computational resources since multiple attack sequences must be simulated and the system functionality be tracked at every stage of degradation, and (2) their results can be influenced by stochastic factors such as random attack patterns or probabilistic strategies, introducing variability into the evaluation. Consequently, repeated simulations with averaging are necessary to ensure reliable and reproducible assessments.

Despite these limitations, *a posteriori* metrics offer notable advantages. They do not rely on strong assumptions about the relationship between structural features and network performance, making them applicable to a wide range of scenarios, including diverse attack models and various network functionalities. Their flexibility enables direct observation of functionality degradation under realistic conditions, providing an empirical basis for robustness evaluation. Although computationally demanding, this challenge can be mitigated through techniques such as sampling strategies or machine learning-based surrogate models [79,80].

In summary, because *a priori* metrics are inherently limited in capturing robustness under diverse conditions, their applicability remains restricted. By contrast, *a posteriori* metrics are generally preferred for practical applications, as they provide empirical evaluations without relying on strong structural assumptions and can adapt to various attack models and network functionalities. Their observational nature ensures higher accuracy and flexibility, making them the dominant choice for robustness assessment in real-world scenarios where reliability and adaptability are critical [42].

3.1.2 *Controllability Robustness Metrics*

Compared to connectivity robustness, or other forms of structural robustness, controllability robustness focuses on the ability of a network to maintain or restore its controllability under adverse conditions such as attacks, failures, or structural disruptions. While controllability robustness shares certain characteristics with structural robustness, it exhibits distinct properties that reflect a functional perspective. Specifically, controllability robustness concerns the preservation of dynamic controllability rather than mere structural integrity, making it a critical metric for networked systems where control performance is as important as structural connectivity.

Robustness of network controllability is primarily evaluated through measures related to control energy or cost, which can be quantified by the proportion of driver nodes required to determine the controllability of the entire network, or a substantial portion of it. In practical applications, some systems permit flexible adjustment of the driver nodes, allowing such nodes to be added or reallocated when some existing ones failed. However, in many scenarios, the configuration of driver nodes must remain fixed or be altered only under strict constraints. Consequently, depending on the context, various metrics are defined and employed to assess the robustness of network controllability, hereafter referred to as the *controllability robustness.*

3.1.2.1 *Percolation-theory-based Metrics*

Percolation-theory-based metrics were originally introduced to evaluate connectivity robustness by analyzing how network structure degrades as nodes or edges are progressively failed or removed [71]. The primary objective in classical percolation models is to determine the critical percolation threshold beyond which a giant connected component (GCC) or the largest connected component (LCC) disintegrates, resulting in the loss of global connectivity. This approach has been widely applied to assess the resilience of complex systems such as communication, transportation, and biological networks under random failures or targeted attacks.

In the context of controllability robustness, percolation-theory-based metrics have been extended to quantify how controllability evolves as network structure varies. Instead of focusing on the connectivity, as reflected by GCC or LCC, these metrics measure the proportion of driver nodes required to maintain complete controllability over the remaining network after each time of node or edge removal. This adaptation enables evaluation of whether the network remains structurally connected and also dynamically controllable.

Specifically, controllability robustness under percolation-based assessment is expressed as

$$R_{PT} = \frac{1}{T}\sum_{i=1}^{T} c_D(i) = \frac{1}{T}\sum_{i=1}^{T} \frac{n_D(i)}{n(i)}, \tag{3.1}$$

where $c_D(i)$ and $n_D(i)$ denote the ratio and number of the driver nodes required to maintain complete controllability after i elements (nodes or edges) have been removed. The term $n(i)$ serves as a normalization factor, which can either be the original network size n (treated as a constant) or the current size under attack $n(i) = n - i$ (treated as a varying term). The parameter T represents the total number of attack steps occurred. A smaller value of R_{PT} indicates a stronger controllability robustness, as fewer driver nodes are needed to maintain or restore the controllability step by step throughout the entire attack process.

3.1.2.2 *Control-centrality-based Metrics*

Unlike Equation (3.1), where the set of driver nodes can be freely adjusted after each attack, control centrality evaluates the control capability of an individual node when it is treated as a fixed driver node [76, 81]. This metric quantifies how effectively a single node maintains its influence on the network throughout a sequence of attacks.

For a single node v, its controllability matrix is defined by

$$\mathbf{C}^v = [\mathbf{b}_v \ \mathbf{A}\mathbf{b}_v \ \mathbf{A}^2\mathbf{b}_v \ \ldots \ \mathbf{A}^{n-1}\mathbf{b}_v],$$

where $\mathbf{b}_v$ is the input vector associated with node v, which is typically a column of $\mathbf{B}$ with a value of 1 at position v and zeros elsewhere, as defined in Equation (2.2).

Then, for this single node v, its controllable subspace is defined as

$$\mathcal{S}^v = \mathrm{col}(\mathbf{C}^v),$$

col(·) represents the column space of a matrix, that is, the subspace spanned by its column vectors.

Further, the control-centrality-based robustness metric for this single node v is defined as

$$R_{CC}^{v} = \frac{1}{T}\sum_{i=1}^{T}\frac{\dim(\mathcal{S}^{v}(i))}{n(i)} = \frac{1}{T}\sum_{i=1}^{T}\frac{\mathrm{rank}_g(\mathbf{C}^{v}(i))}{n(i)}, \tag{3.2}$$

where $\dim(\cdot)$ denotes the dimension of a subspace, defined as the number of linearly independent vectors that span the subspace; $\mathcal{S}^{v}(i)$ denotes the controllable subspace of node v after the i-th attack; $\mathbf{C}^{v}(i)$ denotes the controllability matrix associated with node v after the i-th attack, constructed using the post-attack system matrix and the corresponding input vector $\mathbf{b}_v(i)$; $\mathrm{rank}_g(\mathbf{C}^{v}(i))$ is the rank of the $\mathbf{C}^{v}(i)$ in the network; the denominator $n(i)$ serves for normalization, with the same meaning as that in Equation (3.2).

3.1.2.3 *Reachability-based Metrics*

While the control-centrality-based metrics focus on the controllable subspace associated with a single driver node, the reachability-based metrics consider the controllable subspace associated with a set of driver nodes in two modes: the *free control* mode and the *fixed control* mode.

In the free control mode, a fixed number of n_D controllers are installed on n_D driver nodes before any structural disturbance occurs. These controllers can be reassigned to any nodes in the network without restriction, modeling adaptive control strategies that allow dynamic reconfiguration.

In contrast, the fixed control mode assumes that controllers are pinned to a predetermined set of nodes [82, 83], which cannot be relocated after deployment. This setting is essentially equivalent to the control-centrality-based metric defined in Equation (3.2), where the control capability of each fixed driver node is evaluated under progressive attacks.

The above two modes reflect distinct assumptions about controller flexibility in practical systems. The free control mode captures adaptive strategies, while the fixed control mode represents scenarios constrained by hardware limitations or policy restrictions. Together, they provide complementary perspectives for evaluating controllability robustness under adversarial conditions. In both modes, the number of driver nodes is non-increasing throughout the attack process, since failed controllers are not replaced. The key objective is to evaluate the controllable portion within the network, that is, the portion that remains reachable and influenceable by the given set of controllers under progressive structural degradation.

Given a set of driver nodes $\mathbf{u}$, the controllable subspace, equivalently the reachable subspace associated with this set of driver nodes, is defined as

$$\mathcal{S}^{\mathbf{u}}(i) = \text{col}(\mathbf{C}^{\mathbf{u}}(i)),$$

and accordingly the reachability-based metric is defined as

$$R_{RE}^{\mathbf{u}} = \frac{1}{T}\sum_{i=1}^{T}\frac{\dim(\mathcal{S}^{\mathbf{u}}(i))}{n(i)} = \frac{1}{T}\sum_{i=1}^{T}\frac{\text{rank}_g(\mathbf{C}^{\mathbf{u}}(i))}{n(i)}. \tag{3.3}$$

This formulation applies to the collective sets of driver nodes $\mathbf{u}$; when only one single driver node v is considered, this formula reduces to Equation (3.2).

The extension from Equation (3.2) to Equation (3.3) generalizes the formulation from a single driver node to a set of driver nodes, meanwhile more importantly raising the question of how these driver nodes are selected, namely under free control modes versus under fixed control modes. Different control modes can lead to remarkably different outcomes in terms of controllability robustness. However, if only one single driver node is considered, no such distinction between control modes exists.

By averaging the dimensions of the controllable subspace over repeated attacks, this metric quantifies how effectively the remaining driver nodes maintain effective control over the network. A greater value of R_{RE} indicates a higher level of robustness, as it implies that a larger controllable subspace is preserved after structural perturbations.

The reachability-based approach is particularly suitable for applications where the number of driver nodes is fixed (as in the free control mode) or where both the number and positions are predetermined and unchanged (as in the fixed control mode). Typical examples include power grids, where control centers are located at fixed positions, and sensor networks, where controllers are deployed at specific nodes with limited mobility.

3.1.2.4 *Comparison of Metrics*

Percolation-theory-based metrics assess network robustness from a system-wide perspective by modeling changes in controllability during a node or edge removal process and identifying the critical threshold for maintaining network functionality. Since control inputs can be installed at various nodes in varying quantities, this metric is highly theoretical, aiming to determine the minimum number of control inputs or lowest level of energy required by the entire system throughout the attack process.

In contrast, control-centrality-based metrics and fixed reachability-based metrics evaluate the network controllability robustness due to individual nodes by quantifying the degradation of their control capability under attacks. These metrics are particularly useful for identifying nodes best suited to serve as control nodes from a robustness standpoint. However, if a designated driver node is compromised at the outset, the system may lose controllability entirely, with no fallback options available.

Reachability-based metrics emphasize maintaining controllability within a fixed control energy budget, highlighting the trade-off between resource constraints and system performance. This approach is especially relevant in practical scenarios where the number or placement of controllers is constrained by physical or policy conditions.

There is a conceptual overlap between control-centrality-based metrics and reachability-based metrics, specifically in the case of fixed reachability-based metrics where controllers are pinned to predetermined nodes and cannot be reallocated thereafter.

Since the above three metrics address distinct aspects of the controllability robustness and are tailored to different application contexts, they are not interchangeable. Notably, there is no unified metric capable of comprehensively capturing all concerned aspects simultaneously.

3.2 Attack Strategies

Identifying the most destructive attack on network controllability and designing effective defenses constitute dual challenges that are fundamental for constructing robust network topologies and assessing attack strategies. Given an importance metric $\mathcal{F}$ for nodes or edges, targeted attacks select the element with $\arg\max \mathcal{F}$ as the most critical, whereas random attacks select elements without prioritization.

Based on the nature of the importance measure $\mathcal{F}$, attack strategies can be classified into four categories:

- *Structural feature-based strategies*: The importance measure $\mathcal{F}$ is computed directly from network topology or semantic information, and remains invariant throughout the attack process.
- *Immediate damage-based strategies*: A local damage measure $\mathcal{F}$ is designed to maximize the immediate degradation of network functionality at each step of the attacking process.

- *Computational intelligence-based strategies*: A global damage measure $\mathcal{F}$ is optimized to maximize cumulative damage across a sequence of attacks, which typically incurs high computational complexity.
- *Data-driven strategies*: The importance measure $\mathcal{F}$ is learned from empirical data without relying on predefined assumptions. Although computationally intensive, this approach leverages advances in machine learning to improve adaptability and prediction accuracy, especially in the reinforcement learning framework [21].

3.2.1 *Structural Feature-based Attack Strategies*

Many widely-used attack strategies were originally designed to degrade network connectivity, whereas some are also effective for controllability. These strategies typically rely on structure-centrality-based measures such as degree, betweenness, closeness, eigenvector, Katz index, and PageRank. As discussed in Section 2.2.3, these features may exhibit positive correlations with controllability and connectivity, providing useful guidance for designing efficient attack strategies. For example, the hierarchical structure of a directed network enables upstream or downstream random attacks, which are more destructive to controllability than purely random attacks [76]. Module-based strategies [84, 85] focus on nodes associated with critical inter-community edges that maintain connectivity between communities. In practical scenarios where removal costs vary across nodes, attack strategies can be further optimized to minimize the total disruption cost [86].

Attack strategies constructed based on one or more structural features are generally straightforward: they target components with the highest level of importance according to the selected feature, referred to as *targeted strategies*. Targeted approaches are highly effective, hence widely adopted, due to the significance of degree as a local metric and betweenness as a global one. However, ranking node or edge importance becomes computationally challenging for large-scale networks [21, 87], and most metrics, including degree and betweenness, cannot guarantee that removing a selected component will consistently cause the greatest global damage on the network.

Given the same structural feature, structural feature-based strategies can be implemented in two forms. The first form uses initially computed features to determine a fixed attack sequence in advance, which is computationally efficient but less adaptive. The second form, known as the recalculated approach, updates the features dynamically through the attack process, selecting each target based on the current residual network structure [88]. Although more computationally intensive, the recalculated approach is significantly more effective because many structural features change as nodes or edges are removed. Updating the importance measure at each step enables the strategy to adapt to the evolving network topology, resulting in more accurate targeting with greater overall damage.

Among various structural features, degree and betweenness are the most frequently used ones. Degree is a local feature, while betweenness is global. Iterative recalculation leads to more severe damage than static strategies [89]. A degree-based attack recalculates node degrees after each step and targets the node with the highest degree currently, defined as

$$v^* = \arg\max_{v \in \mathcal{V}(i)} \deg(v)\,, \tag{3.4}$$

where v^* is the node selected at step i, $\mathcal{V}(i)$ is the set of remaining nodes, and $\deg(v)$ denotes the degree of node v in the current residual network. This dynamic selection ensures that the most connected node is always targeted, making the attack increasingly destructive. When multiple nodes share the highest degree, any one can be randomly selected.

Another widely-used strategy is the betweenness-based attack, which targets nodes or edges with the highest betweenness centrality. Betweenness quantifies how frequently a node or edge lies on shortest paths between node pairs, making it a critical indicator of network data and communication flow. Nodes with high betweenness are essential for maintaining connectivity and information transmission across the network. To maximize the impact, the strategy recalculates betweenness after each node or edge removal, ensuring that the most critical node is selected at every step. Formally, the attack is defined as

$$v^* = \arg\max_{v \in \mathcal{V}(i)} \mathrm{bet}(v)\,, \tag{3.5}$$

where v^* is the node selected at step i, $\mathcal{V}(i)$ is the set of remaining nodes, and $\mathrm{bet}(v) = \sum_{s \neq v \neq t} \frac{\sigma_{st}(v)}{\sigma_{st}}$ denotes the betweenness centrality of node v in the current residual network, with σ_{st} representing the number of shortest paths between nodes s and t, and $\sigma_{st}(v)$ the number of those paths passing through v.

3.2.2 *Damage-based Attack Strategies*

Unlike strategies based on structural features, the concept of *damage* refers to the loss of functionality (e.g., controllability, connectivity, or other performance metrics) before and after an attack is executed [90, 91]. The definition of damage is inherently *a posteriori*, typically requiring a trial-and-error evaluation process. Consequently, damage-based strategies provide a more principled basis for assessing attack effectiveness but incur significantly higher computational cost compared to strategies that rely on structural features [91].

A specific formulation for measuring damage depends on the application scenario. For example, if the connectivity robustness is the primary concern, damage is defined as the reduction in the size of the giant connected component [90]. In the context of controllability, following Equation (3.1), damage can be quantified by the increase in the proportion of driver nodes required to maintain full control of the network after each attack [10]. Nodes and edges whose removal leads to an increase in the number of required driver nodes are referred to as critical nodes and critical edges, respectively. Damage-based strategies prioritize these critical components throughout the attack process to maximize controllability loss [91, 92].

Using damage as the importance measure, the most critical node or edge is attacked at each step, forming a greedy strategy aimed at inflicting maximum destruction. This strategy dynamically adapts to the evolving network structure by continuously identifying and targeting the component whose removal results in the highest incremental damage. However, this approach has two notable drawbacks:

- Greedy selection does not guarantee globally maximal destruction over a sequence of attacks, as it only considers the immediate impact of each step rather than the cumulative effect in the whole process. Consequently, the resulting attack sequence may be suboptimal when long-term damage is the objective.
- The computational cost of evaluating damage at each step is substantial, especially for large-scale networks, since it requires recalculating controllability or reevaluating connectivity after each attack. The complexity grows with network size and also with the number of potential targets, making the strategy computationally expensive and often impractical for real-time applications.

Despite these limitations, damage-based strategies provide valuable insights into network vulnerabilities and serve as benchmarks for evaluating the effectiveness of other attack strategies. To mitigate computational overhead, various heuristic approaches have been proposed, including sampling-based methods, incremental update techniques, and surrogate models that estimate potential damage without the need of full recalculation. These approximations aim to balance accuracy and efficiency, enabling scalable implementations for large-scale networks.

3.2.3 *Computational Intelligence-based Attack Strategies*

Identifying an optimal attack sequence constitutes an NP-hard combinatorial optimization problem [93], where the objective is to select one or several sequences of node removals (or edge removals) from a total of $n!$ possible node sequences (or $m!$ edge sequences), such that the overall degradation in network functionality, such as controllability or connectivity, is maximized both as early as possible and to the greatest possible extent. Due to the factorial growth of the search space, exhaustive enumeration becomes computationally infeasible for large-scale networks. In such cases, computational intelligence approaches, particularly evolutionary computation methods, provide an efficient alternative by evolving populations of candidate attack sequences to approximate the optimal solution.

Evolutionary algorithms are inspired by the principles of natural selection and evolution, iteratively improving a population of candidate solutions over successive generations. Each candidate attack sequence, represented as a chromosome, undergoes genetic operations such as selection, crossover, and mutation [94]. The objective is to evolve sequences that maximize a fitness function representing the extent of network degradation. The general process can be summarized as follows:

- *Initialization*: Generate an initial population of candidate solutions, where each solution encodes a sequence of node or edge removals.
- *Fitness Evaluation*: Compute the fitness of each individual sequence by applying the removal sequence to the network and evaluating its impact using a robustness metric, for example Equation (3.1), which quantifies controllability or connectivity loss.
- *Reproduction*: Create new sequences as offspring through genetic operators such as mutation, crossover, and local search applied to parent sequences. These operations effectively reorder the node or edge removal positions within a sequence.
- *Selection*: Choose the most promising candidates for the next generation based on fitness values and selection criteria, ensuring a balance between exploration of new solutions and exploitation of high-quality sequences.
- *Termination*: Repeat the process until a predefined number of generations is reached or a convergence criterion is satisfied.

Although evolutionary algorithms can effectively balance exploration (searching new regions in the solution space) and exploitation (refining existing high-quality solutions), this iterative process is particularly time-consuming for large-scale networks.

Most robust evolutionary algorithms are well-suited for optimization problems with dimensions ranging from tens to several hundreds of variables. For higher-dimensional problems, algorithmic adaptations often introduce additional overhead or lead to performance degradation, as highlighted by the no-free-lunch theorem [95]. Large-scale problems involving thousands or even tens of thousands of variables typically require specialized techniques, such as parallelization, distributed computing, or hybrid heuristics, to maintain efficiency. Since real-world networks frequently exceed tens of thousands of nodes, applying evolutionary algorithms to search for an optimized attack sequence is generally impractical due to the extremely long computational time required.

Nevertheless, evolutionary algorithms provide an effective approach for iteratively optimizing attack sequences and are particularly efficient for small to medium-scale networks. Computational intelligence-based strategies can be regarded as global optimization methods that aim to maximize cumulative damage across an entire sequence, whereas damage-based strategies are inherently greedy, focusing only on the immediate impact of each removal step in the process.

3.2.4 *Data-driven Attack Strategies*

Similarly to computational intelligence-based approaches, machine learning provides valuable guidance for identifying critical components in a network with respect to specific functionalities, such as controllability, connectivity, information flow, or even multiple objectives simultaneously [21, 22, 96].

On one hand, by leveraging large-scale network data, machine learning models can learn complex patterns and relationships that are difficult to capture using traditional analytical methods. On the other hand, the rapid advancement of machine learning algorithms has endowed them with stronger generalization capabilities, enabling models trained on limited data from networks of constrained sizes to be applied effectively to a broader range of network instances, including those with different structures or scales [21]. Learning paradigms differ in their reliance on labeled data and optimization objectives. Building on these foundations, machine learning techniques including supervised, unsupervised, and reinforcement learning have been explored for designing adaptive attack strategies [21, 96].

Under a supervised learning framework, data-driven attack strategies typically involve two main steps [21, 96]:

- *Model Training*: Use network data as input to train a model with labeled outputs or scores obtained from experiments or measurements. These targets represent node or edge importance, vulnerability, or the damage caused by their removal.
- *Prediction*: When new network data, either seen or unseen, are provided, the trained model predicts one or a sequence of nodes or edges expected to yield the maximal attack effect.

Supervised learning approaches rely on labeled data, where nodes or edges are annotated with their importance or impact scores in relation to network functionality. Classical models such as decision trees, random forests, and shallow neural networks can be trained to classify or rank nodes based on their vulnerability [97]. Deep neural networks, including convolutional and graph-based architectures, further extend this capability by leveraging strong expressive power to evaluate controllability attack sequences within a supervised framework [22, 98]. Beyond static prediction, reinforcement learning provides a dynamic paradigm for sequential attack optimization, where an agent interacts with the network environment, learns adaptive attack policies through trial and error, and receives feedback via reward signals such as reductions in network functionality. Deep reinforcement learning models, in particular, have demonstrated remarkable scalability and effectiveness in addressing large-scale networks and complex attack scenarios [21, 99].

Under an unsupervised learning framework, the process differs when no labeled data are available. A possible scheme could be the following:

- *Feature Extraction*: Compute structural or functional features for nodes and edges, such as degree, betweenness, or embedding vectors.
- *Clustering or Representation Learning*: Apply clustering algorithms (e.g., k-means, spectral clustering) or graph embedding methods to group nodes or edges with similar characteristics.
- *Critical Group Identification*: Identify clusters or latent representations that correspond to high-impact components, based on heuristic criteria such as cluster centrality or density.

- *Attack Execution*: Translate identified clusters or representations to actionable attack sequences, prioritizing components predicted to have the greatest possible impact.

Unsupervised methods, such as clustering or representation learning, aim to identify groups of potentially critical components without prior labels. A typical process involves feature extraction, grouping nodes or edges with similar characteristics, and applying heuristic criteria to select high-impact clusters. These approaches are effective for tasks like community detection but generally require additional steps to translate clusters to actionable attack sequences, which limits cost-efficiency compared to supervised or reinforcement learning strategies.

Despite their promise, data-driven approaches face notable challenges. Model performance depends heavily on the quality and quantity of the training data, whereas insufficient or biased data can lead to suboptimal predictions. Training machine learning models for large-scale networks is computationally expensive, imposing significant resource constraints. Furthermore, generalizing learned strategies to unseen networks with substantial structural variance remains difficult and generally requires robust validation and transfer learning techniques.

Nevertheless, these approaches provide a promising direction for developing adaptive and intelligent attack strategies that outperform traditional heuristics. Combining machine learning with domain knowledge and computational intelligence can further enhance efficiency and effectiveness. Future development should focus on improving generalization, reducing computational costs, and integrating hybrid models that combine learning-based methods with classical optimization techniques.

3.2.5 *Comparison of Attack Strategies*

Figure 3.1 compares four types of attack strategies. The structural feature-based approach incurs minimal overhead (assuming structural feature computation is not excessive, which is generally the case), scales well, and does not require a training phase or trial-and-error procedure. However, performance may be limited because predefined structural metrics do not always capture the most critical components throughout the evolving attack process.

The damage-based approach aims to maximize impact at each attack step, which is by nature a greedy method focusing on locally optimal decisions. This requires a trial-and-error process to identify the component

Table 3.1: Comparison of attack strategies based on structural features, damage, computational intelligence, and data-driven approaches with respect to overhead, scalability, performance, and training data requirements.

Attack Strategy	Overhead	Scaling	Performance	Training Data
Feature-based	low	○	×	×
Damage-based	high	×	○	×
Computational Intelligence-based	high	×	○	×
Data-driven	high	○	○	○

causing the highest immediate damage. While overhead for a single step can be small, the cumulative cost becomes substantial for a long attack sequence, especially in a large-scale network, as each step of the process requires repeated evaluation of the concerned network functionality.

The computational intelligence-based approach shares similarities with damage-based methods but adopts a global optimization criterion, considering the entire sequence of node removals. Metaheuristics such as evolutionary algorithms and swarm optimization aim to identify sequences that maximize the cumulative damage. Although this approach improves performance compared to greedy methods, computational overhead grows nonlinearly with network size and complexity.

The data-driven approach offers a promising trade-off between adaptability and effectiveness. Machine learning models can learn structural patterns and predict critical components for targeted attacks. However, this approach incurs high computational overhead and requires a training phase with sufficient, high-quality data under supervised learning. Computational cost can increase further under unsupervised learning due to additional steps for feature extraction and clustering. Its effectiveness depends heavily on representative training data and, for supervised learning, the ability to generalize to unseen networks with different structural properties.

Edge attacks can also be categorized under structural feature-based, damage-based, computational intelligence-based, and data-driven frameworks. Since edge attacks substantially overlap with node attacks, they are not discussed here to avoid redundancy; detailed information is available in [42].

3.3 Hierarchical Attacks to Network Controllability

Recent empirical studies reveal that targeted removals of high-degree nodes or critical edges can severely degrade network controllability [52, 89, 92]. Motivated by this vulnerability, the identification of critical components for maintaining network controllability is explored in [91], with a hierarchical attack (HA) strategy proposed, where nodes and edges are ranked into categories with different priorities for removal. The concept of *critical node* from [10] is adopted, where a node is critical if its removal immediately increases the number of driver nodes required for maintaining the network controllability; otherwise, it is non-critical. Inspired by this, *critical edges* are defined similarly: an edge is critical if its removal immediately increases the number of required driver nodes. From a greedy perspective, these elements are the most influential on the controllability, as their removal causes maximal damage; however, from a global structural perspective, such a strategy may not be optimal. Although suboptimal, the HA strategy remains highly efficient in degrading network controllability.

The HA strategy prioritizes removing critical nodes and edges, and updates their rankings dynamically throughout the attack process. Extensive experiments on synthetic and real-world networks demonstrate that exposing these critical elements helps significantly damage the controllability. From a defensive perspective, concealing critical nodes and edges is essential for designing robust networks.

3.3.1 *Hierarchical Attack Framework*

Since removing an edge or node increases the number of required driver nodes by at most 1, eliminating a critical element always causes the maximum possible damage to controllability. The framework categorizes nodes and edges by attack priority, ensuring that the highest-priority component is removed first in an attack.

3.3.1.1 *Hierarchical Node Attack*

Nodes are classified into three types: (1) *critical nodes*, whose removal increases the number of driver nodes; (2) *normal nodes*, which have no effect; and (3) *redundant nodes*, whose removal conversely improves controllability. Unlike edges, there are no subcritical nodes because a unique perfect matching ensures that all nodes are matched.

3.3.1.2 *Hierarchical Edge Attack*

Edges are similarly classified into three types: (1) *critical edges*, whose removal increases the number of driver nodes; (2) *subcritical edges*, which do not affect driver nodes but increase unmatched nodes; and (3) *normal edges*, which affect neither. Subcritical and normal edges are non-critical. Attack priorities follow this hierarchy: first critical, then subcritical, and finally normal edges. Subcritical edges appear only when a unique perfect matching exists; breaking this matching is more harmful than removing a normal edge.

3.3.2 *Computational Complexity*

Computing network controllability, primarily through determining the number of required driver nodes, has a complexity of $O(m \cdot \sqrt{n})$ using the Hopcroft–Karp algorithm, where n is the number of nodes and m is the number of edges. In hierarchical node or edge attacks, iterative evaluation of criticality introduces additional computational overhead, approximately $O\left(\sum_{i=1}^{|\mathcal{E}^*|}(i \cdot \sqrt{n})\right)$, where $|\mathcal{E}^*|$ denotes the number of edges in the maximum matching. Since critical nodes or edges must belong to the matching set, repeated calculations become a significant burden for large-scale networks. Because such strategies are highly time-consuming, and this book aims to reveal controllability from various perspectives, hierarchical attacks are not included in extensive comparisons in this and subsequent chapters. Instead, commonly adopted random and maximum-degree attacks are employed. For possible interest, detailed results on the performance of hierarchical attacks are reported in [91].

3.4 Attack Simulations and Practical Stopping Criterion

3.4.1 *Attack Simulations*

Attack simulations aim to evaluate controllability robustness by using computer programs to simulate the attack process, which can be extended to investigate other network functionalities.

Given a general attack simulation framework applicable to any robustness metric, such as those defined in Equations (3.1), (3.2) and (3.3), the process can be expressed as

$$g(i) = f(\mathrm{ATK}(\mathcal{G}_{i-1} \setminus \{v_i\}, \{e_i\})), \tag{3.6}$$

where $\mathcal{G}_{i-1} = \{\mathcal{V}_{i-1}, \mathcal{E}_{i-1}\}$ represents the residual network with node set $\mathcal{V}_{i-1}$ and edge set $\mathcal{E}_{i-1}$ before the i-th attack takes place, ATK$(\cdot)$ denotes an attack strategy that purposefully removes nodes $\{v_i\}$ and edges $\{e_i\}$, $f(\cdot)$ represents the measure function for remaining the concerned functionality, and $g(i)$ records the network functionality at step i in the process.

If ATK$(\cdot)$ is a relatively deterministic strategy with minimal randomness, such as maximum-degree attacks, repeated simulations are generally unnecessary. However, for stochastic strategies, such as random attacks, evaluating network robustness based on a single run is unreliable because the randomness such as the attack order can significantly influence the outcome [50]. Therefore, multiple simulation runs are necessary, and the average result should be taken to ensure a robust, consistent and unbiased assessment.

The robustness metric used to measure the average controllability is quantified as $\frac{1}{T}\sum_{i=1}^{T} g(i)$, where T denotes the number of attack steps performed. The choice of T is critical because it determines the extent of evaluation under attack. Commonly, T is set to n, meaning that the robustness is assessed by simulating the removal of all nodes. Some case studies adopt empirical values, such as $T = 0.5n$ in [21], $T = 0.05n$ in [100], or less than $0.2n$ in [89], where n represents the initial number of nodes. In all cases, T is a user-defined hyperparameter chosen empirically based on research goals or network characteristics.

Even if a reliable importance measure $\mathcal{F}$ for nodes or edges can be identified, simulation-based metrics still require careful parameter settings, such as the numbers of attack steps and repeated runs, to reach reasonable results on the robustness. Moreover, determining a truly reliable importance measure $\mathcal{F}$ remains a highly challenging task.

3.4.2 *Practical Stopping Criterion for Attack Simulations*

In network theory, connectedness describes whether nodes are mutually reachable. For undirected networks, a graph is connected if every pair of nodes is linked by at least one path; otherwise, it is disconnected and decomposes into multiple *connected components*, each being a maximal subset of nodes in which every node is reachable. For directed networks, two notions apply: a graph is *strongly connected* if every node can reach every other node via a directed path, and (*weakly*) *connected* if this property holds when edge directions are ignored. Strong connectivity implies weak connectivity, but not vice versa. These concepts, together with connected components, are fundamental for analyzing dynamical cohesion, structural robustness, and information transmission in complex networks.

Successive node attacks progressively disconnect the network, increasing the number of connected components. Network destruction manifests regarding both functional loss and topological fragmentation, which can be quantified by tracking the variation in connected components throughout the attack process. Initially, a connected network consists of a single connected component. As nodes and edges are removed, the network is split into multiple components. Eventually, only isolated nodes remain.

Under targeted attacks, isolated nodes remain unaffected until all adjacent neighbors in every component are removed. The number of connected components typically rises during the early stages of the attack as fragmentation occurs, then declines as most nodes become isolated. The peak of this curve marks the destruction threshold, indicating the point at which the network has fully decomposed into small connected components.

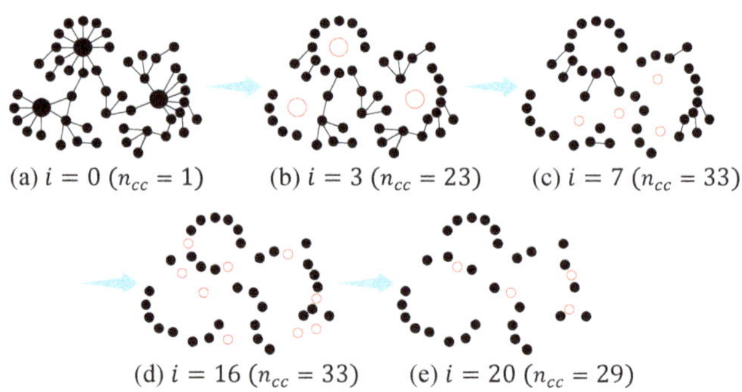

Fig. 3.1: An example of a maximum-degree node attack: i denotes the number of attack steps; the value in parentheses indicates the current number of connected components (n_{cc}); red dashed circles highlight the most recently removed nodes.

As illustrated by Figure 3.1, the network becomes highly fragmented at $i = 7$, where the number of small connected components reaches its peak ($n_{cc} = 33$; and at $i = 16$, all components are isolated, meaning that the structure no longer qualifies as a network. Therefore, in practical evaluations of destruction-based robustness, remaining functionality should not be considered beyond $i = 7$ or $i = 16$ in this example, depending on the application. At this point, the network can be regarded as being destroyed, and the robustness evaluation process should be terminated.

While this example focuses on the number of connected components and primarily addresses controllability, it is unnecessary to extend attack simulations until all nodes are removed. Once the network becomes highly fragmented, e.g. leaving only isolated nodes, the ratio of required driver nodes approaches 100%, which indicates that further evaluation of functionality is meaningless. Figure 3.2 illustrates a typical scenario of evaluating the controllability robustness, where the driver nodes are marked.

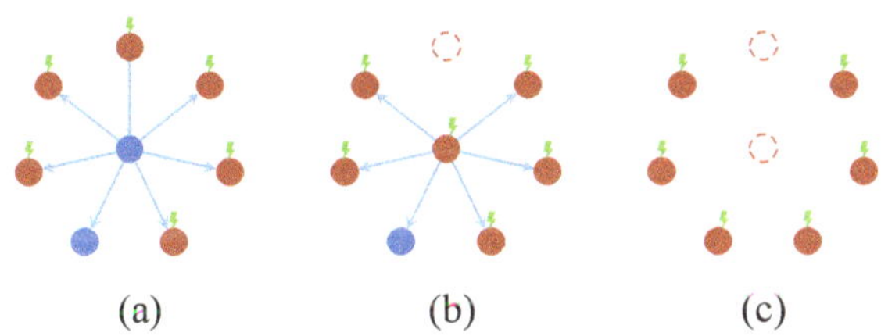

Fig. 3.2: Illustration of node attack simulation: (a) original network; (b) after a node is removed, controllability of the remaining network is recalculated; (c) once the network becomes fully disconnected, further controllability evaluation is unnecessary. Red dashed circles indicate the most recently removed nodes, and green thunder symbols represent control inputs.

A state of severe network destruction is adopted as the *stopping criterion* for robustness measure. The indicator of topological fragmentation is suitable for assessing controllability robustness but is not tied to controllability robustness or any specific network functionality. However, because isolated nodes may appear at any stage of a random attack, this turning point does not represent a precise threshold of destruction. Nevertheless, it provides a practical reference for evaluating topological degradation under various attacks, which typically prioritize node importance disregarding isolated nodes.

Based on the above analysis and discussion, a general-purpose stopping criterion for measuring network functionality robustness is proposed as follows [101]. Let $n_{cc}(i)$ denote the number of *connected components* after i node attacks. The turning point of $n_{cc}(i)$, corresponding to its maximum value, is defined as

$$T_p = \arg\max_i n_{cc}(i)\,, \tag{3.7}$$

where T_p represents the peak position of the n_{cc} curve and serves as a practical *stopping criterion* for robustness measure and attack simulation. When the number of attacks is less than T_p, the networked system is considered intact. When the number of attacks exceeds T_p, the system is deemed to have undergone *severe destruction*, and its functionality should no longer be evaluated.

Substituting $T = T_p$ into Equations (3.1), (3.2), and (3.3) provides a more practical and reasonable stopping criterion for the metrics. Note that $n_{cc}(T_p)$ denotes the maximum number of connected components, which is different from the concept of the largest connected component.

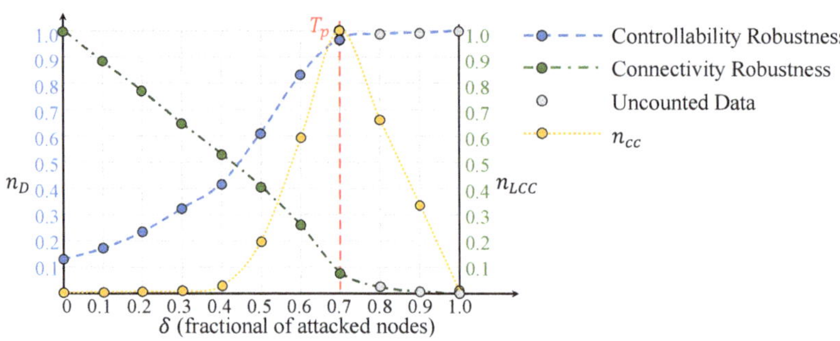

Fig. 3.3: An example of the stopping criterion indicated by the red vertical line at the peak of the normalized number of connected components (yellow circles). Blue and green circles represent data points included in robustness evaluation, whereas gray circles beyond T_p are excluded.

Figure 3.3 illustrates an example of the stopping criterion T_p, shown by the red dashed line, determined at the peak of n_{cc} according to Equation (3.7). Both controllability robustness and connectivity robustness are considered: the blue dashed curve represents controllability robustness, quantified by the ratio of required driver nodes n_D, which increases as the network becomes progressively fragmented, while the green dashed curve represents connectivity robustness, denoted by n_{LCC} as the fraction of nodes in the largest connected component, which decreases monotonically with δ. The yellow dotted curve depicts the normalized number of connected components, reaching its maximum at T_p. This peak serves as the stopping criterion for measuring both robustness indicators, beyond which the network is regarded as severely degraded and further functionality evaluation is no longer needed. Gray circles correspond to data points beyond T_p that are not counted in the robustness measure. As observed, both controllability robustness and connectivity robustness become negligible beyond this point, while including these extreme values could distort the true robustness assessment.

3.5 Analytical Modeling of the Controllability Degeneration Process

Analytical modeling and approximation methods rely on complete knowledge of the network structure, as well as full information about the attack pattern, which is common in many network-related studies, particularly in scenarios such as random attacks that can be effectively represented in mathematical form [92, 102]. By analyzing the network adjacency matrix, initial controllability configurations and critical components can be identified, while knowledge of the attack strategy enables modeling the structural evolution during attacks and thus the degeneration process of the network controllability. This approach allows the controllability curve under random edge-removal attacks to be approximated by modeling the uniform random removal of critical edges [92]. These analytical techniques are essential for estimating both controllability robustness [92] and reachability-based controllability robustness [83] under random edge-removal attacks.

In Erdős–Rényi (ER) model networks [49], analytical approximation benefits from the similarity between their generative process and the reverse process of randomly removing edges from a fully-connected network. Based on average degree, random-graph networks can be classified as dense, median, or sparse. The hybrid approximation (HyA) method incorporates this classification and leverages prior structural knowledge to predict controllability curves with high accuracy [103]. The following discussion focuses on analytical approximation techniques for predicting controllability curves in random-graph networks subjected to random edge-removal attacks. Although these methods provide highly precise predictions, their applicability remains limited to this specific context.

3.5.1 *Initial Critical Edge-based Approximation*

The initial critical edge-based approximation (ICA) introduces a two-stage method for estimating controllability robustness based on initial critical edges [92]. A *critical edge* is defined as an edge whose removal increases the number of driver nodes by exactly one to preserve the full controllability of the network [10].

The ICA scheme operates as follows. Given a network, let the total number of critical edges be m_c, the ratio of critical edges be $r_c = \frac{m_c}{m}$, the ratio of removed edges be $r_i = \frac{i}{m}$ ($i = 0, 1, 2, \ldots, m$, $r_i \in [0, 1]$), and the number of driver nodes in the initial (non-attacked) network be $n_D^{[0]}$. Under this framework, ICA approximates the controllability curve as follows:

$$\hat{n}_D = \begin{cases} \frac{1}{n}\left(n_D^{[0]} + r_i \cdot m_c\right), & \text{if } r_i \le r_c\,, \\ \frac{1}{n}\left(p_0 \cdot \delta^2 + p_1 \cdot \delta + p_2\right), & \text{if } r_i > r_c\,, \end{cases} \tag{3.8}$$

where $\hat{n}_D$ represents the approximation of n_D, with parameters

$$\begin{cases} p_0 = \dfrac{n - n_D^{[0]} \cdot m_c}{n \cdot (1 - r_c)^2}\,, \\ p_1 = \dfrac{m_c}{n} - 2p_0 r_c\,, \\ p_2 = 1 - \dfrac{m_c}{n} + p_0 \cdot (2r_c - 1)\,. \end{cases} \tag{3.9}$$

This formulation is derived from the geometric shape of the controllability curve.

ICA is a two-phase approximation that effectively estimates controllability curves under random edge-removal attacks when the initial network contains a substantial number of critical edges, i.e., r_c is relatively high (for example $r_c > 0.2$). However, the approximation performance deteriorates significantly when r_c is low. Moreover, the ratio of critical edges changes dynamically throughout the attack process [91].

3.5.2 *Similarity between Construction and Attack Processes in ER Networks*

Erdős–Rényi (ER) networks [49] are generated by connecting each pair of the n given nodes with probability $p \in [0, 1]$. For a network with n nodes and m edges, this probability can be approximated as

$$p \approx \frac{m}{\binom{n}{2}} = \frac{2m}{n(n-1)}\,,$$

yielding networks with approximately m edges. Alternatively, ER networks can be constructed by randomly selecting m edges from the $\binom{n}{2}$ possible undirected edges, or equivalently, by removing $\binom{n}{2} - m$ edges from a fully-connected network [104]. Both approaches produce networks with exactly m edges, and the algorithms for edge addition and removal are statistically equivalent, with the latter resembling a random edge-removal attack [104]. According to [105], if $p > \frac{(1+\epsilon)\ln n}{n}$, the network is almost surely connected; if $p < \frac{(1-\epsilon)\ln n}{n}$, it is almost surely disconnected, where $\epsilon = o(1)$.

Now, let $m_1 < m_2$ denote the number of edges in networks $\mathcal{G}_1$ and $\mathcal{G}_2$, respectively, both with n nodes. Performing a uniform random edge-removal attack on $\mathcal{G}_2$ and removing $m_2 - m_1$ edges yields a network $\mathcal{G}_2'$ with n nodes and m_1 edges. Although $\mathcal{G}_2'$ is structurally different from $\mathcal{G}_1$, the uniform random edge addition process used to generate $\mathcal{G}_1$ and $\mathcal{G}_2$ and the inverse process of uniform random edge removal that produces $\mathcal{G}_2'$ make these two networks statistically equivalent. This property is often overlooked when robustness is evaluated using the edge-removal ratio r_i instead of the absolute number of edges removed. Statistically equivalent ER networks exhibit similar robustness under random edge-removal attacks. However, this property is specific to ER networks due to its consistent generation and attack dynamics, which may not be applicable to other network models [103].

3.5.3 *Hybrid Approximation of Controllability Robustness*

The hybrid approximation (HyA) approach leverages the structural similarity between ER network generation and the reverse process of random edge-removal attacks. HyA classifies ER networks into dense, median, or sparse categories, since network density is one of the key major factors that influences the network controllability [67]. Based on this classification, HyA applies a three-phase approximation scheme that integrates analytical modeling with density-aware adjustments to predict controllability curves under random edge-removal attacks with high accuracy [103].

An ER network can be classified into three categories based on two threshold parameters, σ_1 and σ_2, where $\sigma_1 < \sigma_2$:

- **Dense**: If an ER network has an average degree $\langle k \rangle \geq \sigma_2$, it is considered to be dense. Such a network can retain full controllability during the early stage of edge removals, which is typically a short period. To estimate the controllability curve, a three-phase approximation is applied as follows:

$$\hat{n}_D = \begin{cases} \frac{1}{n}, & \text{if } 0 \leq r_i \leq \dfrac{m - \sigma_2 \cdot n}{m}, \\ \frac{1}{n}(q_2 r_i^2 + q_1 r_i + q_0), & \text{if } \dfrac{m - \sigma_1 \cdot n}{m} \leq r_i \leq 1, \\ \frac{1}{n}(p_1 r_i + p_0), & \text{if } \dfrac{m - \sigma_2 \cdot n}{m} < r_i < \dfrac{m - \sigma_1 \cdot n}{m}. \end{cases} \tag{3.10}$$

where $\hat{n}_D$ denotes the approximation of n_D, and $r_i \in [0, 1]$ is the ratio of removed edges. The coefficients q_0, q_1, and q_2 are computed using the following quadratic formula:

$$\hat{n}_D = \frac{1}{n}\left(q_2 r_i^2 + q_1 r_i + q_0\right), \tag{3.11}$$

by substituting $(r_i, \hat{n}_D)$ with the values $(1,1)$, $\left(\frac{m-\sigma_1 n}{m}, n_D^{\left[\frac{m-\sigma_1 n}{m}\right]}\right)$, and $\left(\frac{m-n}{m}, n_D^{\left[\frac{m-n}{m}\right]}\right)$, respectively. Here, $n_D^{[t]}$ represents the ratio of required driver nodes after a proportion t of edges has been removed. The values of q_0, q_1, and q_2 are determined by solving a system of three linear equations:

- $(1,1)$ represents the endpoint of the controllability curve, where $r_i = \frac{m}{m} = 1$ and $\hat{n}_D^{[1]} = 1$. This condition applies to any network, indicating that, when all edges have been removed, the ratio of the required driver nodes reaches 100%.
- $\left(\frac{m-\sigma_1 \cdot n}{m}, n_D^{\left[\frac{m-\sigma_1 \cdot n}{m}\right]}\right)$ represents the controllability of a network with n nodes and $\sigma_1 \cdot n$ edges. Any n-node network with average degree $\langle k \rangle > \sigma_1$ will pass through this state during edge attacks, where a "state" corresponds to a network density or average degree.
- $\left(\frac{m-n}{m}, n_D^{\left[\frac{m-n}{m}\right]}\right)$ indicates the controllability of a network with n nodes and n edges, which is a necessary intermediate state for any dense network.

Alternatively, higher-order equations can be considered, such as

$$\hat{n}_D = \frac{1}{n}\left(q_3 r_i^3 + q_2 r_i^2 + q_1 r_i + q_0\right),$$

where the coefficients q_0, q_1, q_2, and q_3 are determined by solving a system of equations using the points $(1,1)$, $\left(\frac{m-\sigma_1 \cdot n}{m}, n_D^{\left[\frac{m-\sigma_1 \cdot n}{m}\right]}\right)$, $\left(\frac{m-2n}{m}, n_D^{\left[\frac{m-2n}{m}\right]}\right)$, and $\left(\frac{m-n}{m}, n_D^{\left[\frac{m-n}{m}\right]}\right)$.

In Equation (3.10), the transition stage $\frac{m-\sigma_2 \cdot n}{m} < r_i < \frac{m-\sigma_1 \cdot n}{m}$ is linearly approximated by

$$p_1 = \frac{n_D^{[j]} - n_D^{[i]}}{r_j - r_i}, \quad p_0 = n_D^{[i]} - r_i \cdot \frac{n_D^{[j]} - n_D^{[i]}}{r_j - r_i},$$

which defines a straight line between the points $(r_i, n_D^{[i]})$ and $(r_j, n_D^{[j]})$, where $r_i = \frac{m-\sigma_2 \cdot n}{m}$, $n_D^{[i]} = \frac{1}{n}$, $r_j = \frac{m-\sigma_1 \cdot n}{m}$, and $n_D^{[j]} = \frac{1}{n}\left(q_2\left(\frac{m-\sigma_1 \cdot n}{m}\right)^2 + q_1\left(\frac{m-\sigma_1 \cdot n}{m}\right) + q_0\right)$.

- **Sparse**: If an ER network has an average degree $\langle k \rangle < \sigma_1$, it is considered a sparse ER network, for which more than $\frac{1}{n}$ driver nodes are required to ensure the full controllability of the initial network before any attack is performed. For such sparse networks, ICA [92] is used to approximate the controllability curves. Let the number of critical edges be m_c, the ratio of critical edges be $r_c = \frac{m_c}{m}$, and the initial driver node ratio be $n_D^{[0]}$. ICA approximates the curve as follows:

$$\hat{n}_D = \begin{cases} \frac{1}{n}(n_D^{[0]} + r_i \cdot m_c), & \text{if } r_i \le r_c\,, \\ \frac{1}{n}(p_2 r_i^2 + p_1 r_i + p_0), & \text{if } r_i > r_c\,, \end{cases} \tag{3.12}$$

with parameters $p_2 = \frac{n - n_D^{[0]} \cdot m_c}{n(1-r_c)^2}$, $p_1 = \frac{m_c}{n} - 2p_2 r_c$, and $p_0 = 1 - \frac{m_c}{n} + p_2(2r_c - 1)$ [92].

- **Median**: For a median ER network where $\sigma_1 \le \langle k \rangle < \sigma_2$, the initial controllability is $n_D \approx \frac{1}{n}$, but n_D increases immediately once an attack begins. A three-phase approximation is used to model the controllability curve tendency, slightly differing from Equation (3.10), as follows:

$$\hat{n}_D = \begin{cases} \frac{1}{n}(n_D^{[0]} + r_i \cdot m_c), & \text{if } 0 \le r_i \le r_c\,, \\ \frac{1}{n}(q_2 r_i^2 + q_1 r_i + q_0), & \text{if } \dfrac{m - \sigma_1 \cdot n}{m} \le r_i \le 1\,, \\ \frac{1}{n}(p_1 r_i + p_0), & \text{if } r_c < r_i < \dfrac{m - \sigma_1 \cdot n}{m}\,, \end{cases} \tag{3.13}$$

where the coefficients q_0, q_1, and q_2 are computed according to Equation (3.11), by substituting $(r_i, \hat{n}_D)$ with the values $(1, 1)$, $\left(\frac{m-\sigma_1 \cdot n}{m}, n_D^{\left[\frac{m-\sigma_1 \cdot n}{m}\right]}\right)$, and $\left(\frac{m-n}{m}, n_D^{\left[\frac{m-n}{m}\right]}\right)$, respectively. The transition stage $\frac{m-\sigma_2 \cdot n}{m} < r_i < \frac{m-\sigma_1 \cdot n}{m}$ is linearly approximated by

$$p_1 = \frac{n_D^{[j]} - n_D^{[i]}}{r_j - r_i}\,, \quad p_0 = n_D^{[i]} - r_i \cdot \frac{n_D^{[j]} - n_D^{[i]}}{r_j - r_i}\,,$$

which defines a line between $(r_i, n_D^{[i]})$ and $(r_j, n_D^{[j]})$, where $r_i = r_c$, $n_D^{[i]} = \frac{1}{n}(n_D^{[0]} + r_c \cdot m_c)$, $r_j = \frac{m-\sigma_1 \cdot n}{m}$, and $n_D^{[j]} = \frac{1}{n}\left(q_2\left(\frac{m-\sigma_1 \cdot n}{m}\right)^2 + q_1\left(\frac{m-\sigma_1 \cdot n}{m}\right) + q_0\right)$.

Formally, a pseudo-code for the hybrid approximation scheme is presented in Algorithm 1.

The parameter σ_1 is fixed at $\sigma_1 = 3$ for all cases, while σ_2 varies with the network size n and is denoted as $\sigma_2(n)$. Each specific value of $\sigma_2(n)$ is

Algorithm 1: Hybrid Approximation

Input : Number of nodes n; number of edges m; adjacency matrix $\mathbf{A}$; threshold values σ_1 and σ_2

Output: Controllability approximation $\hat{n}_D$

$\langle k \rangle = \frac{2m}{n}$;
if $\langle k \rangle \geq \sigma_2$ **then**
    Calculate $\hat{n}_D$ using Equation (3.10); `// dense case`
else
    if $\langle k \rangle < \sigma_1$ **then**
        Calculate $\hat{n}_D$ using Equation (3.12); `// sparse case`
    else
        Calculate $\hat{n}_D$ using Equation (3.13); `// median case`
    end
end

obtained numerically and empirically. In particular, $\sigma_2(n)$ is fitted using a two-term exponential model:

$$\sigma_2(n) = q_1 e^{q_2 \cdot n} + q_3 e^{q_4 \cdot n} ,$$

where $q_1 = 7.311$, $q_2 = 2.101 \times 10^{-5}$, $q_3 = -2.846$, and $q_4 = -1.143 \times 10^{-3}$. For example, $\sigma_2(2100) \approx 7.3835$. More details can be found in [103].

3.5.4 *Experimental Comparison*

The experimental comparison performed here considers three approaches: the hybrid approximation (HyA), the initial critical edge-based approximation (ICA), and the true controllability curve obtained through attack simulations (Sim). To reduce the impact of randomness, simulation results are averaged over 30 independent runs.

HyA and ICA are compared in approximating the controllability curves of ER networks with scalable sizes $n = 500, 1000, 1500$, and 2000. For each network size, four average degrees are considered: $\langle k \rangle = 2, 5, 8$, and 10, resulting in 16 ER configurations illustrated in Figure 3.4.

When $\langle k \rangle = 2$ (Figure 3.4 (a), (e), (i), and (m)), both HyA and ICA closely approximate the true controllability curves obtained through attack simulations. Since $\langle k \rangle = 2 < \sigma_1$ (with $\sigma_1 = 3$), these networks are classified as sparse, and ICA is applied according to Equation (3.12).

For $\langle k \rangle = 5$ (Figure 3.4 (b), (f), (j), and (n)), the networks exhibit medium density. In this case, the three-phase approximation (Equation (3.13)) significantly improves the accuracy.

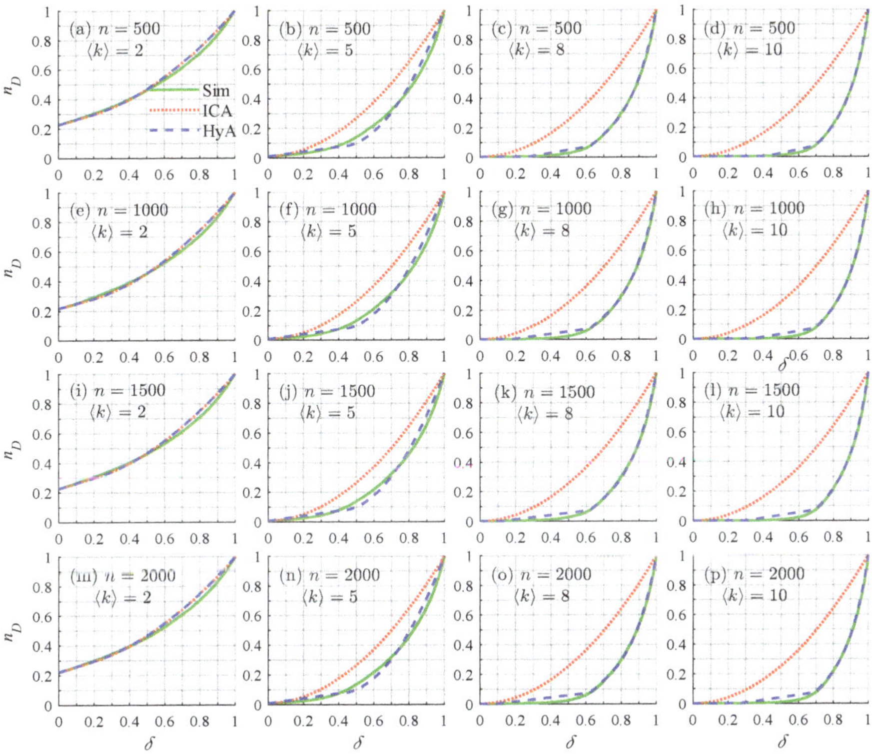

Fig. 3.4: Comparison of controllability curves approximated by ICA and HyA against reference curves obtained from attack simulations (Sim): (a)–(d) $n = 500$ with $\langle k \rangle = 2, 5, 8$, and 10, respectively; (e)–(h) $n = 1000$ with $\langle k \rangle = 2, 5, 8$, and 10; (i)–(l) $n = 1500$ with $\langle k \rangle = 2, 5, 8$, and 10; (m)–(p) $n = 2000$ with $\langle k \rangle = 2, 5, 8$, and 10.

As $\langle k \rangle$ increases further (Figure 3.4 (d), (h), (l), and (p)), the networks become dense, and the controllability curves flatten for $r_i < 0.4$. These cases are treated using Equation (3.10). Under such conditions, ICA fails to approximate controllability robustness, whereas HyA maintains high accuracy.

Beyond visual comparison, Table 3.2 reports the mean-squared error (MSE) and maximum error (MaxE) for quantitative evaluation. Given two sequences of data $\mathbf{y} = \{y_1, y_2, \ldots, y_m\}$ and $\hat{\mathbf{y}} = \{\hat{y}_1, \hat{y}_2, \ldots, \hat{y}_m\}$, MSE is defined as

$$\text{MSE} = \frac{1}{m}\sum_{i=1}^{m}(y_i - \hat{y}_i)^2\,, \tag{3.14}$$

and MaxE is defined as

$$\text{MaxE} = \max_{1\leq i\leq m} |y_i - \hat{y}_i|\,. \tag{3.15}$$

Table 3.2: Comparison of mean-squared error (MSE) and maximum error (MaxE) between ICA and HyA in approximating the controllability curves of ER networks under random edge-removal attacks. Bold values indicate the lower error between the two methods.

Network Size	Method	Error Type	$\langle k\rangle = 2$	$\langle k\rangle = 5$	$\langle k\rangle = 8$	$\langle k\rangle = 10$
$n = 500$	ICA	MSE	$\mathbf{4.37 \times 10^{-4}}$	1.48×10^{-2}	4.90×10^{-2}	6.82×10^{-2}
		MaxE	$\mathbf{4.02 \times 10^{-2}}$	1.91×10^{-1}	3.48×10^{-1}	4.25×10^{-1}
	HyA	MSE	$\mathbf{4.37 \times 10^{-4}}$	$\mathbf{8.76 \times 10^{-4}}$	$\mathbf{1.22 \times 10^{-4}}$	$\mathbf{8.99 \times 10^{-5}}$
		MaxE	$\mathbf{4.02 \times 10^{-2}}$	$\mathbf{6.21 \times 10^{-2}}$	$\mathbf{2.49 \times 10^{-2}}$	$\mathbf{2.30 \times 10^{-2}}$
$n = 100$	ICA	MSE	$\mathbf{3.732 \times 10^{-4}}$	1.494×10^{-2}	5.00×10^{-2}	6.86×10^{-2}
		MaxE	$\mathbf{3.74 \times 10^{-2}}$	1.91×10^{-1}	3.50×10^{-1}	4.28×10^{-1}
	HyA	MSE	$\mathbf{3.73 \times 10^{-4}}$	$\mathbf{8.19 \times 10^{-4}}$	$\mathbf{2.63 \times 10^{-4}}$	$\mathbf{1.77 \times 10^{-4}}$
		MaxE	$\mathbf{3.74 \times 10^{-2}}$	$\mathbf{6.19 \times 10^{-2}}$	$\mathbf{3.18 \times 10^{-2}}$	$\mathbf{2.93 \times 10^{-2}}$
$n = 1500$	ICA	MSE	$\mathbf{4.71 \times 10^{-4}}$	1.45×10^{-2}	4.88×10^{-2}	6.94×10^{-2}
		MaxE	$\mathbf{4.25 \times 10^{-2}}$	1.89×10^{-1}	3.45×10^{-1}	4.29×10^{-1}
	HyA	MSE	$\mathbf{4.71 \times 10^{-4}}$	$\mathbf{8.87 \times 10^{-4}}$	$\mathbf{2.70 \times 10^{-4}}$	$\mathbf{2.53 \times 10^{-4}}$
		MaxE	$\mathbf{4.25 \times 10^{-2}}$	$\mathbf{6.26 \times 10^{-2}}$	$\mathbf{3.07 \times 10^{-2}}$	$\mathbf{3.39 \times 10^{-2}}$
$n = 2000$	ICA	MSE	$\mathbf{5.26 \times 10^{-4}}$	1.52×10^{-2}	4.92×10^{-2}	6.90×10^{-2}
		MaxE	$\mathbf{4.30 \times 10^{-2}}$	1.92×10^{-1}	3.47×10^{-1}	4.30×10^{-1}
	HyA	MSE	$\mathbf{5.26 \times 10^{-4}}$	$\mathbf{9.01 \times 10^{-4}}$	$\mathbf{3.47 \times 10^{-4}}$	$\mathbf{2.72 \times 10^{-4}}$
		MaxE	$\mathbf{4.30 \times 10^{-2}}$	$\mathbf{6.48 \times 10^{-2}}$	$\mathbf{3.51 \times 10^{-2}}$	$\mathbf{3.44 \times 10^{-2}}$

As shown in Table 3.2, HyA and ICA provide similarly accurate approximations when $\langle k\rangle = 2$. However, for $\langle k\rangle \geq 5$, HyA consistently outperforms ICA, achieving lower approximation errors up to three orders of magnitude.

Figure 3.5 compares the MSE of ICA and HyA in approximating ER networks with average degrees $\langle k\rangle = 2, 3, \ldots, 20$ for networks of 200 and 500 nodes. When $\langle k\rangle = 2 < \sigma_1$, both methods yield identical results since the same approach is applied (Equation (3.12)). For $\langle k\rangle = 3, 4 \approx \sigma_1$, HyA based on Equation (3.13) clearly outperforms ICA. As $\langle k\rangle$ increases, the MSE of both methods rises, indicating reduced accuracy in denser networks. When $\langle k\rangle \geq 5 \geq \sigma_1$, HyA using Equation (3.10) significantly outperforms ICA. The performance of ICA continues to degrade with increasing $\langle k\rangle$

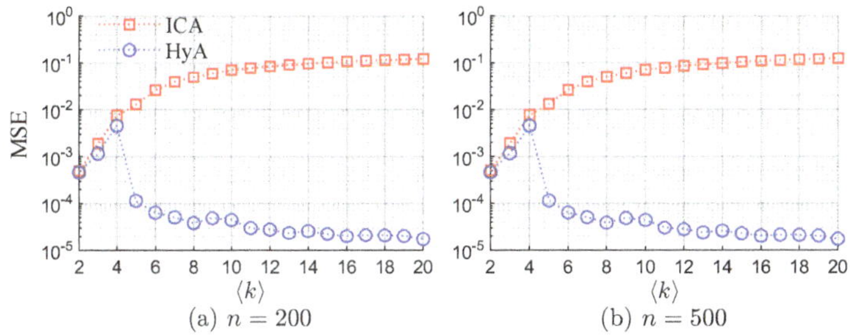

Fig. 3.5: Mean-squared error (MSE) of ICA and HyA as the average degree $\langle k \rangle$ increases from 2 to 20 in increments of 1 for two network sizes: (a) $n = 200$ and (b) $n = 500$.

due to the diminishing proportion of critical edges, which limits the ability to approximate the controllability curve. In contrast, HyA demonstrates robustness and efficiency, as reflected by steadily decreasing MSE values.

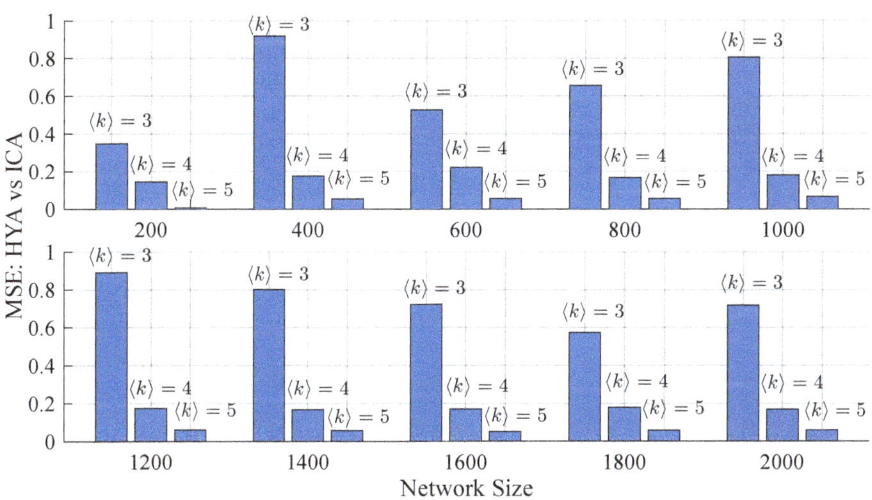

Fig. 3.6: Bar chart comparing the mean-squared error (MSE) ratio between HyA and ICA, where the ratio is computed as the MSE of HyA divided by the MSE of ICA. The average degree $\langle k \rangle$ takes values 3, 4, and 5, and the network size varies as $n = 200, 400, \ldots, 2000$.

The bar chart in Figure 3.6 compares the MSE values for HyA and ICA, where each bar represents the ratio of the MSE of HyA to the MSE of ICA. The comparison is performed for average degrees $\langle k \rangle = 3$, 4, and 5. All bars fall below 1, indicating that HyA consistently achieves lower MSE than ICA across all cases. Moreover, when $\langle k \rangle = 4$ or 5, the ratio decreases substantially, demonstrating that HyA provides significantly better approximation accuracy in networks with higher connectivity. This trend remains stable across different network sizes, confirming the robustness of HyA in denser ER networks.

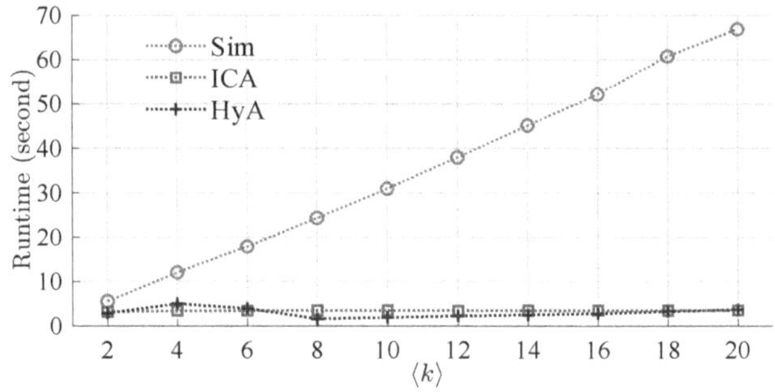

Fig. 3.7: Run-time comparison of attack simulation, ICA, and HyA as the average degree $\langle k \rangle$ varies from 2 to 20 in increments of 2, with the network size fixed at $n = 1000$.

As shown in Algorithm 1, HyA incurs minimal computational cost, which is negligible compared to conventional attack simulations. Figure 3.7 illustrates the average run=time comparison among attack simulations, ICA, and HyA. Both ICA and HyA maintain nearly constant run-time as the average degree increases, whereas the run-time of attack simulations grows significantly with network density. Since edge attacks are considered, scalability is primarily influenced by the number of edges rather than the number of nodes. These results confirm that ICA and HyA, particularly HyA, are highly time efficient approximation methods, making them well suited for large-scale networks where simulation based approaches become computationally prohibitive.

3.6 Controllability Robustness of Synthetic and Real-world Networks

In this book, eight widely-used synthetic network models are employed for simulation studies. These include the Erdős–Rényi (ER) model [49], the extreme homogeneous (EH) model [50], the generic scale free (SF) model [53], the Barabási–Albert (BA) model [51], the Newman–Watts small world (NW) model [56], the Watts–Strogatz small world (WS) model [55], the q-snapback (QS) model [58], and the random triangle (RT) model [62].

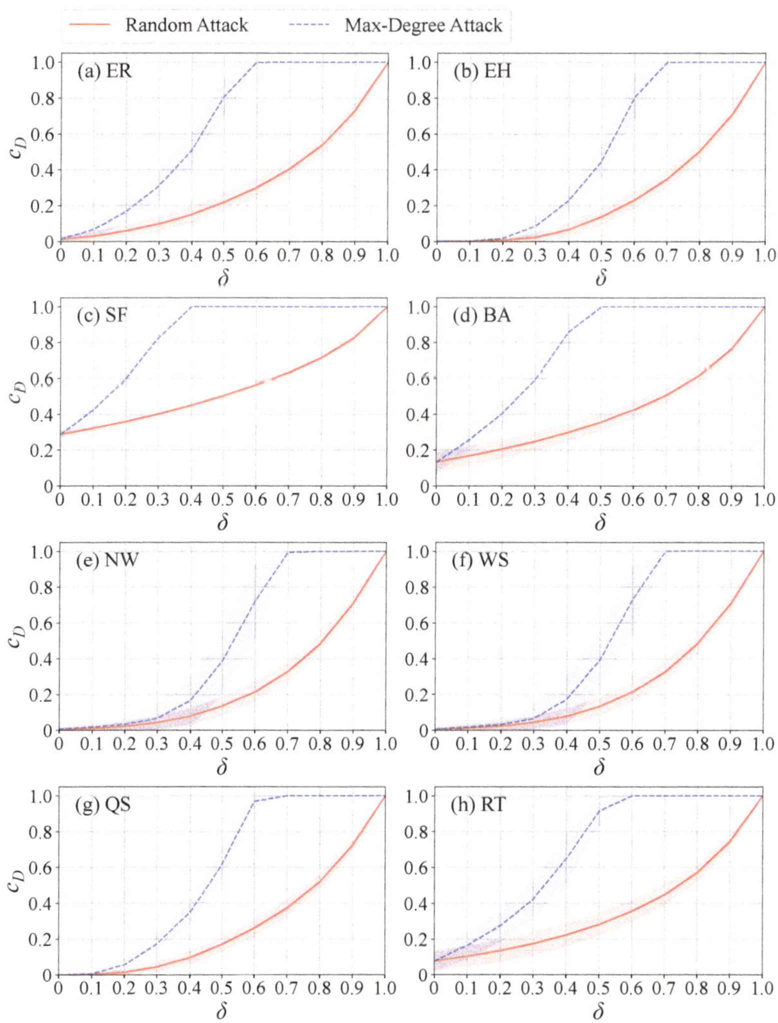

Fig. 3.8: Controllability robustness of synthetic networks with network size $n \in [400, 600]$ and average degree $\langle k \rangle \in [3, 5]$ under random *node*-removal attacks and maximum-degree *node*-removal attacks.

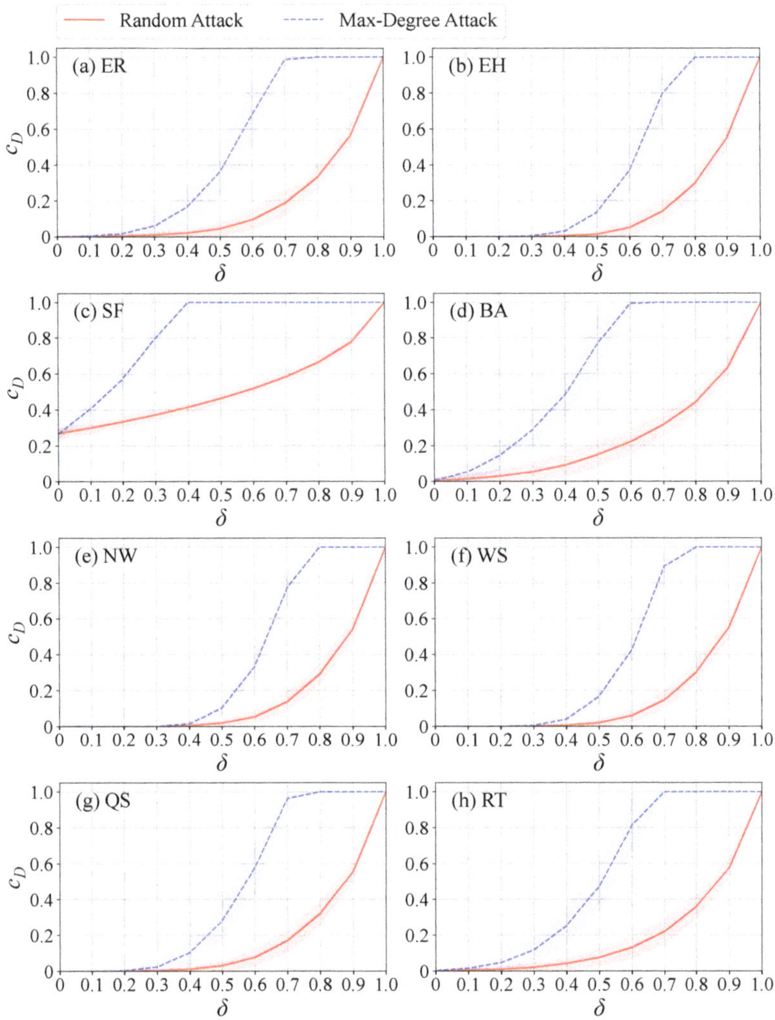

Fig. 3.9: Controllability robustness of synthetic networks with network size $n \in [800, 1200]$ and average degree $\langle k \rangle \in [5, 10]$ under random *node*-removal attacks and maximum-degree *node*-removal attacks.

Six real-world network datasets are used: the Github Stargazers (GIT) dataset [63], the Deezer ego networks (DEE) [63], the protein interaction network (PRO) [64], the Dobson and Doig dataset (DD) [65], the scientific collaboration network (COL) [66], and the Reddit interaction networks (RED) [66].

The generation mechanisms of the synthetic models are described in Subsection 2.2.1, and detailed information on the real-world datasets is provided in Subsection 2.2.2.

Figures 3.8 and 3.9 present the controllability robustness curves of synthetic networks with size $n \in [400, 600]$ (average degree $\langle k \rangle \in [3, 5]$) and $n \in [800, 1200]$ (average degree $\langle k \rangle \in [5, 10]$), respectively. Two node-based attack strategies are considered: random attacks and maximum-degree node-removal attacks. For each synthetic model, 500 randomly generated instances are simulated. In the plots, solid and dotted lines represent the mean controllability values, while shaded regions in matching colors indicate standard deviations. The evaluation metric is defined in Equation (3.1).

Consistent with the observations in Figure 2.1, the initial controllability varies across network types. ER, EH, NW, WS, and QS exhibit relatively strong initial controllability, whereas heterogeneous networks show weaker performance at the outset.

A comparison of Figures 3.8 and 3.9 reveals that increasing the average degree from $[3, 5]$ to $[5, 10]$ enhances initial controllability across all synthetic models. In particular, ER, EH, NW, WS, and QS maintain stable controllability when fewer than 0.2 of nodes are attacked. Regardless of the network size or density, maximum-degree node-removal attacks consistently cause more severe degradation than random attacks, a trend clearly observed from all figures.

Figures 3.10 and 3.11 present the controllability robustness of synthetic networks with size $n \in [400, 600]$ (average degree $\langle k \rangle \in [3, 5]$) and $n \in [800, 1200]$ (average degree $\langle k \rangle \in [5, 10]$), respectively, under edge-based attack strategies. Specifically, random edge-removal attacks and maximum-degree edge-removal attacks are simulated, where edge degree is computed as the sum of the degrees of the two nodes connected by the edge. For each synthetic model, 500 randomly generated instances are evaluated. Similar trends are observed as shown in Figures 3.8 and 3.9, indicating that edge-based attacks produce impacts on controllability robustness comparable to those of node-based attacks.

Figures 3.12 and 3.13 present the controllability robustness of real-world networks. Two randomly selected instances from each dataset are evaluated. Solid and dotted lines represent the controllability trends of individual network instances, assessed using the robustness metric defined in Equation (3.1). Similarly to synthetic networks, different real-world networks exhibit distinct initial controllability levels and varying response behaviors under

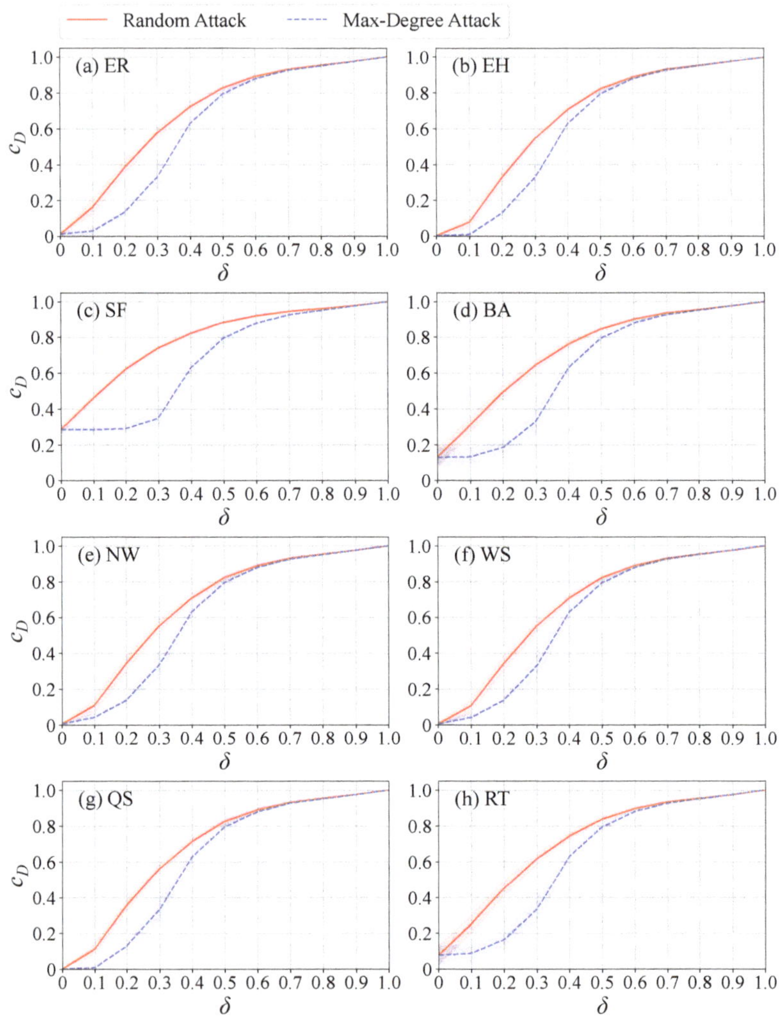

Fig. 3.10: Controllability robustness of synthetic networks with network size $n \in [400, 600]$ and average degree $\langle k \rangle \in [3, 5]$ under random *edge*-removal attacks and maximum-degree *edge*-removal attacks.

attacks. In all cases, attacks targeting nodes or edges with the highest degrees cause more severe degradation of network controllability compared to random attacks.

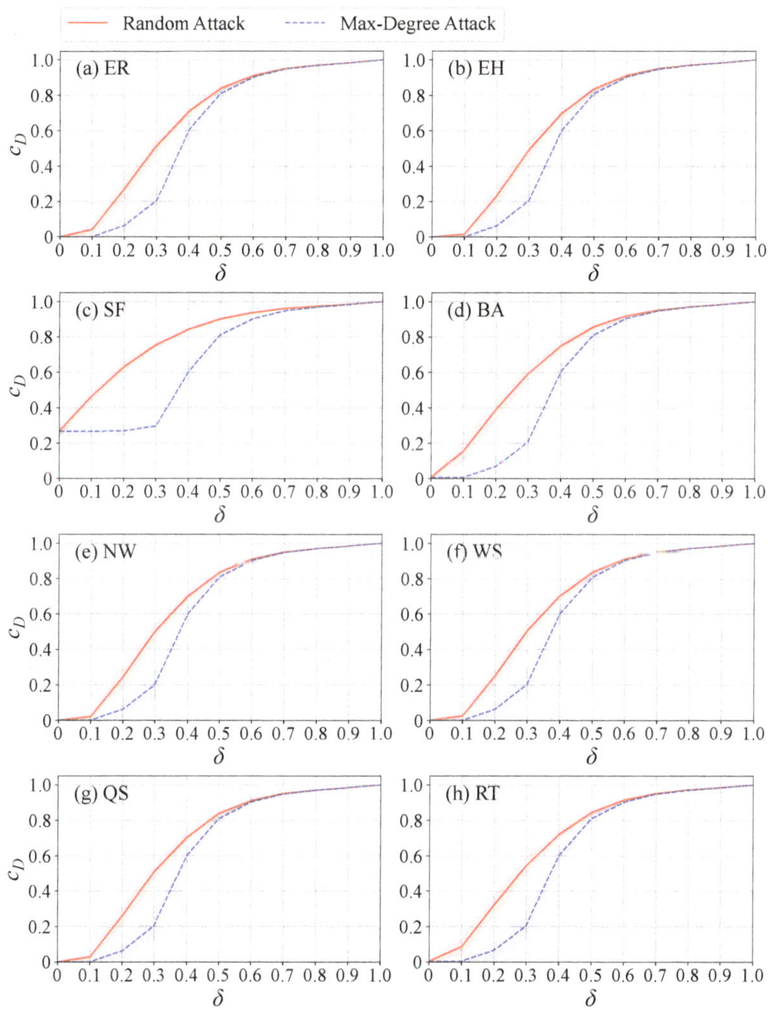

Fig. 3.11: Controllability robustness of synthetic networks with network size $n \in [800, 1200]$ and average degree $\langle k \rangle \in [5, 10]$ under random *edge*-removal attacks and maximum-degree *edge*-removal attacks.

3.7 Summary

This chapter presents a detailed examination of controllability robustness in complex networks under hazardous environments, including random failures, structural perturbations, and malicious attacks. The study formal-

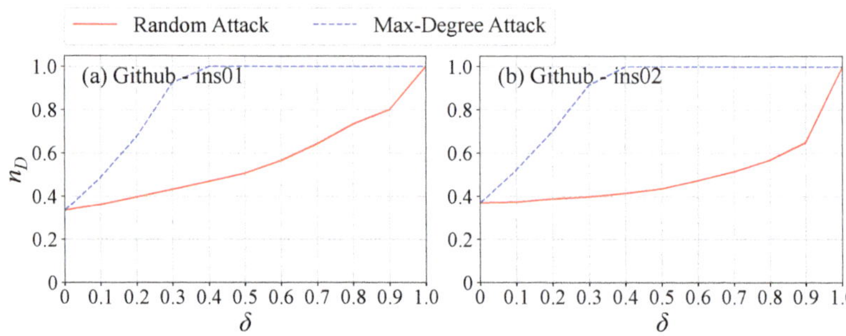

(a) Github

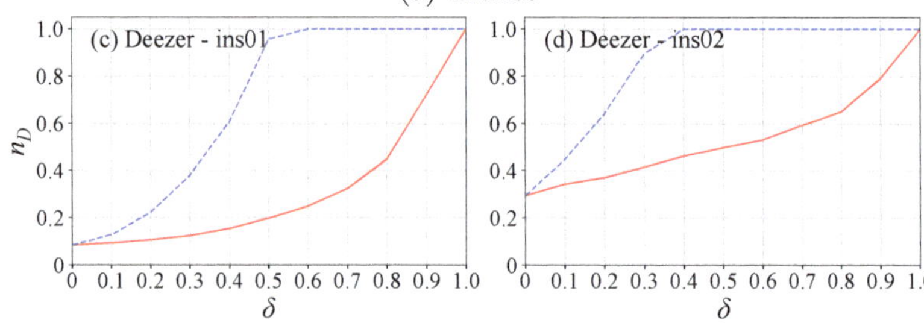

(b) Deezer

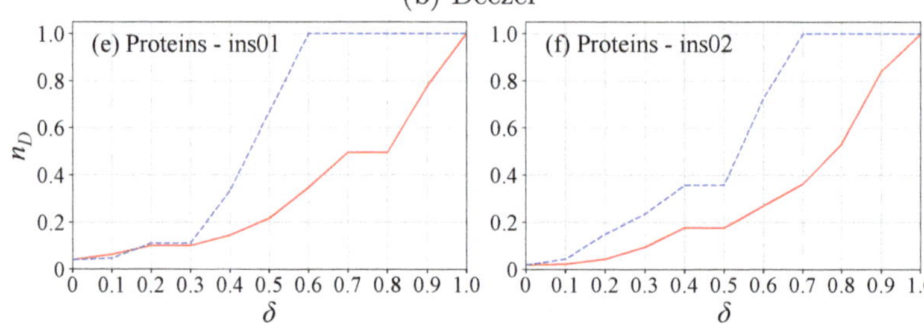

(c) Protein

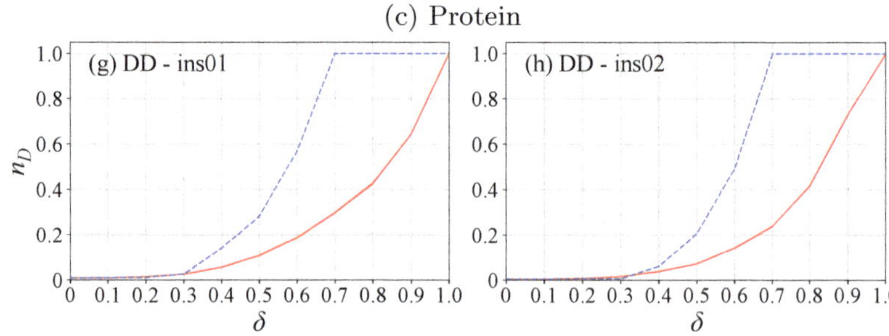

(d) DD

Fig. 3.12: Controllability robustness of real-world networks under random *node*-removal attacks and maximum-degree *node*-removal attacks.

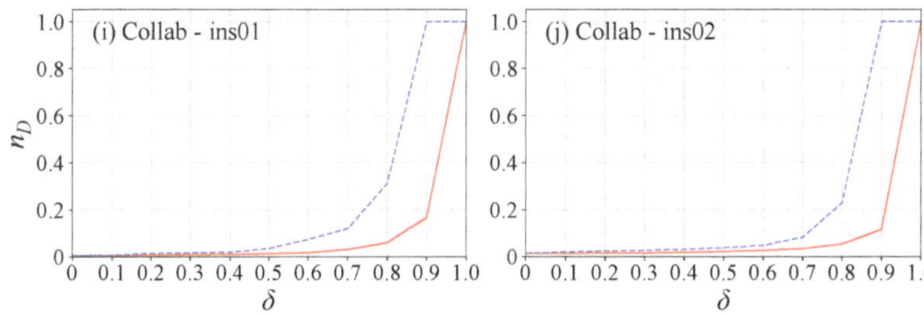

(e) Collab

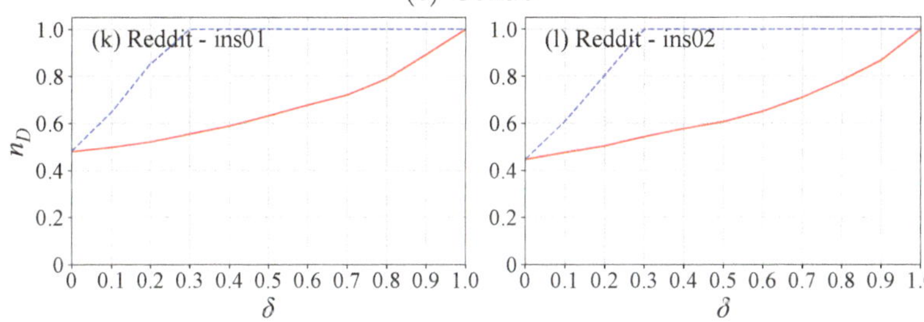

(f) Reddit

Fig. 3.12: (continued)

izes key metrics for assessing network controllability robustness, including percolation-based measures, control-centrality indicators, and reachability-based approaches. It provides a comparative analysis of their theoretical and practical implications. A comprehensive review of attack strategies follows, which includes structural heuristics, damage-based methods, computational intelligence techniques, and data-driven approaches, with particular emphasis on efficiency and effectiveness. Practical aspects of attack simulation are addressed, featuring an adaptive stopping criterion that measures the network functionality when the network becomes severely damaged, ensuring accuracy while reducing computational cost. Analytical models for approximating controllability degradation are introduced, culminating in a hybrid scheme that achieves superior precision and scalability. Extensive experiments on synthetic and real-world networks demonstrate how network density and heterogeneity influence the controllability robustness, exposing critical vulnerabilities but also opportunities for structural optimization. Collectively, these findings establish a rigorous framework for evaluating and improving controllability robustness of large-scale networked systems operating in dynamic and adversarial environments.

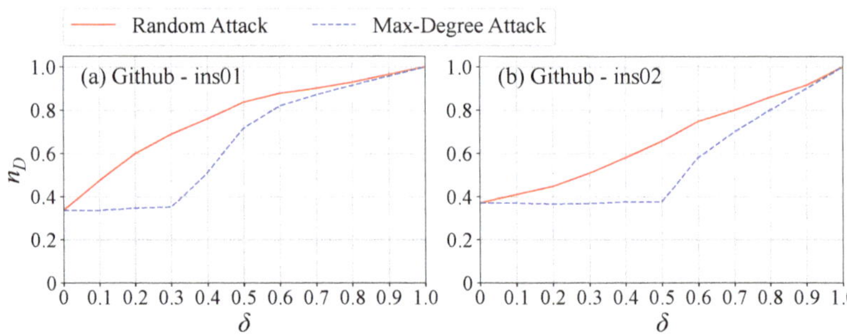

(a) Github

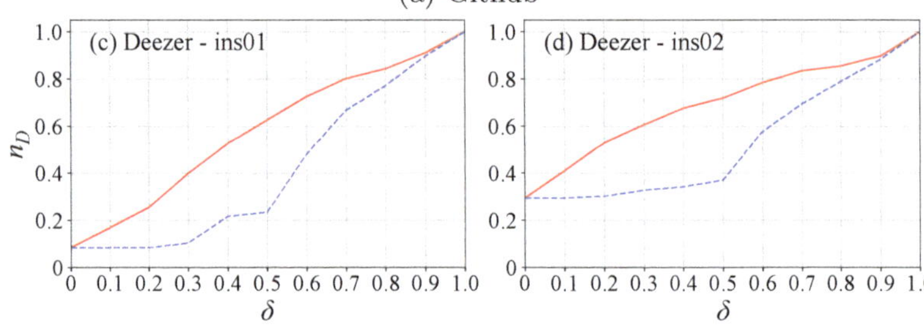

(b) Deezer

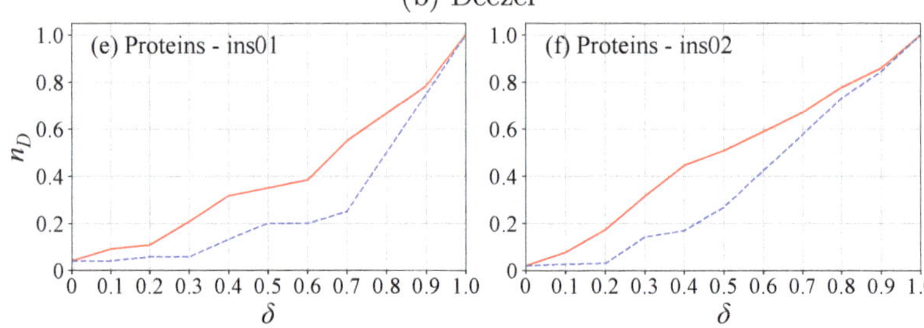

(c) Protein

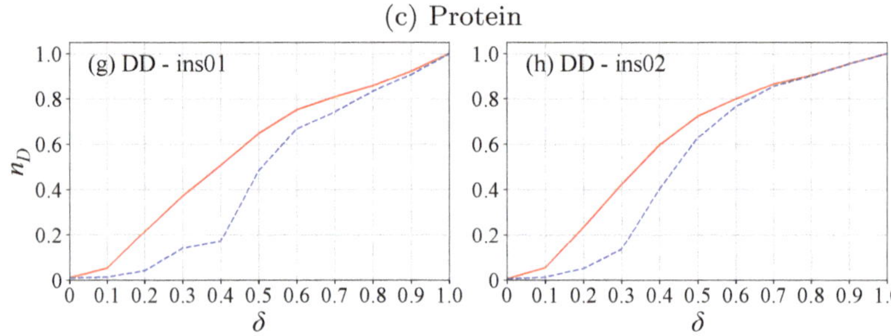

(d) DD

Fig. 3.13: Controllability robustness of real-world networks under random *edge*-removal attacks and maximum-degree *edge*-removal attacks.

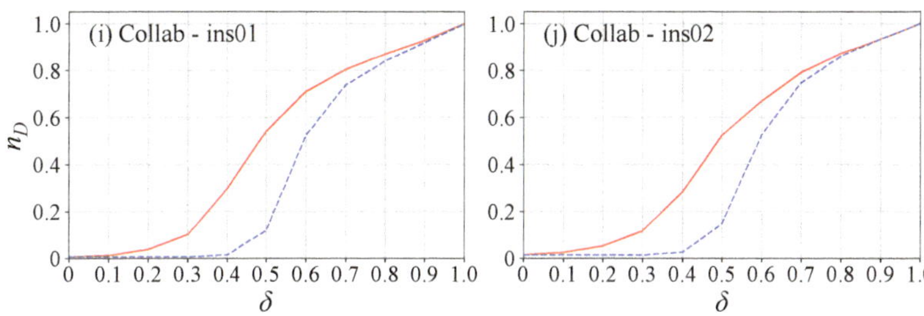

(e) Collab

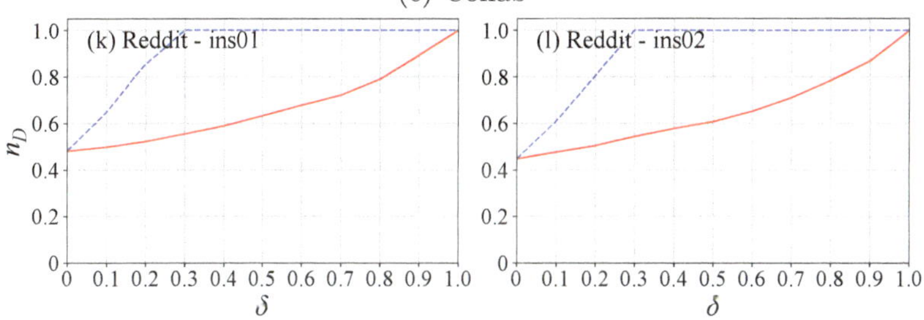

(f) Reddit

Fig. 3.13: (continued)

Chapter 4

Enhancing Controllability Robustness

This chapter investigates some techniques for enhancing network controllability robustness and provides the theoretical foundation, empirical evidence, and practical strategies for improvement. The analysis of correlations between network topology and controllability robustness highlights the absence of a universal theoretical indicator and the limitations of existing structural metrics. Representative robustness-oriented models are introduced, including multiplex congruence networks, q-snapback networks, edge-redirection q-snapback variants, and Henneberg-growth networks. Robustness enhancement approaches based on metaheuristic algorithms are also discussed. Then, an empirical necessary condition (ENC) for optimal controllability robustness is proposed, derived from exhaustive simulations on small networks and validated through extensive experiments on synthetic and real-world networks. Empirical results indicate that homogenized degree distributions, shortened path lengths, and increased number of loop structures enhance the controllability robustness. Random edge rectification (RER) is investigated as a means to reform networks toward ENC satisfaction and robustness improvement. The chapter concludes by demonstrating that RER transforms networks to highly homogeneous structures, providing a practical pathway for designing systems with improved controllability robustness.

The chapter is organized as follows. Section 4.1 gives the motivation and general background information. Section 4.2 presents network topology designs. Section 4.3 discusses robustness enhancement through edge rewiring using metaheuristic algorithms. Section 4.4 introduces an empirical necessary condition for achieving optimal controllability robustness. Finally, Section 4.5 briefly summarize the study.

4.1 Introduction

The existing approaches to enhancing controllability robustness focus on topology design and structural modification through edge rewiring and edge adding. Techniques beyond topology such as key node shielding are outside the scope of this book, since shielding depends strongly on specific schematic network contexts, while the study here is focused on general network topologies.

Although the correlation between topology and controllability robustness under non-ideal conditions has been explored, no single consistent theoretical indicator exists for accurately characterizing network controllability robustness. Over time, structural features have been extensively investigated, including centrality metrics, spectral metrics [77], and other topological properties that partially have the ability to maintain certain network functionalities under random failures or malicious attacks. Some attributes, such as assortativity [106] and natural connectivity [107], often exhibit positive correlations with robustness. High assortativity may indicate well-connected subnetworks that support overall functionality, while greater natural connectivity suggests multiple redundant paths, reducing the likelihood of disconnection when some nodes or edges fail. However, the effectiveness of these features varies with the robustness metric used and the attack strategy taken, and their correlation strengths differ across environmental scenarios. Consequently, no single feature could adequately characterize and represent robustness, and a comprehensive understanding requires jointly considering multiple features.

Moreover, under different attack strategies, controllability robustness behaves differently because the definition of node or edge *importance* changes against the types of attacks. Common measures of importance include degree and betweenness [52]. In [76], control centrality is introduced to quantify node importance, revealing that upstream neighbors are generally more influential than the node itself. Recent studies also indicate that motifs such as rings and chains generally enhance controllability robustness [57–59].

Understanding the intrinsic relationship between topology and controllability of most directed networks requires considerable effort. It was shown that clustering and modularity have little impact on the controllability, whereas degree correlation exerts a measurable effect [108]. Random networks with minimum in- and out-degrees greater than two are controllable by an extremely small fraction of driver nodes [67]. Control centrality was further studied in [76] for its role against random attacks, and controllability properties of canonical graph models were compared in [109]. For growing networks, controllability evolution was analyzed in [31]. Multi-input multi-output networked systems were examined in [32, 110], where necessary and sufficient conditions were derived. A comprehensive survey of these topics is presented in [4].

Regarding the controllability robustness under attacks, including random failures and targeted destructions, numerous studies have been reported [71,76,111–115]. For node or edge removal attacks, the key challenge is to develop measures that reflect how well networks maintain the controllability post-attack. One approach quantifies the controllability by the number of driver nodes required to restore or retain full controllability of the network, while robustness is represented by a sequence of values recording the controllability levels after successive attacks [57]. To optimize robustness, strategies often aim to preserve the highest possible network connectedness subject to attacks [71]. Under degree-preserving constraints, edge rewiring methods have been proposed to increase the connectivity among high-degree nodes, forming larger k-shell components [116]. In [77], degree-preserving rewiring was applied to optimize spectral measures, though the correlation between spectral metrics and robustness remains unclear [117]. When reliable predictive indicators exist, optimization algorithms can be employed [118–121], and multi-objective schemes are applicable with multiple indicators considered [115,122]. Simultaneous enhancement of robustness against node and edge removals was demonstrated in [123]. A common observation is that heterogeneous networks with onion-like structures exhibit strong resilience [71, 124–126]. The dynamics of alternating attack and defense strategies involving edge removal versus replenishment were studied in [127], where the connectedness of the largest cluster is used as a primary robustness measure [71]. Although connectedness robustness correlates positively with controllability robustness, the two exhibit distinct characteristics and require different measures.

4.2 Topology Designs

This section introduces four models developed to enhance controllability robustness: the multiplex congruence network constructed from the congruence theorem, the q-snapback model based on backbone and snapback edges, an improved q-snapback variant employing edge redirection, and the Henneberg growth model.

4.2.1 *Multiplex Congruence Network*

The multiplex congruence (MC) network offers a number-theoretic approach to modeling complex systems, emphasizing controllability and its robustness [68]. It encodes congruence relations among natural numbers into a multi-layered structure, where each layer reflects specific modular relationships, collectively forming a highly organized and analytically tractable network topology.

The generation mechanism of MC is defined as follows. For a given remainder r_{MC}, consider the congruence relation

$$j \equiv r_{\mathrm{MC}} \pmod{i},$$

where i, j $(i < j)$ are natural numbers. For each fixed r_{MC}, all integer pairs (i, j) satisfying this relation are identified, and a directed edge from i to j is established to represent the congruence. Imposing the constraint $j \leq n$ produces a finite layer:

$$\mathcal{G}(r_{\mathrm{MC}}, n).$$

By varying r_{MC} within $1 \leq r_{\mathrm{MC}} \leq n$, multiple layers are generated, collectively forming the multiplex congruence network [68].

Wherein, each layer exhibits a scale-free topology characterized by an out-degree distribution $P(k) \sim k^{-2}$ [68]. Within a layer $\mathcal{G}(r_{\mathrm{MC}}, n)$, nodes are organized into r_{MC} arithmetic sequences forming chains in ascending order. Each chain originates from a distinct root node, creating a hierarchical structure enriched with chains and loops.

MC networks demonstrate remarkably strong controllability: the minimum number of driver nodes equals r_{MC}. Since $r_{\mathrm{MC}} \ll n$, only a small set of controllers is required to govern very large networks, in sharp contrast to conventional scale-free networks that demand control over a substantially large fraction of nodes.

In terms of controllability robustness, targeted attacks on high-degree nodes have limited impact because chains remain intact, whereas random failures are more disruptive as the removal of a node can fragmentate chains thereby increasing the required number of controllers. This is opposite to that of typical scale-free networks, which are resilient to random failures but vulnerable to targeted attacks.

4.2.2 *q-Snapback Networks*

The enhanced controllability and robustness of MC have motivated deeper investigation into the structural factors underlying these properties. The strong controllability of MC originates from its chain-based architecture, where each chain requires only one controller at its root [10]. However, chains in MC primarily form feedforward loops, whereas feedback loops are more prevalent and practical in real-world systems. To address this issue, the snapback model replaces feedforward links with feedback connections, which substitutes congruence-based relations with uniformly random linkages. This modification introduces a large number of feedback loops, which distinguishes the snapback model from the MC model, which significantly improves the controllability robustness. In this approach, the q-snapback network (QS) was proposed by extending the multi-chain structure of MC to a multi-loop structure, incorporating feedback connections called *snapback* links based on a uniform probability distribution [58]. This design markedly enhances the network robustness. Consequent empirical attack-simulation studies demonstrate that QS outperforms MC under random failures and attacks targeting nodes with the highest betweenness, while maintaining comparable robustness to MC against attacks on highest-degree nodes.

A brief overview of the generation process is given in Subsection 2.2.1.6. The detailed mechanism for constructing QS is as follows:

(1) Let $q_{\text{QS}} \in [0, 1]$ denote the preassigned probability parameter. Each layer begins with a directed backbone chain of nodes $1, 2, \ldots, n$.
(2) For layer $r_{\text{QS}} = i$, and for every node $j = i + 1, i + 2, \ldots, n$, create backward connections to all preceding nodes $j - 1, j - 2, \ldots, i + 1$ with probability q_{QS}.
(3) Repeat this process until no additional connections can be formed, then aggregate all layers into a multiplex network:

$$\mathcal{G}(q_{\text{QS}}, n) = \bigcup_{r=1}^{n-1} \mathcal{G}_r(q_{\text{QS}}, n)\,,$$

which is referred to as the q-snapback multiplex network of size n.

For layer r_{QS} ($r_{\text{QS}} = 1, \ldots, n - 1$), the out-degree of node i ($i = 1, 2, \ldots, n$) is given by

$$k_i^{\text{out}} = \begin{cases} 1, & \text{for } i = 1, 2, \ldots, r_{\text{QS}}\,, \\ 1 + \lfloor \frac{i-1}{r_{\text{QS}}} \rfloor \cdot q_{\text{QS}}, & \text{for } i = r_{\text{QS}} + 1, \ldots, n - 1\,, \\ \lfloor \frac{i-1}{r_{\text{QS}}} \rfloor \cdot q_{\text{QS}}, & \text{for } i = n\,, \end{cases} \tag{4.1}$$

where $\lfloor \cdot \rfloor$ denotes the floor function, returning the greatest integer less than or equal to its argument.

Similarly, the in-degree of node i ($i = 1, 2, \ldots, n$) is

$$k_i^{\text{in}} = \begin{cases} \lfloor \frac{n-1}{r_{\text{QS}}} \rfloor \cdot q_{\text{QS}}, & \text{for } i = 1\,, \\ 1 + \lfloor \frac{n-i}{r_{\text{QS}}} \rfloor \cdot q_{\text{QS}}, & \text{for } i = 2, \ldots, n - r_{\text{QS}}\,, \\ 1, & \text{for } i = n - r_{\text{QS}} + 1, \ldots, n\,, \end{cases} \tag{4.2}$$

where $\lfloor \cdot \rfloor$ denotes the floor function, returning the greatest integer less than or equal to its argument.

For a QS multiplex stacked by r_{QS} layers, the out-degree of node i is

$$k_i^{\prime\text{out}} = \begin{cases} 1, & \text{for } i = 1\,, \\ 1 + \sum_{j=1}^{i-1} I_j \cdot q_{\text{QS}}, & \text{for } i = 2, 3, \ldots, n-1\,, \\ \sum_{j=1}^{n-1} I_j \cdot q_{\text{QS}}, & \text{for } i = n\,, \end{cases} \tag{4.3}$$

where I_j is an indicator function specifying whether a snapback link exists in layer j.

Similarly, the in-degree of a QS multiplex is

$$k_i^{\prime\text{in}} = \begin{cases} \sum_{j=2}^{n} I_j \cdot q_{\text{QS}}, & \text{for } i = 1\,, \\ 1 + \sum_{j=i+1}^{n} I_j \cdot q_{\text{QS}}, & \text{for } i = 2, 3, \ldots, n-1\,, \\ 1, & \text{for } i = n\,. \end{cases} \tag{4.4}$$

In Equations (4.3) and (4.4), I_j denotes an indicator variable defined by

$$I_j = \begin{cases} 1, & \text{if there exists an edge } (i, j)\,, \\ 0, & \text{otherwise}\,. \end{cases} \tag{4.5}$$

4.2.3 q-Snapback Networks with Edge Redirections

Prior studies have shown that edge redirection can enlarge maximum matchings and reduce the number of driver nodes, thereby improving the controllability robustness in various attack scenarios [10, 58, 118, 119]. Additionally, introducing randomness into edge connections, as observed from random graphs [49] and small-world networks [55], has been shown to enhance structural properties and resilience.

The QS model is constructed on a backbone chain having snapback edges added with probability $q_{\text{QS}} \in (0, 1)$, forming a directed multi-ring structure [58]. In its edge-redirection variant (QS-R), each snapback edge is reversed with probability $p_{\text{QS-R}} \in [0, 1]$, independently of q_{QS}, while backbone edges remain unchanged. When $p_{\text{QS-R}} = 0$, the network reduces to the original QS; when $p_{\text{QS-R}} = 1$, it becomes a feedforward network. In QS-R, backbone edges are never altered.

Edge redirection in QS-R may break some existing loops but simultaneously introduces new long-range loops relative to the backbone, resulting in an overall increase in loop count and length. As illustrated by Figure 4.1, where redirected edges are highlighted in red, edges $(4, 2)$ and $(7, 3)$ are redirected to $(2, 4)$ and $(3, 7)$, respectively. The redirection of edge $(4, 2)$ destroys the original loop 2–3–4–2 but creates a larger loop 2–4–5–6–2. Such transformations increase both the number and the size of loops, consequently strengthening the network controllability robustness.

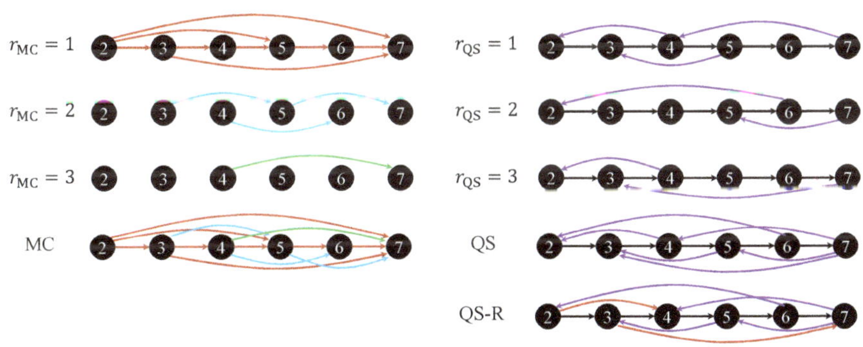

Fig. 4.1: Illustrative examples of MC, QS, and QS-R generation. Left: MC layers construct edges based on congruence relations. Right: QS introduces snapback edges uniformly across layers. Bottom right: QS-R applies edge redirection to snapback links while preserving the backbone structure.

4.2.4 *Henneberg-growth Networks*

Empirical studies have shown that multi-chain and multi-loop structures play a critical role in improving controllability robustness [57–59, 68]. The Henneberg-growth (HG) mechanism, originally developed in graph theory and widely applied to social network modeling, offers a systematic approach for generating multi-clique structures. By assigning suitable edge directions, these cliques can be transformed to interconnected rings and loops, providing a versatile framework for constructing networks with enhanced controllability robustness [60, 128].

Figure 4.2 illustrates four types of random polygon networks generated through the Henneberg-growth process. In (a), a single newcomer connects

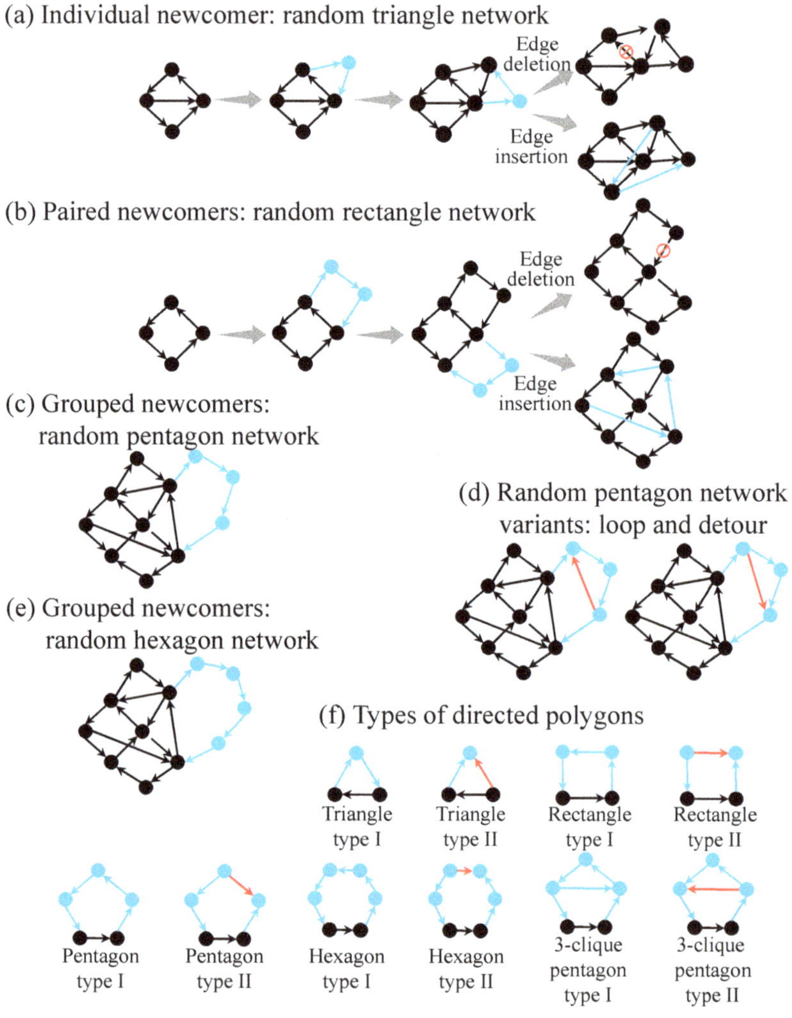

Fig. 4.2: Example of the Henneberg-growth process: (a) RT with newcomers as individuals; (b) RR with paired newcomers; (c) RP with newcomers grouped as 3-chains; (d) two RP variants with newcomers forming a looping triangle (left) and a detouring triangle (right); (e) RH with newcomers grouped as 4-chains; (f) different types of formed polygons. Blue nodes and edges indicate newcomers and new connections, while black nodes and edges represent existing nodes and edges.

to two adjacent existing nodes, forming a triangle referred to as a random triangle (RT). In (b), two newcomers connect to two adjacent nodes, creating a random rectangle (RR). In (c) and (e), newcomers join as 3-node and 4-node chains, forming random pentagons (RP) and random hexagons (RH), respectively. Notably, RP can also be constructed from a 3-clique, as shown in (d), whereas RH is restricted to 4-chains. Panel (f) summarizes the different types of directed polygons formed through these processes. Blue nodes and edges indicate newcomers and newly added connections, while black nodes and edges represent existing elements.

It is important to note that the polygons shown in Figure 4.2 are directed; the undirected case can be obtained by simply removing the arrows from the edges. The HG network family is homogeneous, with both out-degree and in-degree distributions following Poisson statistics.

4.3 Robustness Enhancement via Metaheuristic Edge-rewiring

Understanding the relationship between network structure and robustness is essential. Dense homogeneous networks typically exhibit strong connectivity, controllability, and communication resilience; however, well-designed heterogeneous and even sparse networks can outperform them in robustness [68]. In particular, onion-like heterogeneous networks with high assortativity are widely recognized for their ability to withstand targeted attacks [71, 75, 124–126].

Robustness optimization is commonly addressed through evolutionary algorithms, swarm intelligence, and other metaheuristic approaches, where appropriate robustness metrics serve as optimization objectives [120, 122]. As illustrated by Figure 4.3, edge rewiring is the most frequently employed strategy, although edge addition can be more effective under certain conditions. Structural constraints such as degree preservation are often imposed to maintain network integrity, whereas robustness improvements are typically evaluated using *a posteriori* measures.

Figure 4.3 presents a general flowchart for applying evolutionary and swarm intelligence algorithms to optimize network robustness. Edge rewiring serves as the primary structural modification strategy, although edge addition can be more cost-effective in some scenarios. Structural constraints such as *degree preservation* are typically imposed to maintain predefined properties under a fixed budget for nodes and edges. Important operations of evolutionary operators, including crossover, mutation, and

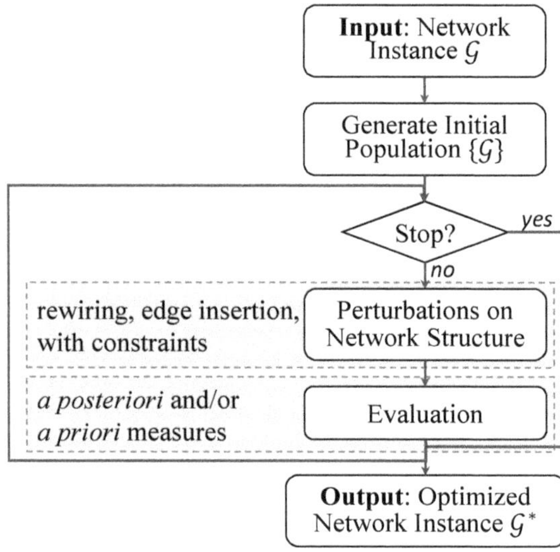

Fig. 4.3: General paradigm for optimizing network functionality robustness using evolutionary algorithms.

local search, are implemented through rewiring steps. After one or more rewiring iterations, the robustness of the modified network must be evaluated either through attack simulation for realistic assessment or using empirical metrics for estimation. Termination criteria are generally based on computational budget rather than robustness improvement, owing to the absence of prior knowledge about the network robustness.

The degree-preserving rewiring strategy operates as follows. For a directed network, it maintains the out-degree and in-degree of each node by reconnecting edges e_{ij} and e_{st} ($i \neq s$ or $j \neq t$) as e_{it} and e_{sj}. For an undirected network, edges $e_{\bar{ij}}$ and $e_{\bar{st}}$ ($i \neq s$ and $j \neq t$) are rewired as $e_{\bar{it}}$ and $e_{\bar{sj}}$, where $e_{\bar{ij}}$ denotes an undirected edge between nodes i and j. This method ensures that the degree of every node remains unchanged. Extended operators build on this principle by allowing clusters of nodes to be treated as "supernodes", which can be rewired while preserving the degree of their external connections.

Table 4.1: Summary of heuristic algorithms for optimizing network robustness. PT: percolation theory-based robustness metric similar to the definition in Equation (3.1); DP: degree preservation for each node; $\langle k \rangle$P: average degree preservation for the entire network; EA: evolutionary algorithm; GA: genetic algorithm; MOEA: multi-objective evolutionary algorithm; AC: algebraic connectivity.

Work	Measure	Algorithm (Constraint)	Object
Schneider [71]	PT	Random Rewiring (DP)	Node
Herrmann [75]	PT	Monte Carlo (DP)	Node
Buesser [129]	PT	Simulated Annealing (DP)	Node
Zeng [123]	PT	Hybrid Greedy (DP)	Nodes & Edges
Peixoto [130]	PT	BFGS [131] & Swarm-based ($\langle k \rangle$P)	Node
Cao [132]	PT	Edge Insertion (N/A)	Node
Zhou [133]	PT	Memetic Algorithm (DP)	Node
Xiao [114]	$\frac{1}{n}\sum_{i=1}^{n}(1-c_D(i))$	Dynamic Optimization (DP)	Node
Bai [134]	PT	Hill-climbing Search (DP)	Node
Yang [135]	PT	Greedy Bypass Rewiring (DP & $\langle k \rangle$P Preservation)	Node
Tang [136]	Cascading Failure-based	Memetic Algorithm (DP)	Node
Ma [127]	PT for Nodes & Edges	Edge-replenishment (Preserve Node & Edge Numbers)	Nodes & Edges
Sun [137]	PT	Tabu Search (DP)	Node
Tang [138]	Cascading Failure-based	Memetic Algorithm (DP)	Node

Continued on next page

Continued from previous page			
Work	Measure	Algorithm (Constraint)	Object
Park [139]	PT	Greedy Bypass Rewiring (N/A)	Node
Wang [140]	Bi-objective: PT & Cooperation	MOEA (DP)	Node
Wang [141]	Community Integrity [142]	GA (DP)	Node
Wang [143]	Normalized Mutual Information [143]	Simulated Annealing (DP)	Node
Wang [115]	Bi-objective: $\frac{1}{n}\sum_{i=1}^{n}\frac{n_L(i)}{n_D(i)}$ & Cooperation	MOEA (DP)	Node
Rong [144]	PT	Heuristic (DP)	Node
Gunasekara [122]	PT & Spectral Measures	MOEA (N/A)	Node
Liu [145]	PT	EA (N/A)	Node
Liu [120]	PT for Nodes & Edges	MOEA (DP)	Nodes & Edges
Qiu [146]	PT	Multi-population Co-evolution (DP)	Node
Cai [147]	Bi-objective: Max AC & Min Edge Removal	NSGA-II, NSGA-III, & MODPSO (N/A)	edge
Wang [79]	PT*	Surrogate-assisted EA (DP)	Node
Wang [80]	PT*	Surrogate-assisted MOEA (DP)	Nodes & Edges
Lou [50]	PT for Edge	Edge Rectification ($\langle k\rangle$P)	Nodes & Edges
Lou [148]	PT for Edge	Random Rewiring ($\langle k\rangle$P & Topology Preservation)	Node

* with the assistance of surrogates & assortativity

Table 4.3 summarizes 29 representative methods for optimizing network functionality robustness, covering such aspects as controllability, connectivity, and other robustness measures. Evolutionary algorithms are the most widely employed tools for structural modification to enhance robustness against node-removal attacks. Robustness is typically quantified by using a percolation theory-based metric similar to the definition in Equation (3.1), which can be applied to controllability, connectivity, and robustness. During optimization, a common practical constraint is degree preservation for every individual node, although in some cases preserving the average degree of the entire network is acceptable. Degree preservation constrains the degree of each node in an undirected network and both in-degree and out-degree in a directed network. Variations among different methods include alternative robustness metrics, advanced algorithmic designs, diverse topological constraints, and different optimization objectives. Since no single metric can fully capture the network robustness [149, 150], multiple measures are often jointly optimized through multi-objective evolutionary algorithms [80, 120, 122].

Table 4.3 includes methods addressing both connectivity robustness and controllability robustness, as these properties are often interrelated, although they are *not* consistently positively correlated. Sometimes, they are optimized simultaneously. For example, [115] formulates a bi-objective function:

$$R = \frac{1}{n}\sum_{i=1}^{n}\frac{n_L(i)}{n_D(i)},$$

where $n_L(i)$ denotes the residual size of the largest connected component and $n_D(i)$ represents the number of driver nodes required for full controllability. This ratio captures the trade-off between structural connectivity and network controllability under node removal, highlighting that research on connectivity robustness and controllability robustness shares common principles and they can mutually inform each other.

4.4 An Empirical Necessary Condition for Achieving Optimal Controllability Robustness

Examining the correlation between network topology and controllability robustness remains a central challenge in network science [4, 5, 9, 10, 67, 108]. Since rigorous theoretical characterization is still infeasible, empirical approaches based on exhaustive optimization have been employed to identify optimal network structures under fixed node and edge counts. Systematic evaluation of all possible network configurations and exhaustive combinations of attack sequences for small-scale networks reveals that optimal robustness is achieved when node degrees are highly homogeneous. This observation forms an empirical necessary condition (ENC), which serves as a practical guideline for designing edge rectification strategies to improve controllability robustness. Simulation results on both synthetic and real-world networks confirm that enforcing the ENC significantly enhances robustness, offering a feasible pathway toward near-optimal network designs [57–59].

4.4.1 *Empirical Necessary Condition for Optimal Controllability Robustness*

To comprehensively evaluate controllability robustness under all possible attack scenarios, node-removal attacks are used as an illustrative example, and exhaustive simulations are performed on small-scale networks.

For a network with n nodes, all $n!$ possible node-removal sequences are considered and recorded. For a specific attack sequence $\omega \in \Omega$, where Ω denotes the set of all $n!$ sequences ($|\Omega| = n!$), applying attack sequence ω on the network generates a corresponding controllability robustness curve R_ω. The overall robustness of this network is then computed as the average over all sequences:

$$\langle R \rangle = \frac{1}{|\Omega|} \sum_{\omega \in \Omega} R_\omega \,. \tag{4.6}$$

Based on exhaustive attack simulations on networks with $n = 4$, 5, and 6, statistical analysis indicates that instances achieving optimal controllability robustness share distinctive structural characteristics. Specifically, such networks contain a directed global loop connecting all n nodes and exhibit highly homogeneous in-degree and out-degree distributions, consistent with previous findings [57–59, 151]. Generally, for a directed network with n nodes and m edges, optimal robustness is achieved when the in-degree and out-degree of every node satisfy

$$\left\lfloor \frac{m}{n} \right\rfloor \le k_i^{\text{in}}, k_i^{\text{out}} \le \left\lceil \frac{m}{n} \right\rceil, \quad i = 1, 2, \ldots, n \,, \tag{4.7}$$

where k_i^{in} and k_i^{out} denote the in-degree and out-degree of node i, and $\lfloor \cdot \rfloor$ and $\lceil \cdot \rceil$ represent the floor and ceiling functions, respectively. Equation (4.7) requires the node degrees to be as close as possible to the average $\frac{m}{n}$: exactly $\frac{m}{n}$ if divisible, or within $\left[\lfloor \frac{m}{n} \rfloor, \lceil \frac{m}{n} \rceil\right]$ otherwise.

Figure 4.4 illustrates the hierarchical relationship among network instances for given n and m. At the outermost level, it includes all possible

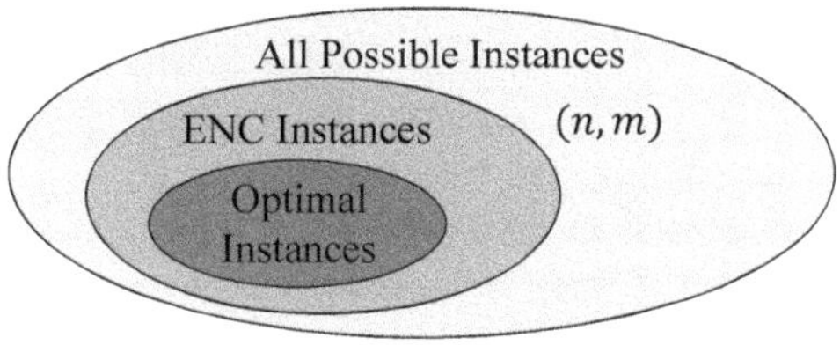

Fig. 4.4: Hierarchical relationship among network instances for given n and m: all possible instances, instances satisfying the empirical necessary condition (ENC), and optimal instances. All optimal instances form a subset of ENC instances, which in turn form a subset of all possible instances.

network configurations with n nodes and m edges. Within this set, there is a subset of instances that satisfy ENC, which possesses near-homogeneous in-degree and out-degree distributions. The innermost subset corresponds to optimal instances that achieve the highest controllability robustness under exhaustive attack evaluations. This hierarchy demonstrates that all optimal networks satisfy the ENC, but not all ENC-compliant networks are optimal. Consequently, the ENC serves as a practical necessary condition for robustness optimization, significantly narrowing down the search space while guiding an efficient network design.

Although exhaustive attacks are feasible for networks with $n = 4$, 5, and 6, the number of possible instances grows exponentially with n. For example, when $n = 6$, there are $2^{\binom{6}{2}} = 32{,}768$ undirected instances and more than one billion directed instances, making exhaustive testing impractical for larger networks. Empirical results show that all optimal instances satisfy ENC, yet not all ENC-compliant instances are optimal (see Figure 4.4); thus, ENC is a *necessary but not sufficient* condition. Applying ENC significantly reduces the candidate space for optimal networks. Although the total number of possible instances increases rapidly with n and m, the proportion of ENC-compliant instances remains small, making ENC an effective filter for large-scale searches.

4.4.2 *Edge Rectification*

Since it is computationally infeasible to enumerate *all* possible instances for large n and m, a simple yet effective strategy, random edge rectification (RER), was proposed to modify synthetic or real-world networks to satisfy the ENC [50]. RER generates a variant network with the same n and m but a different topology.

For any node i in a given network represented by the adjacency matrix $\mathbf{A}$, if its in-degree or out-degree violates Equation (4.7), edge rectification is performed according to the following four possible operations:

(1) If $k_i^{out} < \lfloor m/n \rfloor$, find a node v with $k_v^{out} > \lceil m/n \rceil$, randomly select one of its out-edges $A_{v,l}$, delete $A_{v,l}$, and add $A_{i,l}$.
(2) If $k_i^{out} > \lceil m/n \rceil$, randomly select one of its out-edges $A_{i,j}$, find a node v with $k_v^{out} < \lfloor m/n \rfloor$, delete $A_{i,j}$, and add $A_{v,j}$.
(3) If $k_i^{in} < \lfloor m/n \rfloor$, find a node v with $k_v^{in} > \lceil m/n \rceil$, randomly select one of its in-edges $A_{l,v}$, delete $A_{l,v}$, and add $A_{l,i}$.
(4) If $k_i^{in} > \lceil m/n \rceil$, randomly select one of its in-edges $A_{j,i}$, find a node v with $k_v^{in} < \lfloor m/n \rfloor$, delete $A_{j,i}$, and add $A_{j,v}$.

Each execution of these operations is an RER operation. The RER strategy randomly applies these operations until either the maximum number of operations is reached or the network satisfies the ENC. Between two networks, the one requiring fewer RER operations to exactly satisfy the ENC is considered closer to the condition [50].

4.4.3 *Experimental Validation of the Empirical Necessary Condition*

The change in controllability robustness is examined as the number of RER operations varies. Here, four scenarios are compared: (1) no RER operation, where networks are generated using their original generation methods without modification; (2) 1000 RER operations, approximately one tenth of the number required to fully satisfy ENC. In this case, RER operations are applied repeatedly to the original networks for 1000 iterations, and the controllability robustness of the resulting networks is evaluated; (3) 5000 RER operations, roughly half of the number needed to satisfy ENC; and (4) unlimited RER operations (denoted as Inf) until ENC is exactly satisfied.

The results are shown in Figure 4.5, which demonstrates that the controllability robustness improves as the number of RER operations increases. Subplot (a) displays the initial differences among networks without rectification; subplot (b) indicates that robustness improves and performance gaps narrow after 1000 RER operations; subplots (c) and (d) reveal that robustness is significantly enhanced and differences among networks become negligible. Although theoretical guarantees for optimal robustness are absent, the empirical results clearly demonstrate substantial improvement through RER-based rectification.

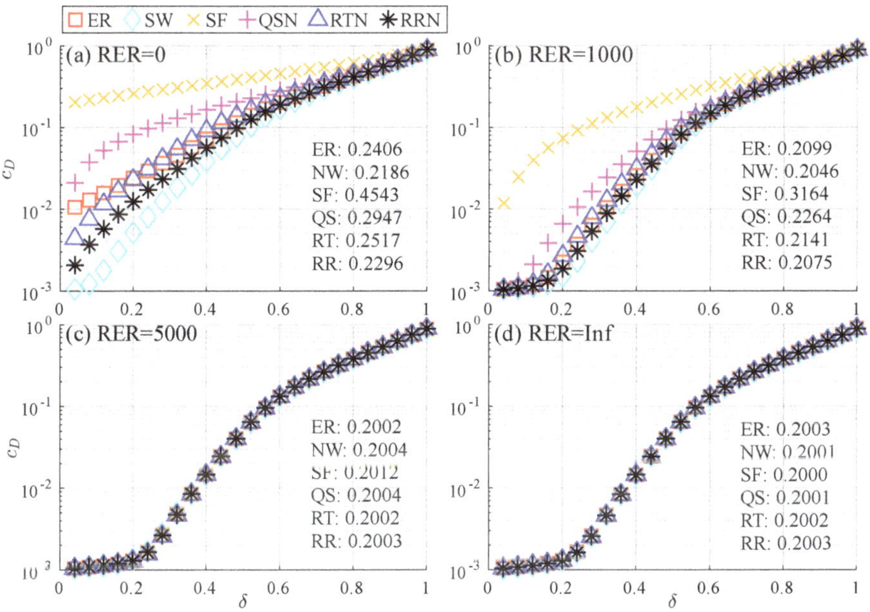

Fig. 4.5: Controllability robustness of six network models under different levels of degree-preserving edge rewiring (RER): (a) without rectification (RER = 0); (b) after 1000 RER operations; (c) after 5000 RER operations; and (d) with unlimited RER operations until ENC is fully satisfied. Here, c_D denotes the density of controlled nodes computed using Equation (3.1), and δ represents the proportion of removed nodes. Each curve is averaged over 1500 independent runs. The corresponding $\langle R \rangle$ values, calculated according to Equation (4.6), are shown beside the curves.

It is important to note that the network structure can change significantly during rectification. For example, an SF network subjected to 1000 RER operations no longer exhibits a scale-free degree distribution (see Figure 4.8(b) and Figure 4.9(b)), although it is still referred to as SF based on its original topology.

Next, only ER and SF networks are simulated. A small step length for increasing RER is used so that the subtle effects of RER on both controllability robustness and connectivity robustness can be clearly evaluated.

Figure 4.6 presents the controllability robustness curves of ER and SF networks as the number of RER operations increases, with RER values set to $\{0, 100, 200, 500, 1000, 2000, 5000, \mathrm{Inf}\}$. The results are obtained by

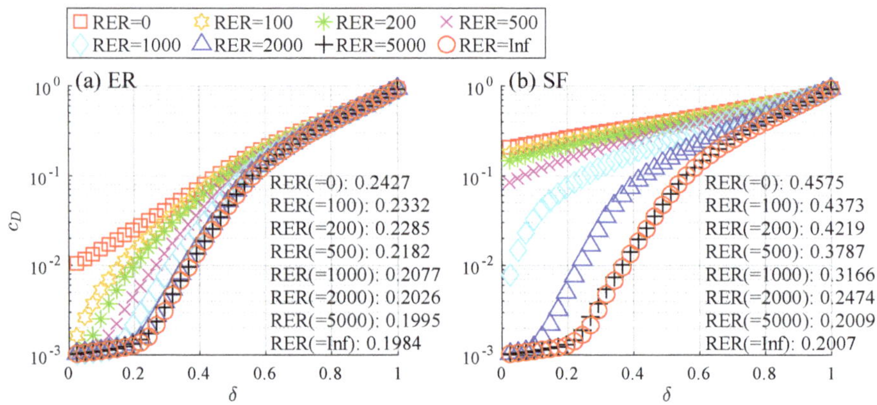

Fig. 4.6: Controllability robustness of (a) ER and (b) SF networks, under different numbers of RER operations. c_D denotes the density of controlled nodes computed using Equation (3.1), and δ represents the proportion of removed nodes. Each curve is averaged over 100 independent runs, and the corresponding $\langle R \rangle$ values, calculated according to Equation (4.6), are shown beside the curves.

averaging 100 independent runs. It is evident that increasing the number of RER operations significantly enhances controllability robustness. The curves are distinguishable even after 100 RER operations, indicating that the effect of RER is substantial even at relatively low levels of rectification.

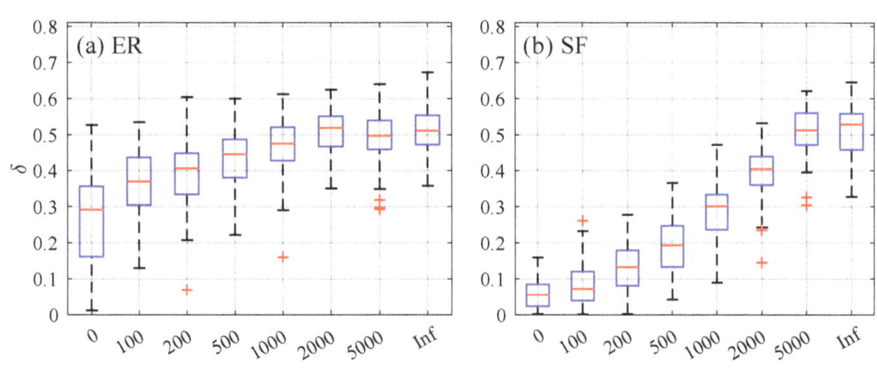

Fig. 4.7: Proportion of random node removals (δ) versus the number of RER operations required to disconnect the network: (a) ER and (b) SF.

Figure 4.7 shows the proportion of random node removals (δ) required to disconnect a network as a function of the number of RER operations. The results are averaged over 100 independent runs. A higher δ value indicates that more nodes must be removed to disconnect the network, meaning that the network has greater connectivity robustness. For both ER and SF networks, connectivity robustness improves consistently as the number of RER operations increases.

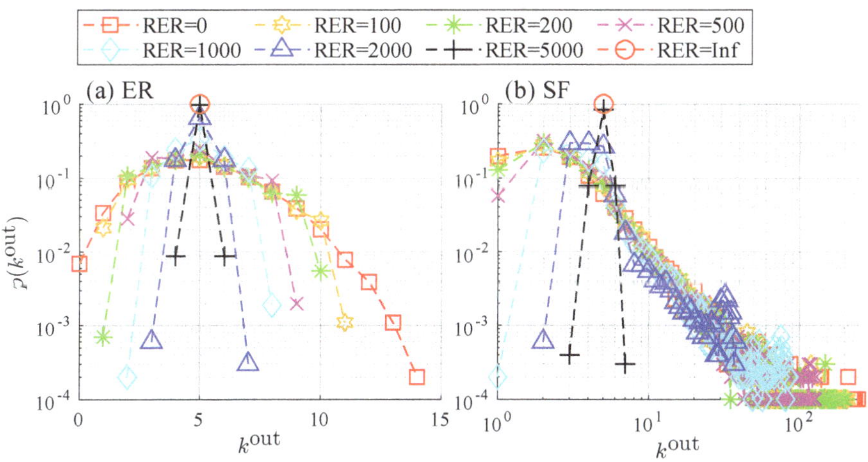

Fig. 4.8: Out-degree distribution changes as the number of RER operations increases: (a) ER and (b) SF networks.

RER operations gradually make a network more homogeneous. Figures 4.8 and 4.9 illustrate the evolution of out-degree and in-degree distributions for ER and SF networks, respectively. In both figures, subplot (a) shows the distributions for ER networks. As the number of RER operations increases, the out-degree and in-degree distributions of ER become increasingly concentrated around m/n ($m/n = 5$ in this example). The original Poisson distribution of ER networks progressively narrows toward the center at $m/n = 5$ and eventually collapses to a single point, a discrete delta distribution, when unlimited RER operations are applied, resulting in that all nodes have identical degrees.

Subplot (b) in both figures shows the corresponding changes in SF networks. The original power-law distribution of SF networks also shifts toward $m/n = 5$ as RER operations increase. Ultimately, an unlimited number of RER operations makes both ER and SF networks, as well as any

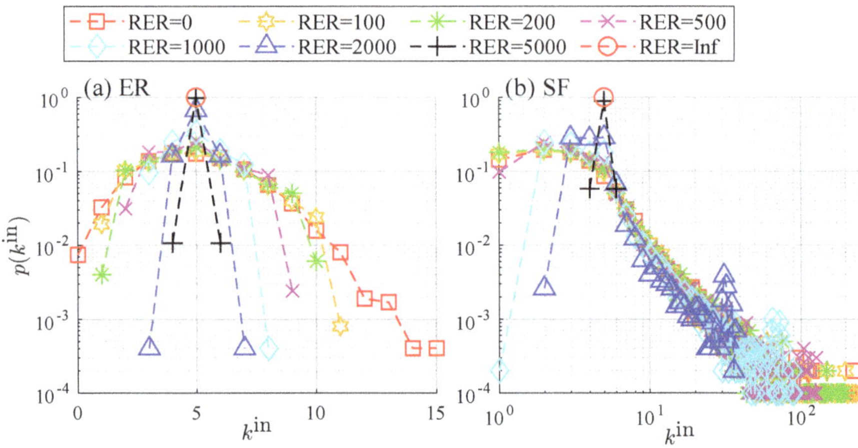

Fig. 4.9: In-degree distribution changes as the number of RER operations increases: (a) ER and (b) SF networks.

other network topology, extremely homogeneous in terms of degree distribution.

Table 4.2: Parameters and descriptions of the two real-world networks. For EE, the number of edges m is 25571 in [152]; after discarding self-loops, it becomes 24929.

Network	Description	n	m
email-Eu-core (EE)	a directed network generated using email data from European research institution	1005	24929
Gnutella peer-to-peer (GP)	a directed network generated by snapshots of Gnutella peer-to-peer file sharing network in August 2002	6301	20777

Now, consider two real-world networks: the email-Eu-core (EE) network and the Gnutella peer-to-peer (GP) network [152]. Their parameters and brief descriptions are presented in Table 4.2.

The original EE and GP networks (with RER $= 0$) are compared to configurations with RER values $\{100, 1000, 5000, 10000, \text{Inf}\}$. The controllability curves are shown in Figure 4.10. A phenomenon similar to that ob-

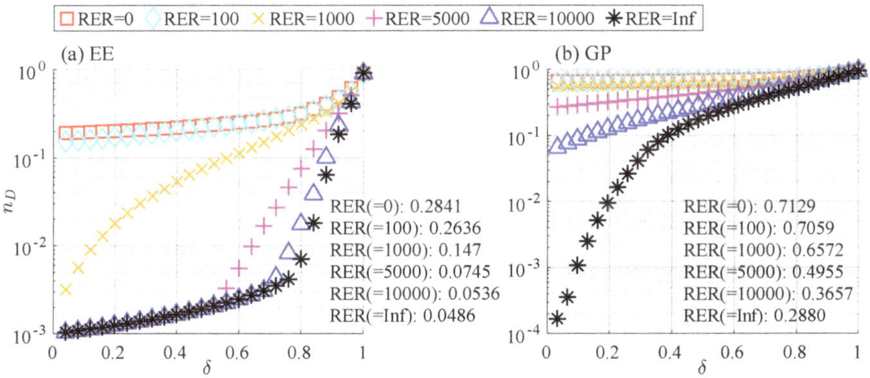

Fig. 4.10: Controllability robustness of (a) EE and (b) GP networks under random node removal. c_D denotes the density of controlled nodes computed using Equation (3.1), and δ represents the proportion of removed nodes. Each curve is averaged over 100 independent runs, and the corresponding $\langle R \rangle$ values, calculated according to Equation (4.6), are shown beside the curves.

served in synthetic networks emerges: controllability robustness improves as the number of RER operations increases. The curves for the original EE and GP networks (RER = 0) are far from those satisfying ENC (RER = Inf), clearly indicating that real-world networks are far from achieving optimal controllability robustness.

It can be observed from Figure 4.6 that, when unlimited RER operations are applied, the resulting extremely homogeneous ER and SF networks exhibit very similar controllability robustness. In contrast, Figure 4.10 shows that applying unlimited RER operations to EE and GP networks produces markedly different levels of controllability robustness.

Table 4.3 summarizes the changes in several basic network features when the number of RER operations is set to 0, 1000, and Inf. The compared features include average degree, average path length, average (node) betweenness centrality, clustering coefficient, number of basic loops, heterogeneity of out-degrees, and heterogeneity of in-degrees.

Clearly, RER does not alter the average degree of a network but significantly reduces the average path length from Inf (which occurs when at least one node i is unreachable from any other node j) to a small finite value. RER slightly decreases the average betweenness centrality in ER networks but increases it in SF, EE, and GP networks. Furthermore, RER reduces

Table 4.3: Changes of basic network features when RER is set to 0, 1000, and Inf, respectively. The compared features include average degree ($\langle k \rangle$), average path length (APL), average (node) betweenness centrality (BET), clustering coefficient (CLU), number of basic loops (NOC), heterogeneity of out-degrees (HO), and heterogeneity of in-degrees (HI). Network sizes are $n_1 = 1000$, $n_2 = 1005$, $n_3 = 6301$.

	$\langle k \rangle$	APL	BET	CLU	NOC	HO	HI
ER (n_1) RER=0	5	Inf	3.4E+03	0.0051	2039.0	1.1992	1.1984
ER (n_1) RER=1000	5	4.3365	3.3E+03	0.0044	2170.9	1.0532	1.0533
ER (n_1) RER=Inf	5	4.2943	3.2E+03	0.0041	2201.2	1	1
SF (n_1) RER=0	5	Inf	2.4E+03	0.0947	1576.3	6.2678	6.1320
SF (n_1) RER=1000	5	3.8097	2.8E+03	0.0334	1832.9	3.0727	2.9580
SF (n_1) RER=Inf	5	4.2943	3.2E+03	0.0040	2187.3	1	1
EE (n_2) RER=0	24.80	Inf	1.3E+03	0.3657	11603.0	2.7831	2.2534
EE (n_2) RER=1000	24.80	Inf	1.8E+03	0.2731	11661.9	2.4983	2.0567
EE (n_2) RER=Inf	24.80	2.5132	1.5E+03	0.0410	12344.0	1.0003	1.0003
GP (n_3) RER=0	3.30	Inf	1.1E+04	0.0054	4572.0	3.0318	4.9266
GP (n_3) RER=1000	3.30	Inf	1.4E+04	0.0047	4817.4	2.7168	4.2411
GP (n_3) RER=Inf	3.30	7.0686	3.8E+04	0.0004	7754.0	1.0192	1.0192

clustering coefficients while increasing the number of basic loops across all four networks. Finally, as expected, RER decreases both in-degree and out-degree heterogeneity for all networks.

Table 4.4: Basic network features, when RER is set to Inf. The compared features include average degree ($\langle k \rangle$), average path length (APL), average (node) betweenness centrality (BET), clustering coefficient (CLU), number of basic loops (NOC), heterogeneity of out-degrees (HO), and heterogeneity of in-degrees (HI). Network sizes are $n_1 = 1005$ and $n_2 = 6301$.

	ER (n_1)	SF (n_1)	EE (n_1)	ER (n_2)	SF (n_2)	GP (n_2)
RER	Inf	Inf	Inf	Inf	Inf	Inf
$\langle k \rangle$	24.80	24.80	24.80	3.30	3.30	3.30
APL	2.4954	2.4957	2.5132	7.0693	7.0677	7.0686
BET	1.50E+03	1.50E+03	1.52E+03	3.82E+04	3.82E+04	3.82E+04
CLU	0.0238	0.0238	0.0410	0.0003	0.0004	0.0004
NOC	12388.7	12242.7	12344.0	7716.0	7813.0	7754.0
HO	1.0003	1.0003	1.0003	1.0192	1.0192	1.0192
HI	1.0003	1.0003	1.0003	1.0192	1.0192	1.0192

It is notable that unlimited RER operations make the basic features of ER and SF networks almost identical. This observation confirms that RER can rectify any network toward an extremely homogeneous structure, or at least a very similar one, regardless of its original topology. However, this phenomenon is not observed for EE and GP networks. Due to differences in size and in average degree, the basic features of EE and GP cannot be uniformly rectified in the same way as ER and SF networks with identical n and m values. For example, when RER is set to Inf, the number of basic loops differs significantly between EE and GP. As previously noted, multi-loop structures are highly beneficial for controllability robustness [57–59].

Table 4.4 further demonstrates that, regardless of the original topology, RER rectifies networks toward an extremely homogeneous structure or very similar configurations. In this comparison, both ER and SF are configured with $n_2 = 1005$ and $\langle k \rangle = 24.80$, matching the configuration of EE. After unlimited RER operations, most basic features of the three networks become nearly identical, except for minor differences in clustering coefficients. Similarly, when ER and SF are configured to match GP ($n_3 = 6301$ and $\langle k \rangle = 3.30$), all basic features of the three networks converge to very similar values.

4.5 Summary

This chapter presents a comprehensive study on controllability robustness and its enhancement through structural optimization. After introducing the theoretical background and indicating the limitations of existing indicators, several network models designed to improve the robustness are discussed, including multiplex congruence networks, q-snapback networks, their edge-redirection variants, and Henneberg-growth networks. The chapter then focuses on optimization strategies based on metaheuristic algorithms, with degree-preserving edge rewiring (RER) as the core technique. An empirical necessary condition (ENC) for optimal controllability robustness is proposed and verified through exhaustive simulations on small-scale networks with extensive experiments performed on both synthetic and real-world networks. Results show that RER progressively homogenizes network degree distributions, reduces path lengths, and increases loop structures, leading to significant improvements in both controllability and connectivity robustness. Comparative analyses reveal that networks with identical size and average degree converge toward similar structural properties under unlimited RER operations, while networks with heterogeneous configurations exhibit persistent differences. The chapter concludes by demonstrating that RER rectifies networks toward extremely homogeneous structures, providing practical guidelines for robust networks design.

Chapter 5

Data-driven Approaches for Controllability Robustness Assessment

This chapter provides a systematic and comprehensive study of data-driven approaches for evaluating network controllability robustness, addressing three key issues: input representation, model architecture, and output interpretation.

From the input perspective, various graph representation paradigms are examined, ranging from structure-based representations including adjacency, incidence and modularity matrices to graph embedding such as learning-based features, DeepWalk, LINE, `node2vec`, SDNE, and `struc2vec`, as well as one-dimensional embedding derived from node-level features. Experimental results show that adjacency-matrix-based representations are particularly suitable for describing and evaluating network controllability robustness. Along this line of investigation, the impact of training data distribution is also analyzed for CNN models.

From the modeling perspective, the chapter introduces machine-learning-based, CNN-based, and GNN-based frameworks under consistent experimental conditions across synthetic and real-world networks. Advanced CNN architectures, including spatial pyramid pooling (SPP) and learning feature representation (LFR)-based models, are discussed alongside a multi-task framework based on the graph isomorphism network (GIN), which is selected for its strong discriminative capability and theoretical expressiveness in capturing structural patterns relevant to robustness prediction. A multi-expert system is also discussed, where each trained model specializes in a specific type of input representation.

From the output perspective, machine-learning-based and CNN-based methods generally predict controllability robustness as a single task, whereas the GIN-based approach extends the task to multi-task learning and achieves superior performance.

Extensive experiments show that structure-preserving representations, particularly adjacency and modularity matrices, consistently outperform general-purpose embedding, underscoring the need for task-oriented designs. Machine-learning-based methods, although limited in expressive power, can achieve strong performance when combined with high-quality features, while highly expressive GNN models remain the most effective. The findings underscore the critical role of structure-preserving representations and advanced GNN models in achieving accurate and reliable controllability robustness evaluation.

The chapter is organized as follows. Section 5.1 introduces network representation methods, ranging from matrices to graph embedding models. Section 5.2 discusses the advantages and limitations of machine-learning-based approaches for controllability robustness analysis. Section 5.3 presents CNN-based approaches, including advanced variants such as SPP and LFR. Section 5.4 introduces GNN and multi-task learning for robustness evaluation. Section 5.5 provides a systematic experimental comparison, first among different representation methods, then across machine learning, CNN and GNN approaches for robustness prediction. Finally, Section 5.6 provides a summary of the study.

5.1 Network Representation Methods: From Matrices to Graph Embedding

This section introduces network representation methods, from matrix representations to graph embedding models.

5.1.1 *Graph Structure-based Representations*

Structure-based graph representations are first discussed.

5.1.1.1 *Adjacency Matrix*

The adjacency matrix is a fundamental representation of a graph, which is used for describing the topology of a network. For a graph $\mathcal{G} = (\mathcal{V}, \mathcal{E})$ with n nodes, representing an unweighted and undirected network, the adjacency matrix $\mathbf{A} \in \mathbb{R}^{n \times n}$ is defined in such a way that its entry $A_{ij} = 1$ if an edge exists between nodes i and j, and $A_{ij} = 0$ otherwise. For weighted networks, A_{ij} stores the corresponding edge weight, which can represent distance, capacity, or interaction strength, etc. For undirected networks, the adjacency matrix is symmetrical, satisfying $A_{ij} = A_{ji}$, whereas for directed networks, in general $A_{ij} \neq A_{ji}$. Since self-loops are not considered in basic graph theory, $A_{ii} = 0$. The adjacency matrix captures the complete connectivity structure of a network and serves as the basis for numerous graph-theoretic and spectral analyses.

5.1.1.2 *Higher-order Adjacency Matrices*

High-order adjacency matrices, denoted as $\mathbf{A}^{(k)}$, extend the concept of the standard adjacency matrix by capturing connectivity through paths of length k $(k = 1, 2, \cdots)$ within a network. Formally, the entry $A_{i,j}^{(k)}$ specifies the number of distinct walks of length k between nodes v_i and v_j. These matrices offer a comprehensive view of global connectivity patterns, uncovering indirect relationships that the first-order adjacency matrix cannot reveal. For $k > 1$, higher-order adjacency matrices provide valuable information and insights about structural characteristics such as reachability and path diversity. Nevertheless, they cannot serve as stand-alone representations because they exclude direct edge information contained in the original adjacency matrix $\mathbf{A}$. Therefore, $\mathbf{A}^{(k)}$ is typically employed along with $\mathbf{A}$ in tasks involving network analysis and higher-order structural characterization.

5.1.1.3 *Incidence Matrix*

The incidence matrix $\mathbf{B} \in \mathbb{R}^{n \times m}$ represents the relationships between nodes and edges, where each row corresponds to a node and each column to an edge. An entry $B_{i,j}$ indicates whether node v_i is incident to edge e_j. Each adjacency matrix is bijective to its corresponding incidence matrix, so the incidence matrix also contains complete information about the network structure. However, its relevance to controllability is limited, and it introduces variability in input size while requiring additional steps to recover node-node connectivity, making it less practical for large-scale network analysis. In contrast, the adjacency matrix directly captures node interactions, supports efficient message passing and spectral analysis, and integrates smoothly with GNNs and other deep learning frameworks. Therefore, throughout this book, the adjacency matrix is frequently used, but not the incidence matrix.

5.1.1.4 *Modularity Matrix*

Modularity matrices, denoted by $\mathbf{H}$, play a key role in modularity-based community detection algorithms. They are computed as $H_{i,j} = A_{i,j} - \frac{k_i \cdot k_j}{2m}$, where $A_{i,j}$ is the adjacency matrix entry, k_i and k_j are the degrees of nodes v_i and v_j respectively, and $m = |\mathcal{E}|$ is the total number of edges. These matrices enable algorithms to identify communities, which are groups of nodes with dense internal connections and sparse external links, by maximizing their modularity scores.

5.1.1.5 *Laplacian Matrix*

The most commonly used representation is the Laplacian matrix $\mathbf{L} \in \mathbb{R}^{n \times n}$, which serves as a fundamental representation that integrates both connectivity and node degree information. It is defined as $\mathbf{L} = \mathbf{D} - \mathbf{A}$, where $\mathbf{D}$ is the degree matrix with $D_{ii} = \sum_j A_{ij}$. The Laplacian is central to algebraic graph theory and widely applied in diffusion, synchronization and controllability. Its spectral properties reveal key structural features such as connectivity, robustness, and community structure. For graph learning, it offers advantages over the adjacency matrix by encoding node degrees, supporting spectral clustering via the Fiedler value, namely its smallest nonzero eigenvalue, and enabling formulations for random walks and consensus dynamics, making it well-suited for various control and optimization tasks. Both adjacency and Laplacian matrices serve as the foundation for many algorithms in network science and machine learning, including spectral clustering, graph signal processing, and robustness optimization.

5.1.2 *Gray-scale Image Representation*

Converting an adjacency matrix, or any matrix introduced in Subsection 5.1.1, to a gray-scale image enables the application of image-based deep learning models for graph classification, regression, and other analytical tasks. This approach bridges graph representation learning with established computer vision techniques, allowing convolutional neural networks (CNNs) to extract structural patterns directly from matrix-encoded connectivity.

Notably, this representation introduces spatial locality and pixel-based positional information, which do *not* naturally exist in graph-structured data due to its non-Euclidean nature. To address this mismatch, some techniques were developed, aiming to filter out such spatial locality to better preserve the intrinsic graph topology. For example, to make these images meaningful for machine learning, network nodes are reordered using a permutation-invariant method, such as breadth-first search ordering starting from the highest-degree node, so that structural patterns become visually apparent and consistent across samples [153, 154].

However, it is also observed that randomly shuffling the pixels does not substantially influence the performance of network controllability robustness prediction. When gray-scale images are fed into CNNs, the local pixel adjacency is more strongly associated with the controllability robustness [98]. Nevertheless, features such as local connectivity, symmetry, and intensity variation can still be effectively captured and mapped to performance metrics. This representation is particularly useful for large-scale or heterogeneous graphs, where traditional graph learning methods may face challenges in scalability or generalization. Moreover, gray-scale encoding facilitates integration with standard image processing pipelines, enabling efficient training and inference under the deep learning framework.

Converting matrices to gray-scale images involves several independent techniques based on different philosophies. Each matrix entry can be directly mapped to a pixel intensity, where binary graphs typically use values zero and one, with weighted graphs normalized to the gray-scale range. Matrix values may be scaled using minimum-maximum or Z-score normalization [155] to enhance contrast and ensure consistency. Node reordering methods, such as degree-based sorting, breadth-first search, and spectral arrangement, are then applied to improve spatial coherence in the resulting images [153, 154]. Adjacency matrices may be padded or resized to fixed dimensions to meet the input requirements of image-based models. With appropriate sorting, less important pixels can be omitted from the representation. Upsampling and downsampling [98] are also used to adjust the sizes of graph-converted images, whereas the CNN input size is fixed. Multiple graph-related matrices, including adjacency, Laplacian and degree matrices, can be stacked as separate channels to enrich the image representation. These techniques are conceptually distinct but do not imply any specific order or dependency.

Figure 5.1 shows an illustrative example of converting adjacency matrices from various network models to gray-scale images. Both unweighted and weighted versions of four network types are presented: Erdős–Rényi (ER) [49], generic scale-free (SF) [51], q-snapback (QS) [58, 59], and Newman–Watts (NW) [56]. For unweighted networks (top row), each adjacency matrix is visualized as a binary image, where black pixels represent zero entries (no edge) and white pixels represent one entries (edge presented).

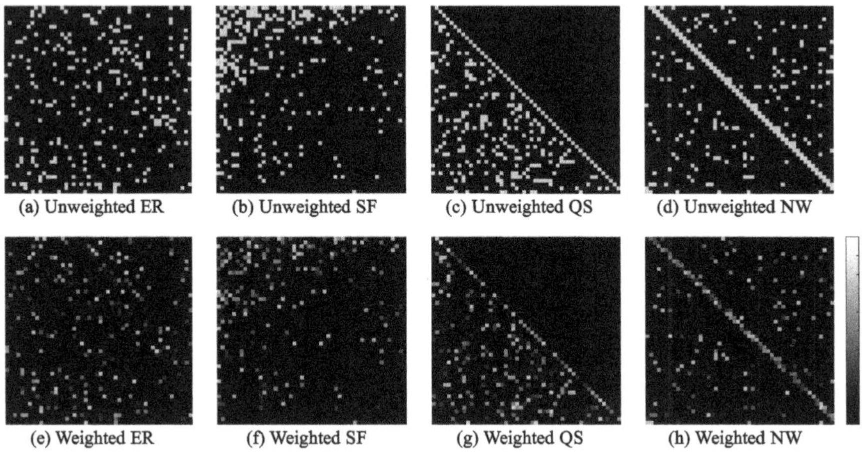

Fig. 5.1: An illustrative example of converting an adjacency matrix to a gray-scale image for both weighted and unweighted networks. The network size is $n = 50$ with average degree $\langle k \rangle = 5$. In each image, a black pixel represents a zero element in the adjacency matrix, while a white pixel represents a one element in the unweighted network. For a weighted network, the non-zero elements are normalized to the range $(0, 1]$ to form a gray-scale image.

For weighted networks (bottom row), nonzero elements are normalized to the range $(0, 1]$ and mapped to corresponding gray-scale intensities, as indicated by the color bar. The gray-scale images in Figure 5.1 are generated according to the original network construction schemes without any additional node sorting or pixel shuffling. As a result, for QS and NW networks, the backbone structure is clearly visible in the images.

5.1.3 *Graph Embedding*

Graph embedding provides a powerful framework for representing complex network structures in a form amenable to quantitative analysis and machine learning [156]. In the context of controllability robustness, graph embedding techniques capture essential topological features that influence a network's ability to maintain controllability subject to structural perturbations or failures. By transforming graphs to structured representations such as vectors, matrices, or images, these methods enable systematic feature extraction for robustness evaluation. Formally, graph embedding maps nodes of a graph $\mathcal{G} = (\mathcal{V}, \mathcal{E})$ to vectors in a continuous vector space through an embedding function $\Phi : v \in \mathcal{V} \rightarrow \mathbb{R}^{|\mathcal{V}| \times d}$, where v denotes a node and d is the embedding dimension.

This section introduces the principles and methodologies of graph embedding with application to controllability robustness analysis, highlighting how different strategies facilitate the assessment and prediction of robust controllability properties in diverse networked systems.

5.1.3.1 *Learning Feature Representation*

Learning feature representation (LFR) reduces higher-dimensional network data to lower-dimensional representations through three operations: selection, assembly, and normalization [157,158].

In the selection step, important nodes are identified based on centrality measures such as degree, betweenness, or closeness. Assembly constructs receptive fields for each selected node using breadth-first search to capture local neighborhood structures, and normalization ensures scale consistency for downstream learning tasks. This process compresses an $n \times n$ adjacency matrix into a structured representation of size $\ell \cdot g \cdot h$, where $\ell \leq n$ is the number of selected nodes, and $g, h \ll n$ represent the dimensions of the receptive field grid. The resulting representation supports dimensionality reduction (from n^2 to $\ell \cdot g \cdot h$), size regulation (fixed input size regardless of n), and feature extraction, by associating structural patterns with robustness-oriented embedding.

5.1.3.2 *DeepWalk*

DeepWalk [159] learns node embedding by leveraging co-occurrence relationships through truncated random walks, analogous to sentences in `word2vec` [160,161]. The method generates sequences of nodes by performing multiple random walks over a graph and then applies the skip-gram model [160] to maximize the likelihood of predicting context nodes within a fixed window. This approach captures both local and global structural contexts, enabling embedding that preserves neighborhood similarity and higher-order proximity.

DeepWalk has become a foundational technique for unsupervised graph representation learning, particularly valued for simplicity and scalability in large-scale networks.

5.1.3.3 *LINE*

Large-scale information network embedding (LINE) [162] emphasizes preserving node proximity in a continuous vector space by modeling both first-order and second-order similarities with explicit optimization objectives. First-order proximity captures direct connections between nodes, while second-order proximity reflects similarities in neighborhood structures.

LINE employs edge sampling and negative sampling to ensure scalability and efficiency, making it suitable for large-scale and heterogeneous networks. The resulting embedding is well-suited for applications that require accurate modeling of both local and global connectivity patterns.

5.1.3.4 *node2vec*

`node2vec` [163] extends DeepWalk by introducing a flexible biased random walk strategy that interpolates between breadth-first search and depth-first search. This design allows `node2vec` to balance local neighborhood exploration with global structural discovery, capturing both community-based homophily and role-based structural equivalence. After generating node sequences through these biased walks, `node2vec` applies the skip-gram model to learn an embedding that preserves the sampled context.

The flexibility of `node2vec` makes it particularly effective for tasks requiring nuanced structural representations across diverse graph types.

5.1.3.5 *SDNE*

Structural deep network embedding (SDNE) [164] employs a deep autoencoder architecture to jointly preserve first-order and second-order proximities, capturing both local connectivity and global structural patterns. The model incorporates nonlinear activation functions to learn complex feature interactions and uses a semi-supervised approach by integrating node labels into the training process for enhanced representation quality. By combining reconstruction objectives with neighborhood constraints, SDNE delivers robust embeddings that excel in scenarios where noise resilience and structural fidelity are critical.

5.1.3.6 *struc2vec*

`struc2vec` [165] addresses the limitations of neighbor-based similarity by defining node similarity through structural roles rather than direct adjacency. The method constructs a multi-layer weighted network where each layer encodes structural similarity at different scales, enabling the comparison of nodes with similar roles even when they are far apart in the original graph. After building this hierarchical structure, `struc2vec` performs biased random walks over the multi-layer network to generate node sequences and then applies `word2vec` to learn embeddings. This role-oriented perspective makes `word2vec` particularly useful for uncovering functional equivalence and detecting structural anomalies in complex networks.

5.1.3.7 *Local Degree Profile*

Local degree profile (LDP) [166] characterizes nodes using degree-based statistics that capture local structural properties. These statistics include the degree of a focal node as well as the minimum, maximum, mean, and sum of the degrees of its neighbors. The computed values are typically represented as histograms or concatenated feature vectors, providing a simple yet effective embedding that preserves the neighborhood degree distribution.

5.1.3.8 *Betweenness, Clustering Coefficient, and Degree*

A simple embedding approach summarizes global and local structural features using betweenness, clustering coefficient and degree (BDC), providing a compact representation of network topology. Betweenness centrality reflects the extent to which a focal node lies on shortest paths between other nodes, capturing its role as a bridge in the network. The clustering coefficient measures the tendency of neighbors of a focal node to form tightly connected groups, indicating local cohesiveness. Degree represents the number of direct connections associated with the focal node, serving as a fundamental indicator of connectivity. Combining these three metrics into one embedding vector yields an interpretable representation that captures both global influence and local structure.

5.1.3.9 *Applications in Network Robustness Evaluation*

The graph embedding methods introduced above are primarily designed for general graph tasks such as node and graph classification or link prediction, with limited direct application to network controllability, robustness, or controllability robustness.

SDNE is employed in evolutionary optimization for network robustness [79, 80], to map each node from a higher-dimensional adjacency matrix of size $n \times n$ to a lower-dimensional continuous vector of size $n \times d$ (typically $d = 2$). The embedding is further processed using principal component analysis, k-means clustering, and selection of higher-degree nodes to form heterogeneous feature sets. The resulting representation captures structural properties relevant to robustness and serves as surrogate decision variables for evolutionary optimization, enabling efficient estimation and search for robust network topologies.

An LFR-based convolutional neural network framework was proposed for robustness prediction [158]. The framework leverages LFR to generate structured embedding that enable dimensionality reduction, size regulation, and extraction of robustness-related features, providing fixed-sized inputs for convolutional architectures regardless of the network scale. Experimental results demonstrate that the LFR-based framework achieves superior performance with lower prediction errors compared to straightforward CNN approaches without feature learning representations.

Graph embedding offers significant advantages by transforming complex network structures to lower-dimensional representations, facilitating efficient feature extraction, scalability, and integration, with quantitative analysis and machine learning. However, when embedding is applied as a separate pre-processing step, the training process becomes partitioned, and the learned representation may not align with the downstream objective, potentially losing critical information relevant to controllability or robustness. In contrast, end-to-end approaches jointly optimize both the embedding and the target objective, allowing representations to adapt specifically to task requirements. This integrated optimization enhances performance by ensuring that learned features are directly aligned with robustness analysis and control tasks in complex networks.

As shown in Figure 5.2, a given network is processed by a deep neural network (DNN) for robustness performance prediction. In the first paradigm, indicated by blue arrows, graph-structured data are transformed into graph embedding (GE) and then fed into the DNN. In this design, GE is generated independently of the DNN, serving primarily for dimensionality reduction and generic feature extraction. As a result, robustness-related features cannot be effectively learned because the optimization process is partitioned. In contrast, the second paradigm, indicated by green arrows, adopts an end-to-end approach, enabling the DNN to directly learn features associated with the robustness performance.

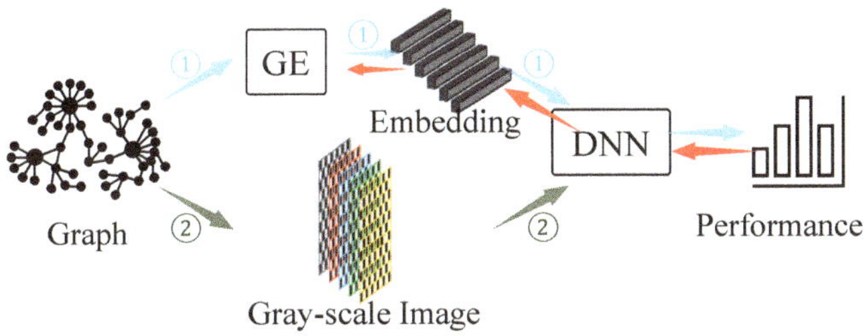

Fig. 5.2: Illustration of two paradigms for network robustness evaluation and optimization: (1) graph embedding combined with deep neural network (DNN) modeling, and (2) gray-scale image representation integrated with DNN for performance prediction.

Several studies have highlighted the limitations of the above two-step paradigm, where GEs are precomputed and then used for downstream tasks. Such separation often produces embedding optimized for general objectives like dimensionality reduction rather than task-specific objectives, resulting in suboptimal performances in robustness prediction. Early work revealed that shallow embedding methods lack joint optimization, motivating the development of end-to-end GNNs that learn representations and task-specific features simultaneously [159]. Subsequent research demonstrated that decoupling embedding generation from learning objectives restricts adaptability, with attention-based mechanisms proposed to mitigate this issue [167]. More recent advances emphasized that task-agnostic embedding fails to capture critical features for specialized applications, advocating for integrated approaches [168].

5.2 Machine Learning-based Approaches

As summarized in Section 3.1, metrics for network robustness, related to controllability or other functionalities, can be broadly categorized into two types: *a priori* metrics and *a posteriori* metrics [42]. The *a priori* metrics require only a one-time computation and typically exhibit lower time and computational complexities [77,78]. However, their predictive scope is limited, particularly in capturing diverse attack strategies and scenarios [117]. In contrast, *a posteriori* measures are quantified through a sequence of values that reflect the functionality of the remaining network after successive node- or edge-removal attacks. Ideally, an *a posteriori*-like approach should be employed to describe controllability robustness, but computed in an *a priori*-like manner. This strategy is suitable and commonly implemented using machine learning techniques.

Supervised machine learning algorithms, such as K-nearest neighbors (KNN) [169], linear regression (LR) [170], decision tree (DT), random forest (RF) [171], and multi-layer perceptron (MLP) [172], have proven effective for predicting controllability robustness. For example, in [97], models including LR, RF, and MLP are trained to estimate the minimum number of driver nodes required to maintain the structural controllability after random, targeted, or degree-based edge-removal attacks. The inputs to these models consist of network-level features such as the numbers of nodes and edges, average degree, clustering coefficient, and the number of critical links. The output is a continuous value representing the predicted number of driver nodes post-attack. While these traditional models demonstrate reasonable predictive performance, their reliance on handcrafted features and limited scalability underscores the need for more expressive graph-based learning approaches.

In [101], MLP, KNN, LR, DT, and RF are employed for network robustness prediction using handcrafted features such as network size, average degree, and assortativity [106]. The output is a robustness curve representing the predicted evolution of controllability or connectivity as nodes are removed under various attacks. Similarly, radial basis function (RBF), inverse distance weighting (IDW), and least-squares (LS) are combined into a surrogate ensemble to estimate robustness values, supporting evolutionary optimization of network structures [79, 173]. However, due to limited expressive power for graph-structured data, these methods are effective only when representative features can be accurately extracted; otherwise, they face performance limitations and scalability challenges for large-scale networks.

Traditional supervised machine learning methods rely on handcrafted features and are often favored for their interpretability, computational efficiency, and strong performance on small datasets. These methods perform well when meaningful structural and semantic features are available, particularly for tasks related to network controllability and robustness. However, their ability to capture complex dependencies inherent in graph topologies is limited, constraining their expressive power in scenarios involving diverse structures or multiple tasks. Performance can also degrade significantly when key features are missing. Consequently, these approaches face notable limitations in large-scale or irregular graph settings and typically require extensive preprocessing such as feature extraction, graph flattening, and vectorization, to transform graph data into formats compatible with conventional learning pipelines.

Deep learning approaches, particularly GNNs, address many limitations of traditional methods by learning representations directly from graph structures and node attributes. GNNs have demonstrated superior performances in tasks such as link prediction and graph classification. However, these models often require large datasets and substantial computational resources, while sacrificing interpretability. When high-quality structural and semantic features are available, deep learning models may underperform compared to traditional methods because these models are not always optimized to leverage predefined features effectively. The choice between machine learning and deep learning depends on task complexity, data availability, and feature quality, as well as the need for model transparency.

The above discussions highlight two complementary research directions: developing more informative structural and semantic *features* tailored to specific network tasks, and advancing more expressive deep learning *models* capable of generalizing in the absence of such features. In addition, unsupervised learning over networks represents a promising avenue for future exploration.

5.3 Convolutional Neural Network-based Approaches

CNN-based approaches approximate robustness performance by representing network data as gray-scale images [22]. Although effective, this methodology struggles with varying network sizes. Graph representation learning [158,174,175] addresses this limitation by compressing adjacency matrices into fixed-sized lower-dimensional representations, enabling consistent input and improved extraction of topological features.

This section reviews the evolution of CNN-based methods, including straightforward CNN, spatial pyramid pooling-based CNN, and learning feature representation-based CNN.

5.3.1 *Straightforward CNN*

To efficiently evaluate controllability robustness without performing costly attack simulations or relying on handcrafted features, a straightforward CNN-based predictor was introduced [22]. This approach is motivated by four key observations: (1) there is no clear correlation between simple topological features and controllability robustness in general networks; (2) an adjacency matrix can be equivalently represented as a gray-scale image (see Section 5.1.2); (3) CNNs have proven highly effective for image processing and related tasks; (4) prior knowledge can be incorporated through preprocessing and filtering.

In implementation, the adjacency matrix is converted to a gray-scale image and processed by a CNN in an end-to-end manner. The output is a controllability curve, a sequence of values indicating the remaining controllability (measured by the number or density of driver nodes required) after successive node removals. Validation across various network types, both weighted and unweighted, and under multiple attack strategies, demonstrates high prediction accuracy and significant computational efficiency of the CNN-based predictor.

Due to the nature of data-driven algorithms, CNN-based predictor can occasionally generate outputs that violate fundamental logical constraints. Several objective principles govern network robustness analysis. First, network scale decreases through an attack process, meaning that the number of nodes, edges, or both is reduced. Second, for controllability robustness, the number of required driver nodes must be non-decreasing as nodes are removed gradually, whereas for connectivity robustness, the size of the largest connected component must be non-increasing. The CNN-based predictor may fail to satisfy these monotonicity requirement, resulting in unrealistic robustness curves.

To address this issue, a filtering mechanism inspired by the principles of physics-informed neural networks (PINNs) [176] was introduced, leveraging prior knowledge to enforce logical consistency in predictions. The filter incorporates two key components: (1) enforcing upper and lower bounds on predicted values at each attack step, and (2) applying monotonicity constraints to guarantee non-decreasing behavior for controllability robustness and non-increasing behavior for connectivity robustness [72]. This integration ensures obtaining physically plausible robustness curves and significantly enhancing the prediction reliability without increasing computational complexity.

Figure 5.3 presents a schematic overview of the straightforward CNN framework for controllability robustness prediction. The process begins with an input graph, which is transformed to a gray-scale image representation of the adjacency matrix, as illustrated in Section 5.1.2. This image is processed by a CNN to extract structural patterns and generate preliminary predictions. To ensure logical consistency and physical plausibility, the CNN output is refined using a filter that incorporates prior knowledge,

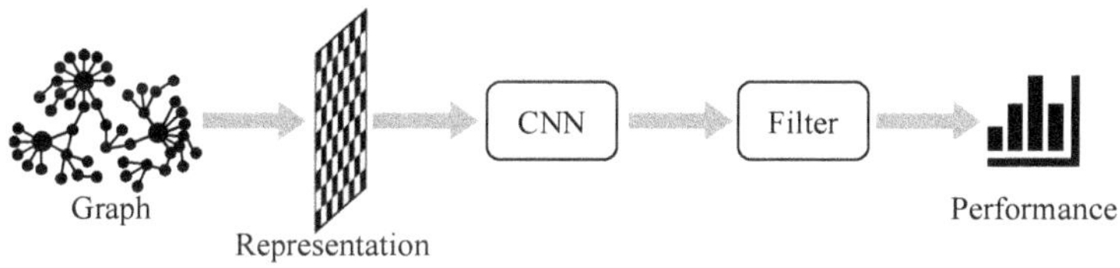

Fig. 5.3: A schematic illustration of the straightforward CNN framework. The input graph is converted to a gray-scale image representation and processed by a CNN. The CNN output is refined using a filter based on prior knowledge, producing the final robustness evaluation. This framework does not prescribe a specific CNN architecture; various CNN models can be integrated into this design.

enforcing constraints such as monotonicity and boundedness. In this design, the filter operates outside the CNN model; however, integrating such constraints within the CNN architecture and training jointly would be a more promising approach. The final output is a robustness curve that reflects controllability performance under successive node-removal attacks. The framework is architecture-agnostic, allowing the integration of different CNN designs without prescribing specific hyperparameters. In practice, deeper CNN architectures are generally preferred for large graphs to capture complex structural dependencies, whereas shallower models offer faster computation for smaller-scale graphs [22, 72].

5.3.2 *Spatial Pyramid Pooling-based CNN*

The above straightforward CNN-based methods predict network robustness by representing adjacency matrices as gray-scale images and processing them with CNNs to approximate measures such as connectivity and controllability in various attack scenarios [22]. These methods offer computational efficiency and eliminate the need for costly attack simulations, while remaining adaptable to different network types and attack strategies. However, a major limitation is the fixed input size required by standard CNN architectures. This constraint arises because fully connected layers in CNNs expect a constant-length input vector, which is derived from feature maps of a predefined size. Without a fixed input dimension, the weight matrices in these layers cannot be properly initialized or trained. For image-based tasks, resizing is straightforward because pixel grids can be scaled proportionally without altering semantic meaning. In contrast, for graph-structured data, resizing the adjacency matrix through upsampling or downsampling is problematic: it can distort topological relationships, remove existing nodes, or introduce artificial ones, leading to misleading representations. Such distortions are particularly harmful when critical structural elements, such as hubs or articulation points, are involved. Consequently, resizing compromises prediction accuracy and limits the generalizability of CNN-based approaches for networks with sizes that deviate significantly from the training data [158].

To overcome the fixed-size constraint of standard CNN architectures, a spatial pyramid pooling (SPP) layer [177] can be incorporated into the CNN framework. SPP enables the model to process networks of arbitrary sizes without cropping, warping or resizing, thereby preserving structural integrity and avoiding distortion of critical topological features. By converting variable-sized feature maps from convolutional layers to fixed-length representations suitable for fully connected layers, SPP resolves the size mismatch problem and enhances both structural flexibility and prediction accuracy.

SPP is built on the spatial pyramid matching concept in computer vision [178, 179], which partitions an image into spatial bins and aggregates local features to capture multi-scale spatial information. By extending this principle, SPP applies max pooling within each bin to generate a fixed-length feature vector regardless of input dimensions. This design allows CNN-based robustness predictors to handle diverse network sizes while maintaining topological fidelity and computational efficiency, making the approach more generalizable across heterogeneous graph structures.

Figure 5.4 illustrates a CNN architecture enhanced with a spatial pyramid pooling (SPP) layer for robustness prediction [180]. The input graph is first converted to a gray-scale image representation of its adjacency matrix and processed by the convolutional layers to extract local structural features. The SPP layer partitions the resulting feature maps into multiple spatial bins at different scales (e.g., 1×1, 2×2, 4×4) and applies max pooling within each bin. The pooled outputs are concatenated to form a fixed-length feature vector, which is then fed into fully connected layers for robustness performance evaluation. This design eliminates the need for resizing, allowing the model to handle networks of arbitrary sizes while preserving topological integrity and capturing multi-scale structural information. By integrating SPP, the framework improves generalizability across heterogeneous networks and mitigates distortions caused by conventional resizing operations, ensuring both computational efficiency and prediction accuracy.

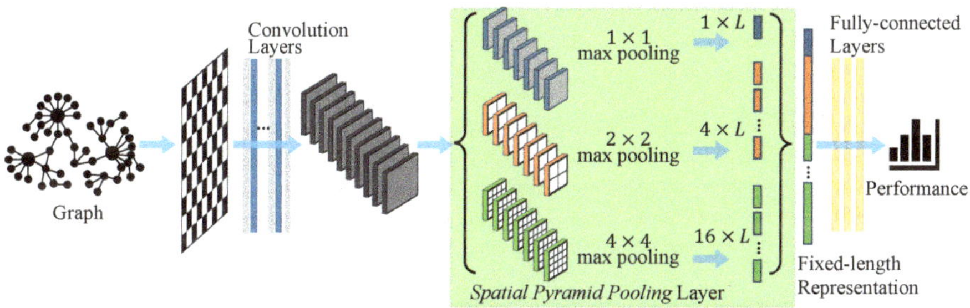

Fig. 5.4: Illustration of a CNN architecture with an embedded spatial pyramid pooling (SPP) layer. The input graph is converted to a gray-scale image-based representation, processed by convolutional layers, and passed through the SPP layer, which applies multi-scale max pooling to produce fixed-length feature vectors. These vectors are then fed into fully connected layers for robustness performance evaluation.

5.3.3 *Multi-expert Controllability Robustness Predictor*

To improve efficiency and avoid the limitations of a single CNN while effectively utilizing prior knowledge such as network topology, the multi-expert CNN robustness predictor (mCNN-RP) is proposed to enhance prediction accuracy and scalability [98, 181]. The core idea of mCNN-RP is a multi-CNN architecture designed as follows. One CNN functions as a classifier, performing expert selection by categorizing networks into predefined or clustered types based on structural features. Each remaining CNN then acts as a specialized predictor for a specific network category, enabling tailored robustness estimation. An optional data-driven filter further refine the predictions by leveraging prior knowledge and training data. The overall structure of mCNN-RP is illustrated by Figure 5.5.

This design enables the mCNN-RP to perform classification (or clustering) and regression simultaneously, predicting controllability robustness under diverse conditions, including various network types, functionalities, and attack patterns. Moreover, the framework is highly extensible. The multi-expert approach can also be applied to other models, such as graph neural networks and hybrid architectures, making it broadly useful for complex networks analysis. In addition, it supports multi-objective robustness prediction, allowing simultaneous evaluation of controllability, connectivity, and other performance measures.

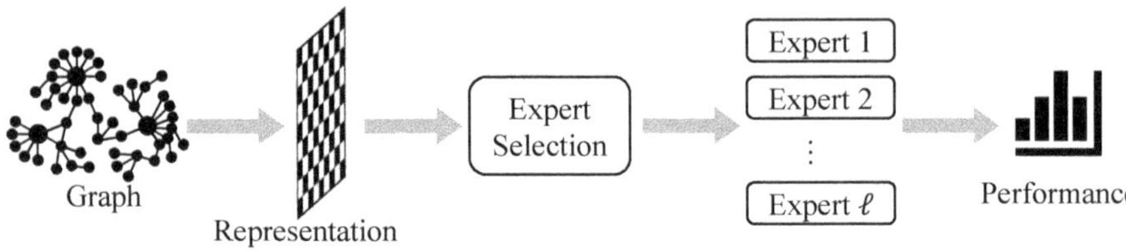

Fig. 5.5: Architecture of the multi-expert CNN robustness predictor (mCNN-RP). A network graph is first converted to a structured representation, followed by expert selection. Each expert CNN specializes in predicting robustness for a specific network category, and the aggregated output shows the final robustness performance.

5.3.4 *Learning Feature-based CNN*

The aforementioned CNN-based approaches treat the graph adjacency matrices as gray-scale images, offering simplicity and shift-invariance. However, these methods suffer from performance degradation when input sizes differ significantly from training samples and from inefficiency caused by sparse network structures [22]. The SPP-based method partially alleviates this limitation by introducing spatial pyramid pooling, which improves the CNN flexibility in handling variable-sized inputs without the need of resizing [180]. Beyond this, graph representation learning provides a more principled solution to the input size mismatch problem. Building on the same idea, the learning feature representation (LFR)-based CNN architecture is proposed [158]. LFR incorporates a feature representation module that compresses higher-dimensional network data into informative lower-dimensional embedding, enhancing learning efficiency and predictive accuracy. This design addresses input size variability while preserving structural fidelity and achieves a favorable balance between model complexity and parameter count compared with straightforward CNN-based predictors [22,98,181]. Extensive experiments demonstrate that LFR outperforms existing methods in predicting connectivity robustness and provides a more reliable indicator than classical spectral measures.

Graph neural networks (GNNs) [174, 175] are inherently suited for graph-structured data, enabling end-to-end learning and generation of lower-dimensional representations. In the LFR architecture, GNNs are employed exclusively for representation learning. Specifically, PATCHY-SAN [157], a representative and influential approach, is integrated to process graph data through three key operations: selecting, assembling, and normalizing (SAN). These operations construct regulated-size representations enriched with learned structural features, which are then fed into the CNN for robustness performance regression. The details of SAN are described below.

- *Node Sequence Selection:* From the n nodes in the network, a fixed-length sequence of ℓ nodes is selected based on importance scores computed using centrality measures such as degree and betweenness. Nodes are ranked in descending order of these scores, and the top ℓ nodes are chosen. For each selected node, a receptive field of size g is created; if $n < \ell$, zero-padding is applied to maintain consistency.
- *Neighborhood Assembly:* For each node in the selected sequence, a neighborhood is constructed using breadth-first search (BFS). The process continues until at least g neighboring nodes are collected or no additional nodes remain, ensuring coverage of local structural context.
- *Normalization:* The assembled neighborhood is ordered using a labeling procedure based on centrality, mapping the unordered neighborhood into a normalized vector space. The root node is placed first, followed by its neighbors in ranked order up to the g-th node, producing a consistent representation for subsequent processing.

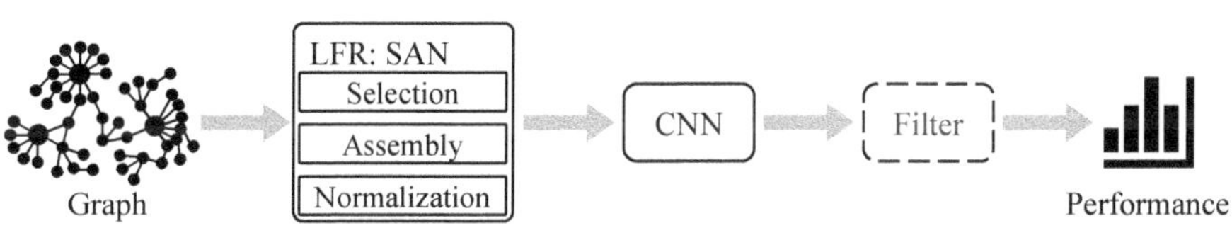

Fig. 5.6: Workflow of the LFR architecture. A graph is first converted to a structured representation through the LFR module, which performs three operations: selection, assembly, and normalization (SAN). The resulting representation is processed by a CNN to extract features, followed by filtering to enforce logical constraints, and finally used for robustness performance evaluation.

Figure 5.6 illustrates the workflow of the LFR architecture. The process begins with a graph represented as an image, which is then converted into structured receptive fields through the LFR module. This module performs three operations: selection, assembly, and normalization. The result of LFR is a compact and informative representation derived from high-dimensional graph data. The structured representations are subsequently processed by a CNN, typically a 1D-CNN, to extract hierarchical patterns and perform controllability robustness regression. An optional filtering step may be applied to enforce logical constraints such as monotonicity and boundedness, ensuring physically consistent robustness curves. In practice, LFR-based approaches generally deliver more accurate and reliable predictions than straightforward CNN methods, reducing the need for extensive post-processing and improving generalizability across diverse network structures.

The LFR module can be substituted with other representation learning techniques to generate structured and reliable inputs from graph-based data. However, as discussed in Subsection 5.1.3, such alternatives typically operate in separate preprocessing steps, whereas an end-to-end architecture is generally more favorable for downstream tasks because it enables joint optimization of representation learning and prediction objectives, improving adaptability and overall performance.

5.3.5 *Influence of Training Data Distributions*

Data-driven approaches for predicting controllability robustness offer a cost-efficient solution but require substantial training data, which can significantly influence the overall performance. This section examines the impact of training data size distribution, including uniform, Gaussian and extra distributions, and the relationship between CNN input size and network dimension.

The learning feature representation (LFR)-based CNN and PATCHY-SAN methods are employed for evaluation. Experiments show that Gaussian and extra distributions significantly improve the prediction accuracy and generalizability compared to uniform distribution for both LFR and PATCHY-SAN. LFR demonstrates superior extension capability and overall performance, thereby becoming the most commonly recommended approach, although optimal CNN input size settings are suggested for different configurations.

Figure 5.7 illustrates three training data size distributions: uniform, Gaussian, and extra. For uniform and Gaussian distributions, network size n is symmetrically centered around the mean size, whereas the extra distribution is asymmetrical because one-sided additional samples help CNN distinguish cases. w denotes the fixed input size of the CNN.

Table 5.1 compares the average ranks of prediction errors for different training data distributions for controllability robustness evaluation. Two

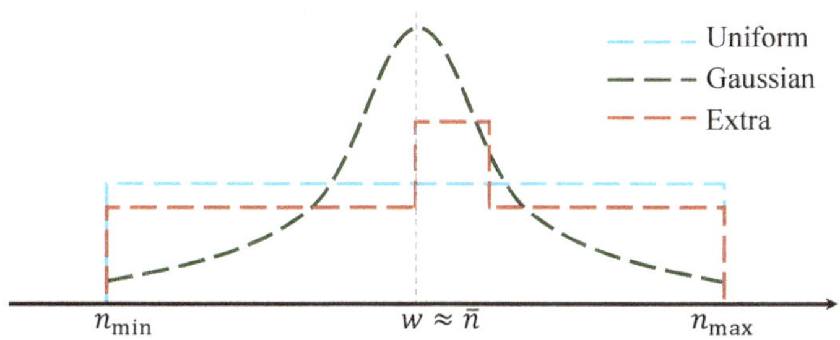

Fig. 5.7: Illustration of three training data size distributions: uniform, Gaussian, and extra.

Table 5.1: Average ranks of prediction errors for different training data distributions. Bold values indicate the best performance.

Measure		Controllability robustness	
Input Size		$w = 500$	$w = 1000$
LFR	Uniform	2.43	1.92
	Gaussian	**1.64**	**1.84**
	Extra	1.93	2.25
PATCHY -SAN	Uniform	2.39	1.98
	Gaussian	1.99	**1.94**
	Extra	**1.62**	2.08

CNN-based approaches, LFR and PATCHY-SAN, are tested with input sizes $w = 500$ and $w = 1000$. Lower rank values indicate better performance, and bold entries highlight the best results within each configuration.

For $w = 500$, each rank value is averaged over 9 network types $\times 33$ network sizes $\times 100$ random instances, where the 9 network types include the 8 types introduced in Section 2.2.1 plus random hexagon (RH) [62]. The 33 network sizes are $n = 100, 125, 150, \ldots, 900$ with an increment of 25, resulting in 33 test sets with different n values.

For $w = 1000$, each rank value is averaged over 9 network types $\times 21$ network sizes $\times 100$ random instances, where the 21 network sizes are $n = 500, 550, 600, \ldots, 1500$ with an increment of 50, resulting in 21 test sets with different n values.

The results show that Gaussian and extra distributions generally outperform uniform distribution, with LFR achieving superior accuracy and generalizability compared to PATCHY-SAN.

Table 5.2: General recommendations for training data distributions and hyperparameter w. Here, U, G, and E represent uniform, Gaussian, and extra distributions, respectively. The symbol $\succ$ indicates that the item on the left is preferred over the item on the right, while $\approx$ indicates that the two items are equally recommended.

	LFR	PATCHY-SAN
Given w	$G \succ E \succ U$	$E \succ G \succ U$
Given distribution	Uniform: Larger w	Uniform: Larger w
	Gaussian: Smaller w	Gaussian: Larger w
	Extra: Either	Extra: Larger w
For unseen data	$G \approx E \succ U$	$G \approx E \approx U$

Since the input sizes of LFR, PATCHY SAN, and many other CNN models are fixed, general recommendations for data distributions and the hyperparameter w are summarized in Table 5.2. When w is given, Gaussian-distributed training data is preferred for LFR, whereas extra-distributed data is recommended for PATCHY SAN. With a given distribution, w should be set as follows: LFR benefits from a larger w for uniform data and a smaller w for Gaussian data, while PATCHY SAN consistently favors a larger w. Finally, both Gaussian and extra distributions enhance generalizability for unseen data.

This highlights the importance of carefully designing training data for controllability robustness analysis, not only for CNN models but also for any other data-driven frameworks.

5.4 Graph Neural Networks and Multi-task Learning

Traditional machine learning methods lack sufficient expressive power for graph-structured data and struggle to scale efficiently to large-sized networks. Deep neural networks (DNNs) enable cost-effective robustness prediction by approximating *a posteriori* metrics in an *a priori*-like manner [182]. However, CNN-based approaches remain sensitive to the input size and exhibit inefficiency when processing sparse graphs [22, 98].

Representation-based methods and spatial pyramid pooling (SPP) layers alleviate these issues by either sacrificing end-to-end learning or introducing additional complexity [158, 180].

Graph neural networks (GNNs) have emerged as one of the most effective tools for processing graph-structured data. By leveraging both topological and attribute information, GNNs ensure permutation invariance, capture complex dependencies, and support end-to-end learning [183]. These advantages motivate the development of a multi-task GNN-based framework for comprehensive and efficient network robustness evaluation. Recent studies confirm that GNN-based approaches for robustness analysis and prediction consistently deliver superior performance compared to traditional and CNN-based methods [184].

5.4.1 *A Brief Introduction to Graph Neural Networks*

GNNs are a class of advanced deep learning models that operate directly on graph structures, making them highly effective for analyzing and processing graph-structured data [183, 185]. Through a message-passing mechanism, GNNs enable nodes to iteratively aggregate and update their representations by exchanging information with neighboring nodes according to the network topology [186]. After L iterations of aggregation, each node incorporates information from its L-hop neighborhood, allowing the model to capture both local and higher-order structural dependencies.

Consider a graph or network denoted by $\mathcal{G} = (\mathcal{V}, \mathcal{E})$, where $\mathcal{V} = \{v_1, v_2, \ldots, v_n\}$ is the node set and $\mathcal{E} = \{(v_i, v_j) \mid v_i, v_j \in \mathcal{V}\}$ is the edge set. A general message-passing GNN consists of two core modules: aggregation and combination, defined as

$$\begin{aligned} h_{\mathcal{N}_v}^{(\ell+1)} &= \mathrm{AGGREGATE}\big(\{h_u^{(\ell)} \mid u \in \mathcal{N}_v\}\big), \\ h_v^{(\ell+1)} &= \mathrm{COMBINE}\big(h_v^{(\ell)}, h_{\mathcal{N}_v}^{(\ell+1)}\big), \end{aligned} \tag{5.1}$$

where $h_v^{(\ell)}$ denotes the representation of node v at layer ℓ, $\mathcal{N}_v$ refers to the neighborhood of v excluding v itself, AGGREGATE$(\cdot)$ computes a summary from the neighboring nodes, and COMBINE$(\cdot)$ integrates this summary with the current representation of node v.

If node v is considered part of its own neighborhood, i.e., $u \in \mathcal{N}_v \cup \{v\}$, the AGGREGATE$(\cdot)$ and COMBINE$(\cdot)$ can be merged into a single update function. For example, the graph convolutional network (GCN)

[187] applies an element-wise mean pooling aggregator, defined as

$$h_v^{(\ell+1)} = \sigma\left(\sum_{u\in\mathcal{N}_v\cup\{v\}} a_{(v,u)}\, h_u^{(\ell)}\mathbf{W}^{(\ell)}\right), \tag{5.2}$$

where $a_{(v,u)}$ is a normalization coefficient derived from the symmetrically normalized adjacency matrix $\tilde{\mathbf{D}}^{-\frac{1}{2}}\tilde{\mathbf{A}}\tilde{\mathbf{D}}^{-\frac{1}{2}}$, $\mathbf{W}^{(\ell)}$ is the learnable weight matrix at layer ℓ, and $\sigma(\cdot)$ denotes a nonlinear activation function.

GraphSAGE [174] introduces several neighborhood aggregation strategies, including MEAN, LSTM, and POOLING. The POOLING aggregator is defined as

$$h_{\mathcal{N}_v^*}^{(\ell+1)} = \mathrm{MAX}\left\{\sigma\left(h_u^{(\ell)}\mathbf{W}^{(\ell)} + b\right) \,\middle|\, u \in \mathcal{N}_v^*\right\}, \tag{5.3}$$

where $\mathcal{N}_v^*$ denotes a fixed-size sampled subset of the neighborhood $\mathcal{N}_v$, $\mathbf{W}^{(\ell)}$ is the learnable weight matrix at layer ℓ, b is the bias term, and $\sigma(\cdot)$ is a nonlinear activation function. After aggregation, the node representation is updated by concatenating the original node embedding with the aggregated neighborhood vector, as follows:

$$h_v^{(\ell+1)} = \mathrm{CONCAT}\left(h_v^{(\ell)}, h_{\mathcal{N}_v^*}^{(\ell+1)}\right)\mathbf{W}^{(\ell)}, \tag{5.4}$$

where CONCAT$(\cdot)$ denotes the concatenation operation that combines the current node representation $h_v^{(\ell)}$ with the aggregated neighborhood representation $h_{\mathcal{N}_v^*}^{(\ell+1)}$, and $\mathbf{W}^{(\ell)}$ is the learnable weight matrix applied after concatenation.

The graph attention network (GAT) [188] enhances message passing by introducing attention weights for neighbors:

$$h_v^{(\ell+1)} = \sigma\left(\sum_{u\in\mathcal{N}_v\cup\{v\}} \alpha_{(u,v)}^{(\ell)} h_u^{(\ell)}\mathbf{W}^{(\ell)}\right), \tag{5.5}$$

where $\alpha_{(u,v)}^{(\ell)}$ are attention coefficients computed by

$$\alpha_{(u,v)}^{(\ell)} = \mathrm{SOFTMAX}\left(\tau\left(h_u^{(\ell)}\mathbf{W}^{(\ell)}, h_v^{(\ell)}\mathbf{W}^{(\ell)}\right)\right), \tag{5.6}$$

with $\tau(\cdot)$ denoting a shared attention mechanism (typically a feed-forward network) and SOFTMAX applied over all neighbors of v to normalize attention scores.

For graph-level tasks such as graph classification or performance regression, node representations h_v (with $v \in \mathcal{V}$) are aggregated into a graph-level representation $H_{\mathcal{G}}$ using a permutation-invariant READOUT function, as follows:

$$H_{\mathcal{G}} = \text{READOUT}\big(\{h_v^{(L-1)} \mid v \in \mathcal{V}\}\big)\,, \tag{5.7}$$

where READOUT can be a simple function such as SUM or MEAN, or advanced pooling methods like SortPooling [189]. Alternatively, models such as DGCNN [189], Jumping Knowledge Networks [190], and GIN [191] concatenate outputs from all layers:

$$H_{\mathcal{G}} = \text{CONCAT}\big(\text{READOUT}(H^{(\ell)}) \mid \ell = 0, 1, \ldots, L-1\big), \tag{5.8}$$

which preserves multi-scale structural information for graph-level tasks.

5.4.2 *Graph Neural Networks for Controllability Robustness Analysis*

A spatial GNN framework was proposed for generating robustness-oriented embedding of complex networks [25]. The embedding generation module is built upon a customized graph convolutional layer for controllability robustness learning (CRL), which aggregates both topological structure and degree-based node attributes. Initial node features are constructed from normalized in-degree and out-degree values. The CRL layer employs two parallel heads: one for extracting global and dynamic topological features, and the other for capturing degree-related node attributes using attention mechanisms. Node representations are updated as

$$h_i^{(\ell+1)} = t_i^{(\ell)} + a_i^{(\ell)}\,,$$

where $t_i^{(\ell)}$ and $a_i^{(\ell)}$ denote topological and attribute information, respectively. Embedding dimensions vary across layers (e.g., $d_\ell \neq d_{\ell+1}$), and residual connections are incorporated to mitigate oversmoothing. The resulting embedding is tailored for controllability robustness, which is transferable across networks of different sizes and types.

Another approach introduces a customized graph transformer to generate robustness-oriented graph embedding for complex networks [192]. Initial node features are constructed via degree centrality encoding, combining in-degree and out-degree information into a learnable embedding of dimension d, typically $d = 10$. The core transformer layer integrates multi-head attention with inner heads for local neighbor aggregation and outer heads for global structure integration, while explicitly encoding edge features and node-edge dependencies through trainable weights. Unlike standard transformers, attention is restricted to local neighborhoods, preserving graph sparsity and enabling efficient message passing. The embedding is designed to capture robustness-related topology rather than for general-purpose representation or dimensionality reduction.

5.4.3 *Multi-task Learning*

While most supervised learning approaches are designed for a single prediction objective, a multi-task GNN-based framework was developed to evaluate multiple network robustness metrics simultaneously [101]. The framework integrates a graph isomorphism network (GIN) backbone with a multi-task learning module, enabling shared representation learning across tasks. This framework reduces parameters and improves efficiency while maintaining accuracy. Shared embedding enables joint prediction of multiple robustness metrics, and multi-task optimization captures correlations and accelerates convergence.

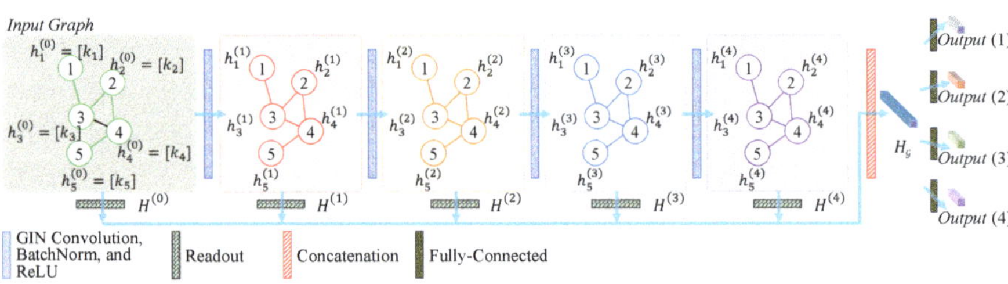

Fig. 5.8: Architecture of the multi-task GIN-based framework for network robustness evaluation. The input graph is processed through multiple GIN convolution layers with BatchNorm and ReLU activation, followed by READOUT and concatenation (CONCAT). Fully-connected layers then produce multiple outputs corresponding to different robustness metrics.

Figure 5.8 illustrates the architecture of the multi-task GIN-based framework for network robustness evaluation. The input graph is processed through a sequence of GIN convolution layers, each followed by Batch Normalization and ReLU activation, to learn node-level representations. A READOUT operation aggregates node features into graph-level embedding, which is concatenated across layers to capture multi-scale structural information. This concatenated embedding is then passed through fully-connected layers to produce multiple outputs, each corresponding to a different robustness metric, enabling simultaneous evaluation within a multi-task learning scheme.

5.4.4 *Discussion and Insights on Data-driven Approaches for Controllability Robustness*

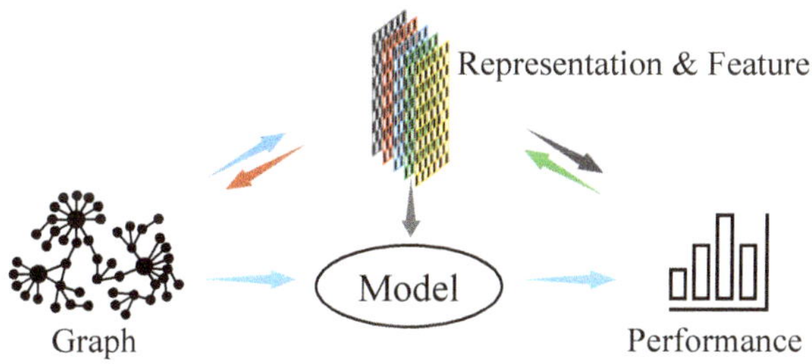

Fig. 5.9: Overview of the data-driven modeling pipeline: Graph structures are transformed to representations and features, which are fed into the model to predict or evaluate performance.

As shown in Figure 5.9, the pipeline illustrates the data-driven paradigm for evaluating controllability robustness.

Following the blue arrows, graph-structured data can either be fed directly into a model or be transformed to structured representations such as handcrafted features or learned embedding. These representations serve as inputs to machine learning models, CNNs, GNNs, or other predictive tools, which then output robustness performance metrics. This process enables an *a priori*-like evaluation of *a posteriori* metrics, reducing reliance on costly simulations.

The red arrow highlights graph representation learning as an independent research topic. Representations can be designed for general-purpose applications or tailored for specific tasks. Learned embedding often provides lower-dimensional, information-rich representations that capture structural patterns, node dependencies, and global properties, making them highly suitable for downstream tasks such as prediction, classification, and robustness evaluation.

The gray arrow indicates an alternative approach that bypasses the full data-driven pipeline by using individual features as proxies for controllability robustness. As discussed in Section 5.1 and further in Section 6.2, no single feature reliably reflects robustness. Nevertheless, features can serve as cost-efficient surrogates for approximate estimation when precision requirements are relaxed.

Finally, the green arrow points to the ultimate goal: understanding the relationship between network characteristics and robustness performance.

This involves uncovering associations between structural properties, learned representations, and controllability metrics, which can inform theory-driven insights, improve interpretability, and guide the design of robust networked systems.

Now, recall the questions to be investigated in this book, presented in Chapter 1:

- *How can complex networks maintain and retain their intended functions such as the controllability under structural disturbances or attacks?*
- *How can this capability be evaluated, analyzed, and optimized?*

Using feature-based or data-driven approaches to analyze controllability robustness is one way to achieve an initial objective recalled above. The ultimate goal is to answer the questions by uncovering associations among structural properties, learned representations, and controllability metrics, which ultimately disentangle these relationships to explain why and how structural characteristics influence network performance.

5.5 A Systematic and Comprehensive Comparison

In this section, the common components for the previously mentioned data-driven approaches are first discussed, including the loss functions used for training, followed by the error metrics for evaluating predicted results. Then, different graph representations are generated, including various structure-based and embedding-based approaches, used as inputs for machine learning and deep neural networks. Finally, a comprehensive comparison of machine learning-based, CNN-based, and GNN-based methods are presented, under fair conditions for controllability robustness prediction across diverse networks.

5.5.1 *Loss Function*

5.5.1.1 *Loss Function for Single-task Learning*

The output of a single-task CNN-based robustness predictor is a T-dimensional vector representing a controllability robustness curve for a network with n nodes, denoted by

$$\hat{\mathbf{v}}_n = [\hat{v}_n(1), \hat{v}_n(2), \ldots, \hat{v}_n(T)],$$

where T denotes the number of sampled functionality values, which typically satisfies $T \leq n$.

The mean-squared error (MSE) between the predicted curve $\hat{\mathbf{v}}_n$ and the true curve,

$$\mathbf{v}_n = [v_n(1), v_n(2), \ldots, v_n(T)],$$

typically obtained from attack simulations, is used as the loss function:

$$\mathcal{L} = \frac{1}{T}\sum_{i=1}^{T}\left(\hat{v}_n(i) - v_n(i)\right)^2, \tag{5.9}$$

where $\hat{v}_n(i)$ and $v_n(i)$ represent the predicted and true values of residual controllability (or connectivity) after removing i nodes from the original network of size n.

For large-scale networks, a relatively smaller $T \ll n$ can be chosen to reduce the dimensionality. During training, model parameters are optimized to minimize $\mathcal{L}$.

5.5.1.2 *Loss Function for Multi-task Learning*

When dealing with multiple tasks, it is essential to ensure that the tasks are non-conflicting; multi-task learning is applicable only under this condition. For a set of non-conflicting tasks, the multi-task learning framework integrates them into a unified objective with weighted losses. The homoscedastic uncertainty-based weighting system [193] assigns adaptive weights to each task, enabling simultaneous learning of quantities with different units and scales. This approach has demonstrated excellent performance in both classification and regression tasks.

Since the adopted robustness metrics may include vectors, scalars, or other forms with significantly different units and scales, an uncertainty-based weighting system is employed. The overall loss function is defined as

$$\mathcal{L} = \sum_{i}\frac{\mathcal{L}_i}{\omega_i}, \tag{5.10}$$

where $\mathcal{L}_i$ represents the loss of the i-th task, and the weight ω_i is computed by

$$\omega_i = \frac{\gamma_i}{\sum_j \gamma_j}, \tag{5.11}$$

where γ_i denotes the variance of $\mathcal{L}_i$ within the current training epoch [193]. Tasks with higher uncertainty receive smaller weights, while tasks with lower uncertainty are assigned larger weights. This adaptive mechanism ensures balanced learning across tasks with heterogeneous scales and units.

In [101], four robustness metrics, including connectivity robustness, controllability robustness, threshold of destruction, and maximum number of connected components, are evaluated simultaneously with a multi-task learning scheme. Each objective minimizes the mean-squared error between predicted and true values obtained from attack simulations. The training process optimizes the overall loss function $\mathcal{L}$, while adaptively adjusting task weights according to uncertainty, as defined in Equation (5.10).

5.5.2 *Error Measures*

One advantage of using data-driven approaches to evaluate controllability robustness (or other network functionalities) is that *a posteriori* metrics can be predicted in an *a priori* manner, making the process simple and computationally efficient.

The output of a data-driven approach can use either an *a posteriori* metric represented as a controllability curve in vector form, or an *a priori* metric represented by a scalar. Among these, *a posteriori* metrics are generally preferable because they provide more detailed information about the attack process and controllability degradation.

For controllability robustness prediction, similar to the loss function, let $\hat{\mathbf{v}}_n = [\hat{v}_n(1), \hat{v}_n(2), \ldots, \hat{v}_n(T)]$ and $\mathbf{v}_n = [v_n(1), v_n(2), \ldots, v_n(T)]$ denote the predicted and true curves, respectively. The mean prediction error $\bar{\xi}$ is computed by

$$\bar{\xi} = \frac{1}{T}\sum_{i=1}^{T} \xi(i)\,, \tag{5.12}$$

where $\xi(i) = |v_n(i) - \hat{v}_n(i)|$ and $i = 1, 2, \ldots, T$. Given two prediction errors from different robustness predictors, denoted by $\bar{\xi}_1$ and $\bar{\xi}_2$ respectively, the predictor with a smaller error ($\bar{\xi}_1 < \bar{\xi}_2$) is considered better.

For predicted scalar values, such as *a priori* metrics and integer outputs like ranks, the prediction error is evaluated by comparing the predicted value with the true value using their absolute difference. This provides a simple and consistent measure of accuracy across tasks involving both discrete and continuous outputs, ensuring that performance comparisons remain interpretable.

5.5.3 *Comparing Graph Representations in Machine Learning for Network Robustness Evaluation*

The evaluation includes both synthetic and real-world networks, considering three representation paradigms: (1) structure-based representations, including adjacency, incidence, and modularity matrices; (2) graph embedding, including LFR, DeepWalk, LINE, `node2vec`, SDNE, and `struc2vec`; (3) one-dimensional graph embedding derived from node-level features, such as degree and clustering coefficient.

Graph representations are categorized into three groups, as follows:

5.5.3.1 *Group#1*

Six structure-based representations: adjacency matrix ($\mathbf{A}$); a combination of adjacency and its $\{2,3\}$-order adjacency matrices ($\mathbf{A}^{\{1,2,3\}}$); incidence matrix ($\mathbf{B}$); modularity matrix ($\mathbf{H}$); a combination of adjacency and modularity matrices ($\mathbf{A}$ & $\mathbf{H}$); a combination of adjacency, second-order adjacency, and modularity matrices ($\mathbf{A}^{\{1,2\}}$ & $\mathbf{H}$).

5.5.3.2 *Group#2*

Six graph embedding: LFR, DeepWalk, LINE, `node2vec`, SDNE, and `struc2vec`, used as input for the CNN-based evaluator. The generated representations have size $n \times d$, where $d = 256$.

5.5.3.3 *Group#3*

By setting the embedding dimension $d = 1$, one-dimensional representations are generated for DeepWalk, LINE, `node2vec`, SDNE, and `struc2vec`. Additionally, one-dimensional representations for LDP and BDC are included. These representations serve as inputs for the MLP-based evaluator.

In the experimental studies, SPP is employed as the benchmark CNN-based evaluator, with parameter settings following [180]. Controllability robustness is computed using Equations (3.1). The random targeted attack (RTA) strategy is adopted, where at each attack iteration, RTA randomly selects either the highest-degree node or the highest-betweenness node for removal. This mixed strategy is chosen because machine learning-based robustness evaluators are inherently invariant to attack strategies, demonstrating broader applicability of such methods.

For synthetic networks, node sizes are uniformly sampled within the range $[700, 1300]$, and the average degree $\langle k \rangle$ lies within $[4, 12]$ for each

Table 5.3: Average ranks for evaluating network controllability robustness (lower values indicate better performance). The top-3 best-performing representations are highlighted in bold.

Group	Representation	Synthetic Networks	Real-world Networks
Group #1	$\mathbf{A}$	4.4	8
	$\mathbf{A}^{\{1,2,3\}}$	**2.2**	5
	$\mathbf{A}$	10.7	9
	$\mathbf{A}$	**2.8**	**1**
	$\mathbf{A}$ & $\mathbf{H}$	**3.1**	4
	$\mathbf{A}^{\{1,2\}}$ & $\mathbf{H}$	4.4	6
Group #2	LFR	9.7	14
	DeepWalk	8.6	**3**
	LINE	8.8	11
	`node2vec`	6.7	7
	SDNE	5.4	**2**
	`struc2vec`	11.8	12
Group #3	DeepWalk (1D)	15.8	10
	LINE (1D)	14.4	19
	`node2vec` (1D)	18.7	18
	SDNE (1D)	15.3	16
	`struc2vec` (1D)	17.0	17
	LDP (1D)	15.8	13
	BCD (1D)	14.4	15

instance. The training dataset consists of 9000 instances, with an additional 900 reserved for testing.

In addition, a set of 1012 real-world network instances is selected from REDDIT-BINARY [194], where network sizes range from 300 to 3782 nodes (average 737), and the number of edges varies from 1248 to 16284 (average 3389). Networks with fewer than 300 nodes are excluded, so as to maintain consistency with the synthetic dataset range.

For comparison, a multi-layer perceptron (MLP) architecture is implemented with four hidden layers containing 512, 1024, 1024, and 512 neurons, respectively.

Table 5.3 summarizes the average ranks of different graph representation paradigms for evaluating network controllability robustness across synthetic and real-world networks. Lower ranks indicate better performance, and the top-3 representations in each category are highlighted in bold.

As can be seen, overall structure-based representations (Group #1) achieve the best performance, consistently outperforming graph embedding (Group #2) and one-dimensional embedding (Group #3). Within Group #1, the modularity matrix (**H**) ranks first for real-world networks, while adjacency-based combinations such as $\mathbf{A}^{\{1,2,3\}}$ and **A** & **H** also perform remarkably well. These results confirm that adjacency and modularity matrices provide rich structural information that CNNs can effectively exploit.

Graph embedding in Group #2 shows moderate performance compared to structure-based representations. Among them, SDNE and DeepWalk achieve competitive ranks, particularly on real-world networks, while other embedding such as LINE and `node2vec` perform less favorably. This indicates that general-purpose embedding, although versatile, is not optimized for robustness evaluation tasks.

Group #3, which includes one-dimensional embedding, performs the worst overall. Methods such as DeepWalk (1D), LINE (1D), and `struc2vec` (1D) exhibit significantly higher ranks, indicating that extreme dimensionality reduction compromises the ability to capture essential structural features. Additionally, the use of MLP for these representations, which is less powerful than CNN, further contributes to their inferior performance.

Table 5.4 provides a comprehensive comparison of prediction performance for real-world networks under the controllability robustness metric defined in Equation (3.1). Each cell reports the average prediction error with its standard deviation in the upper row, followed by the rank in parentheses on the lower row. A lower rank indicates a smaller prediction error and hence a better performance.

Structure-based representations (Group #1) dominate the ranking, with the adjacency matrix (**A**) achieving the lowest prediction error and thus ranks first, while its higher-order variant ($\mathbf{A}^{\{1,2,3\}}$) ranks second. Modularity-based representations (**H** and $\mathbf{A}+\mathbf{H}$) also perform remarkably, confirming that structural information is highly effective for CNN-based prediction.

Graph embedding (Group #2) exhibits moderate performance compared to structure-based representations. Among them, DeepWalk and SDNE achieve relatively competitive ranks, whereas LINE and `node2vec` perform less favorably. This suggests that general-purpose embedding, although widely used in graph learning, is not optimized for robustness evaluation tasks.

Table 5.4: Comparison of controllability robustness prediction for real-world networks. Upper row shows the average prediction error ± standard deviation. Lower row indicates the rank as an integer in parentheses.

Representation	R_{PT}	Representation	R_{PT}
A	0.060 ± 0.040 (1)	SDNE	0.276 ± 0.078 (14)
$\mathbf{A}^{\{1,2,3\}}$	0.071 ± 0.042 (2)	`struc2vec`	0.320 ± 0.123 (15)
B	0.091 ± 0.093 (4)	DeepWalk (1D)	0.275 ± 0.070 (12)
H	0.104 ± 0.041 (6)	LINE (1D)	0.320 ± 0.050 (16)
A & **H**	0.100 ± 0.042 (5)	`node2vec` (1D)	0.360 ± 0.060 (17)
$\mathbf{A}^{\{1,2\}}$ & **H**	0.111 ± 0.045 (7)	SDNE (1D)	0.374 ± 0.137 (18)
LFR	0.276 ± 0.117 (13)	`struc2vec` (1D)	0.414 ± 0.059 (19)
DeepWalk	0.121 ± 0.065 (8)	LDP (1D)	0.073 ± 0.064 (3)
LINE	0.197 ± 0.084 (11)	BDC (1D)	0.177 ± 0.042 (10)
`node2vec`	0.127 ± 0.052 (9)		

One-dimensional embedding (Group #3) performs the worst overall. Methods such as DeepWalk (1D), LINE (1D), and `struc2vec` (1D) show significantly larger prediction errors, indicating that extreme dimensionality reduction severely limits the ability to capture essential structural features. Interestingly, LDP (1D) achieves the third-best rank among all methods, demonstrating that simple statistical features can outperform complex embedding in certain scenarios. These findings highlight the advantage of structure-preserving representations for CNN-based robustness prediction and underscore the importance of maintaining rich structural information for accurate performance estimation.

The above comparative analysis underscores the critical role of representation complexity and structural richness in network robustness evaluation.

Structure-based representations, particularly adjacency matrices and modularity matrices, consistently deliver superior performance for CNN-based prediction tasks. Combinations, such as $\mathbf{A}^{\{1,2,3\}}$ and $\mathbf{A}$ & $\mathbf{A}$, further enhance accuracy by incorporating higher-order connectivity and community structure information. In contrast, graph embedding, while flexible and widely adopted for general graph learning, exhibits lower accuracy in robustness prediction, and one-dimensional embedding performs the worst due to excessive information loss. These findings highlight that preserving detailed structural characteristics is essential for reliable robustness assessment, demonstrating the advantage of using rich structure-preserving representations over abstracted or highly compressed alternatives.

5.5.4 *Comparing Machine Learning, CNN, and GNN Approaches for Network Robustness Evaluation*

In this section, the performances of three machine learning approaches, three CNN-based approaches, and two GNN-based approaches for network controllability robustness evaluation, are compared under fair and consistent conditions.

Eight network models are employed: Erdős–Rényi (ER) [49], extremely homogeneous (EH) [50], generic scale-free (SF) [51–54], Barabási–Albert (BA) [51], two small-world models including Watts–Strogatz (WS) [55] and Newman–Watts (NW) [56], q-snapback (QS) [58, 59], and random triangle (RT) [62]. Details of these models and their generation mechanisms are provided in Subsection 2.2.1.

The three machine learning approaches include K-nearest neighbors (KNN) [169], multi-layer perceptron (MLP) [172], and random forest (RF) [171]. The three CNN-based approaches consist of the straightforward robustness predictor (RP) [22], learning feature representation (LFR) [157, 158], and spatial pyramid pooling (SPP) [177, 180]. The two GNN-based approaches use the graph isomorphism network (GIN) [101, 191] and the graph convolutional network (GCN) [187].

For the three machine learning approaches, namely KNN, MLP, and RF, the following six features are employed as input: number of nodes, number of edges, average degree, global efficiency, size of the largest connected component, assortativity [106], and algebraic connectivity [77, 107]. For the three CNN-based approaches and two GNN-based approaches, adjacency matrices serve as input, which are subsequently converted to gray-scale images, transformed to feature representations, or utilized directly, depending on the mechanism of the approach used.

The average prediction errors with standard deviations are summarized in Table 5.5, Table 5.6, and Table 5.7. In these tables, colors highlight the four top-performing methods for each network topology: red indicates first place, blue indicates second place, green indicates third place, and yellow indicates fourth place. All other methods remain in black without special coloring.

Table 5.5: Prediction error (average prediction error ± standard deviation) for controllability robustness evaluation under maximum node-degree attacks using machine learning, CNN, and GNN approaches. Network size $n \in [400, 600]$. FGor each network type, color coding: red indicates first place, blue indicates second place, green indicates third place, and yellow indicates fourth place.

	ER	EH	SF	BA
RP	49.2 ± 49.2	80.9 ± 32.3	21.3 ± 12.2	36.3 ± 19.5
LFR	13.5 ± 7.8	9.0 ± 5.3	35.2 ± 5.3	24.0 ± 10.0
SPP	66.3 ± 25.5	48.6 ± 18.6	10.9 ± 6.2	22.1 ± 13.1
GIN	7.5 ± 3.6	9.5 ± 6.0	4.2 ± 3.2	5.8 ± 3.7
GCN	301.4 ± 17.2	244.0 ± 20.8	397.0 ± 11.4	358.2 ± 20.7
KNN	15.2 ± 12.2	8.5 ± 7.7	8.6 ± 5.9	9.8 ± 7.4
MLP	41.7 ± 10.0	55.8 ± 20.7	50.1 ± 9.4	43.1 ± 17.2
RF	16.5 ± 14.8	8.8 ± 8.0	7.6 ± 5.1	10.4 ± 7.5
	NW	WS	QS	RT
RP	35.5 ± 21.9	32.2 ± 20.1	26.0 ± 12.2	43.1 ± 27.7
LFR	9.2 ± 6.8	9.2 ± 6.0	11.6 ± 7.5	22.4 ± 10.5
SPP	14.5 ± 10.1	14.4 ± 8.6	14.4 ± 8.5	24.8 ± 15.5
GIN	7.6 ± 4.7	7.7 ± 4.7	7.7 ± 4.9	6.2 ± 3.2
GCN	238.3 ± 23.0	231.9 ± 17.3	269.4 ± 13.0	334.3 ± 21.2
KNN	8.4 ± 7.4	7.5 ± 5.3	8.0 ± 7.3	12.7 ± 9.4
MLP	39.9 ± 14.0	37.8 ± 13.9	39.1 ± 12.9	51.7 ± 17.0
RF	7.8 ± 6.0	6.9 ± 5.7	7.6 ± 5.6	15.3 ± 17.0

Table 5.5 presents the comparison scenario under maximum node-degree attacks. The experiments are conducted on networks of sizes $n \in [400, 600]$ across eight network types. GIN achieves the lowest prediction error in five of the eight network types, RF leads in two, and KNN ranks first in

one. Both RF and KNN frequently appear in top three following GIN, whereas MLP and RP consistently exhibit higher errors compared to GIN, RF, and KNN. Moreover, LFR and SPP show moderate performance in occasional second or third places, while GCN records the largest errors across all network types. Overall, GIN is the most reliable method across heterogeneous networks, KNN and RF serve as strong classical baselines, CNN-based methods vary in effectiveness with RP being the weakest, and GCN underperforms significantly, suggesting a mismatch between its message-passing mechanism and the task or feature representation.

Table 5.6: Prediction error (average prediction error ± standard deviation) for controllability robustness evaluation under maximum node-betweenness attacks using machine learning, CNN, and GNN approaches. Network size $n \in [400, 600]$. For each network type, color coding: red indicates first place, blue indicates second place, green indicates third place, and yellow indicates fourth place.

	ER	EH	SF	BA
RP	52.4 ± 20.6	58.7 ± 24.3	58.2 ± 14.3	50.9 ± 22.1
LFR	29.2 ± 11.1	23.9 ± 10.0	52.1 ± 10.3	39.8 ± 14.9
SPP	63.5 ± 23.9	57.5 ± 20.5	27.2 ± 10.7	35.0 ± 16.3
GIN	24.9 ± 7.7	41.3 ± 30.6	23.7 ± 8.6	24.6 ± 10.4
GCN	133.2 ± 18.2	122.2 ± 11.0	142.0 ± 14.4	130.8 ± 14.7
KNN	39.3 ± 30.1	23.8 ± 13.2	26.9 ± 11.8	26.4 ± 11.2
MLP	39.0 ± 17.1	49.6 ± 20.3	34.8 ± 13.5	38.4 ± 13.7
RF	39.1 ± 31.9	25.9 ± 16.6	24.5 ± 9.6	25.9 ± 10.9
	NW	WS	QS	RT
RP	50.4 ± 29.2	39.8 ± 29.6	33.3 ± 15.6	49.4 ± 20.9
LFR	38.3 ± 21.1	36.6 ± 21.4	30.7 ± 14.6	35.3 ± 11.9
SPP	56.8 ± 25.1	53.0 ± 25.9	31.6 ± 13.1	41.3 ± 19.1
GIN	37.3 ± 21.8	34.6 ± 24.8	27.2 ± 12.6	25.9 ± 11.0
GCN	65.4 ± 20.7	58.4 ± 19.8	96.8 ± 14.1	133.5 ± 24.1
KNN	36.1 ± 23.5	32.7 ± 27.0	28.3 ± 13.0	30.3 ± 14.0
MLP	49.2 ± 27.3	46.8 ± 28.3	52.6 ± 21.3	49.5 ± 19.4
RF	33.7 ± 17.8	30.9 ± 24.2	26.2 ± 12.1	32.3 ± 23.3

Table 5.6 summarizes the results from the scenario under maximum node-betweenness attacks. GIN achieves the lowest prediction error in four

of eight network types, demonstrating superior overall performance. RF ranks first in three network types, while KNN leads in one. Both RF and KNN frequently appear in the top three, following GIN. LFR and SPP perform moderately in occasional second or third places, whereas RP shows consistently larger errors. GCN records the largest errors across all network types, indicating severe underperformance. Overall, GIN remains the most reliable method, RF and KNN serve as competitive alternatives, CNN-based methods vary in effectiveness, and GCN underperforms significantly, suggesting a mismatch between its architecture and the task requirements.

Although different attack strategies are applied in Table 5.5 and Table 5.6, the performance remains consistent across both scenarios. Data-driven methods based on CNN and GNN are largely invariant to attack strategies. While machine learning-based methods are theoretically independent of attack strategies, their input feature vectors may or may not align well with certain attack patterns in specific cases. Overall, data-driven approaches for controllability robustness evaluation exhibit strong invariance to attack patterns and other variable factors.

Table 5.7 evaluates the scalability of data-driven methods on networks with sizes $n \in [800, 1200]$. GIN achieves the lowest prediction error in seven out of eight network types, confirming superior performance at larger scales. RF ranks first for one network type, and both RF and KNN frequently appear in the top three, following GIN. LFR delivers moderate results with occasional high positions, whereas SPP and RP remain less competitive. GCN continues to produce the largest errors across all network types, indicating poor adaptability. Overall, GIN demonstrates superior scalability, RF and KNN remain to be reliable alternatives, CNN-based methods show mixed effectiveness, and GCN exhibits persistent limitations that suggest architectural constraints.

For clearer demonstration, while Tables 5.5, 5.6, and 5.7 present the average prediction errors with standard deviations, the corresponding predicted controllability degeneration processes are shown in Figure 5.10 (for Table 5.5), Figure 5.11 (for Table 5.6), and Figure 5.12 (for Table 5.7), respectively.

5.6 Summary

This chapter presents a systematic evaluation of data-driven approaches for network controllability robustness prediction. The study examines multiple representation paradigms, including structure-based matrices, graph

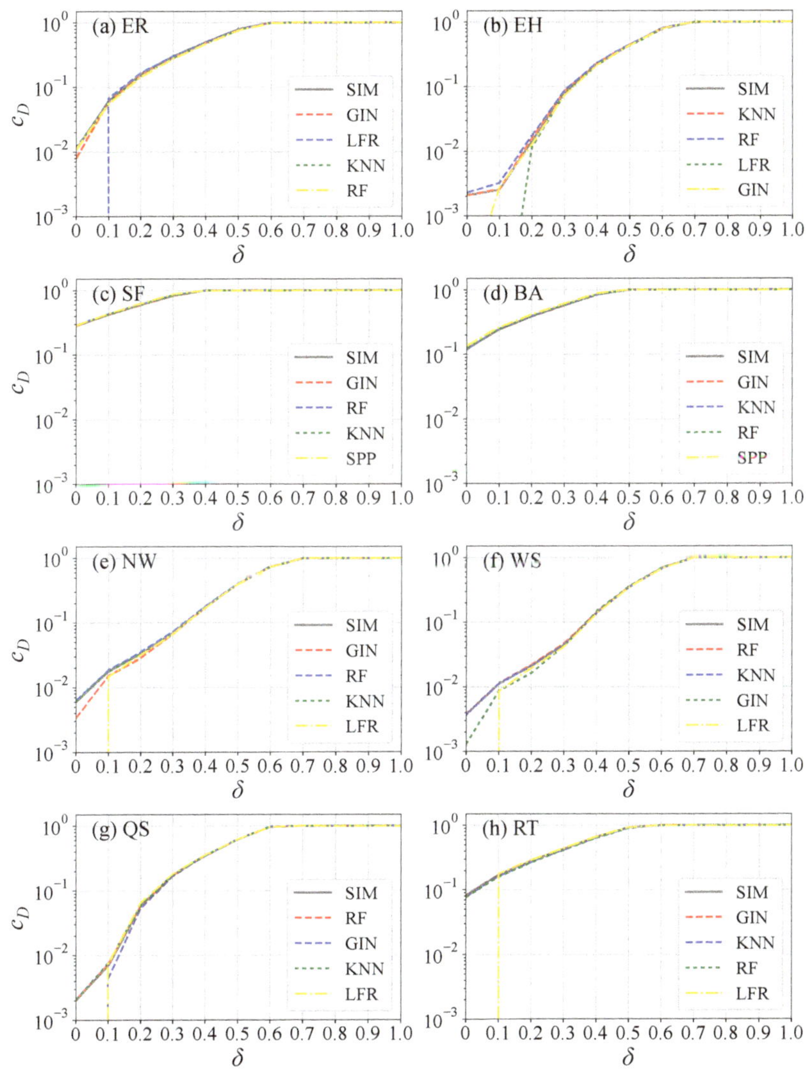

Fig. 5.10: Comparison of controllability robustness process prediction corresponding to data in Table 5.5. For clarity, only the top four performing methods are shown, with attack simulation (SIM) results included as a reference. Gray solid line represents simulation results. Line colors correspond to rankings in the table: red dotted line indicates first place, blue dotted line indicates second place, green dotted line indicates third place, and yellow dotted line indicates fourth place.

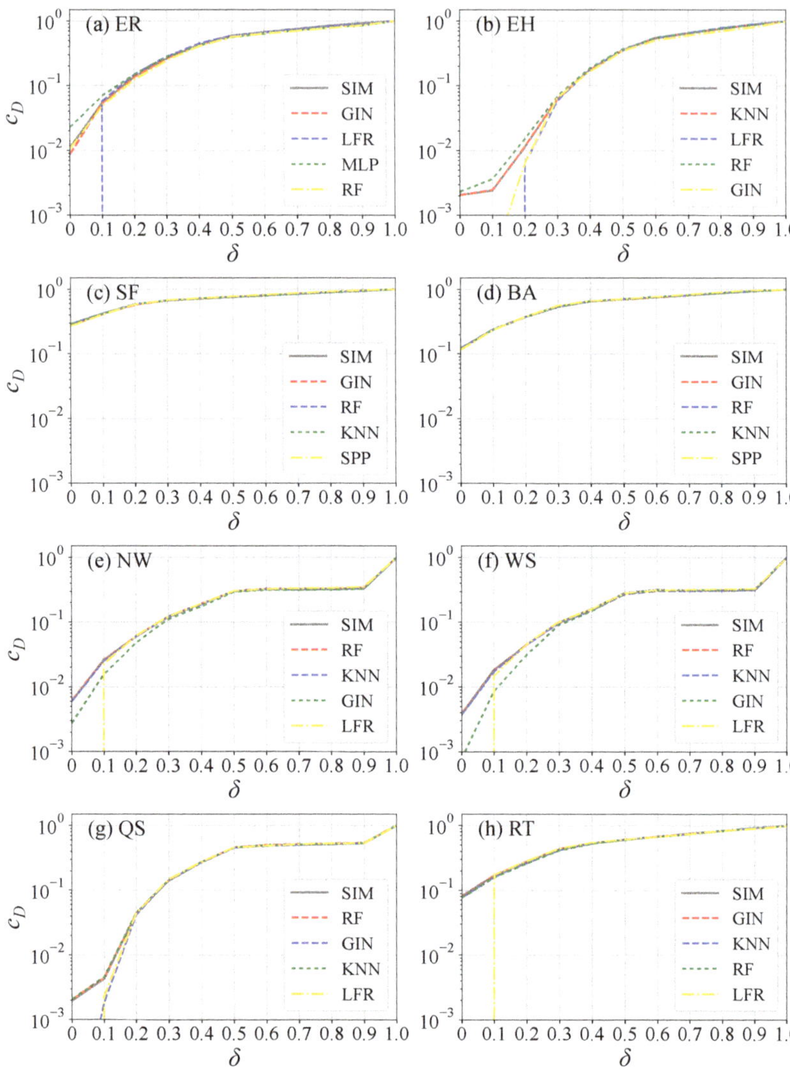

Fig. 5.11: Comparison of controllability robustness process prediction corresponding to data in Table 5.6. For clarity, only the top four performing methods are shown, with attack simulation (SIM) results included as a reference. Gray solid line represents simulation results. Line colors correspond to rankings in the table: red dotted line indicates first place, blue dotted line indicates second place, green dotted line indicates third place, and yellow dotted line indicates fourth place.

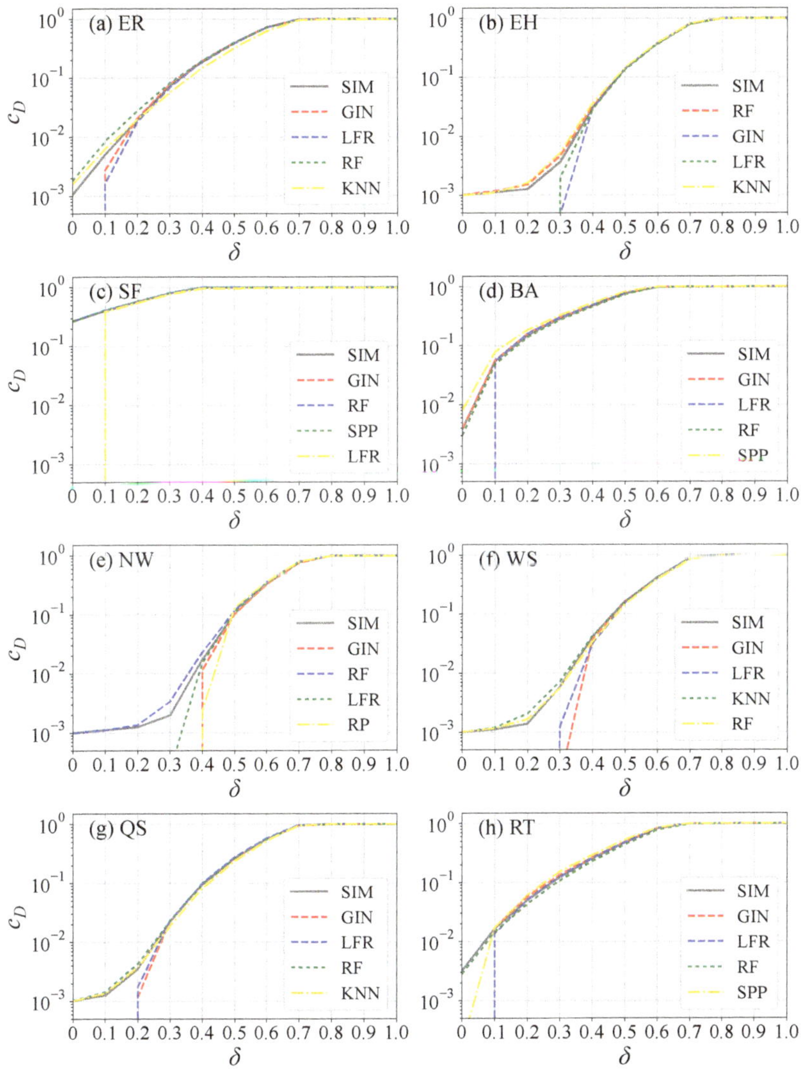

Fig. 5.12: Comparison of controllability robustness process prediction corresponding to data in Table 5.7. For clarity, only the top four performing methods are shown, with attack simulation (SIM) results included as a reference. Gray solid line represents simulation results. Line colors correspond to rankings in the table: red dotted line indicates first place, blue dotted line indicates second place, green dotted line indicates third place, and yellow dotted line indicates fourth place.

Table 5.7: Prediction error (average prediction error ± standard deviation) for controllability robustness evaluation under maximum node-degree attacks using machine learning, CNN, and GNN approaches. Network size $n \in [800, 1200]$. For each network type, color coding: red indicates first place, blue indicates second place, green indicates third place, and yellow indicates fourth place.

	ER	EH	SF	BA
RP	31.5 ± 17.6	59.5 ± 12.1	77.1 ± 8.5	31.7 ± 17.9
LFR	9.6 ± 5.4	7.2 ± 3.4	45.0 ± 12.5	13.4 ± 7.4
SPP	33.6 ± 21.6	62.1 ± 20.0	7.2 ± 5.5	30.5 ± 16.7
GIN	7.4 ± 4.1	5.8 ± 3.7	5.0 ± 3.4	6.6 ± 3.7
GCN	324.1 ± 22.1	282.7 ± 22.7	441.6 ± 13.6	373.1 ± 12.1
KNN	25.9 ± 15.9	9.7 ± 6.6	71.1 ± 58.6	57.4 ± 35.3
MLP	225.6 ± 22.3	220.4 ± 20.8	283.6 ± 10.9	279.0 ± 18.9
RF	14.0 ± 9.8	5.6 ± 3.7	6.0 ± 4.7	13.9 ± 26.1
	NW	WS	QS	RT
RP	13.9 ± 6.6	22.3 ± 8.9	16.1 ± 8.5	24.6 ± 13.1
LFR	7.9 ± 4.5	9.5 ± 5.0	9.5 ± 5.9	12.2 ± 8.2
SPP	31.4 ± 12.6	16.7 ± 7.3	19.6 ± 11.5	23.6 ± 14.8
GIN	6.2 ± 4.0	7.7 ± 4.3	7.0 ± 3.8	7.2 ± 3.6
GCN	281.4 ± 17.1	290.9 ± 15.9	299.1 ± 16.0	343.1 ± 19.9
KNN	19.4 ± 8.3	11.3 ± 8.8	15.7 ± 12.7	47.7 ± 21.0
MLP	223.9 ± 15.7	230.4 ± 17.5	205.3 ± 31.8	288.0 ± 24.1
RF	7.5 ± 7.2	14.2 ± 10.5	10.6 ± 11.3	16.7 ± 14.6

embedding, and one-dimensional feature vectors, with analysis of their impact on the prediction accuracy. Comparative experiments across synthetic and real-world networks demonstrate that representation complexity and structural richness play a critical role in robustness evaluation.

Among the learning frameworks, GNN-based models built on the graph isomorphism network (GIN) consistently achieved superior performance, followed by CNN-based models that leverage structure-preserving representations and traditional machine learning methods with well-selected features. In contrast, general-purpose embedding and shallow machine learning models with poorly selected features exhibited lower accuracy, while one-dimensional embedding performed the worst due to excessive information loss. These findings highlight the importance of maintaining detailed structural information and adopting advanced architectures for reliable robustness assessment.

The data-driven pipeline enables an *a priori*-like evaluation of *a posteriori* metrics by transforming graph structures to representations and feeding them into predictive models, reducing reliance on costly simulations. This paradigm also emphasizes the role of representation learning as an independent research topic and the ultimate goal of uncovering associations among structural properties, learned embedding, and controllability metrics. These useful insights not only improve interpretability but also guide the design of robust networked systems.

Chapter 6

Enhancement Potential for Controllability Robustness

Since the techniques for enhancing controllability robustness introduced in Chapter 4 are inevitably time-consuming, this chapter introduces more efficient edge-cutting techniques for robustness potential assessment leveraging data-driven methods. This framework, termed the robustness potential explorer (RPE), is designed to evaluate and visualize the potential for controllability robustness enhancement in complex networks.

RPE leverages a data-driven approach for estimating whether further optimization is worthwhile, which consists of three components: RPE-F, which extracts features and performs task-oriented feature selection; RPE-V, which visualizes feature distributions before and after enhancement using dimensionality reduction techniques; RPE-P, which predicts robustness enhancement potential through machine learning models. Extensive experiments demonstrate that RPE-P achieves higher predictive accuracy with significantly lower computational cost compared to state-of-the-art methods, while RPE-V offers interpretability and diagnostic insights into feature adequacy. Feature selection using RFE-V further improves efficiency without sacrificing accuracy. Comparative analyses confirm the robustness and scalability of RPE. The chapter concludes by highlighting the effectiveness of RPE in accurately predicting robustness enhancement potential with low computational cost, offering interpretability through visualization and outlining future directions for feature refinement with advanced learning paradigms.

The chapter is organized as follows: Section 6.1 introduces the motivation and background; Section 6.2 reviews network features associated with the controllability robustness; Section 6.3 provides a detailed description of the RPE framework; Section 6.4 presents extensive experimental verification of RPE, including feature selection, visualization, and predictive performance; Section 6.5 summarizes the investigation.

6.1 Introduction

Enhancing the controllability robustness of a specific networked system requires domain-specific knowledge. When critical components such as nodes, edges, connections, and clusters are identifiable, they can be strengthened, shielded and protected to improve robustness [195, 196].

To address controllability and develop a general understanding of controllability robustness under structural disturbances in adverse conditions, such as structural perturbations and malicious attacks, it is effective to focus on improving topological structures under realistic constraints, for example a modest total budget of nodes and edges or a more restricted budget for every node. In this setting, the criticality of a node or edge is determined solely by its structural position, and it is generally assumed that individual nodes and edges have equal sturdiness and cannot be shielded.

Following the second technical question raised in Section 1.1, the study of network robustness primarily encompasses assessment, analysis and optimization, for which optimization is widely regarded as the ultimate objective. Controllability robustness optimization aims to identify a network structure that maximizes a robustness metric under diverse attack scenarios, generally formulated as

$$\mathcal{G}^* = \arg\max_{\mathcal{G}\in\Omega} R\,, \tag{6.1}$$

where Ω denotes the feasible solution space, wherein all network instances $\mathcal{G}$ satisfy the prescribed constraints, and R represents a robustness metric specifically related to maintaining controllability subject to failures and attacks. Determining or constructing the optimal network instance $\mathcal{G}^*$ constitutes an NP-hard problem [79]. Consequently, pursuing a cost-efficient approximation $\hat{\mathcal{G}}^*$ is more practical and computationally feasible, particularly for large-scale networks. Various computational intelligence algorithms were employed for this purpose [79, 80, 197]. However, due to the diversity of disturbance forms, including heterogeneous attack strategies and varying damage types, identifying a universally optimal controllability-robust network instance remains both theoretically and practically infeasible [50]. Therefore, the focus of the concern here shifts from theoretical optimization toward achieving substantial robustness enhancement under realistic constraints.

As summarized in Chapter 4, general robustness optimization strategies can generally be classified into three categories:

(1) *Model design*, which is a conceptually straightforward yet labor-intensive approach grounded in fundamental principles, such as congruence theory [68], Henneberg theory [62], and empirical domain expertise. This method typically involves constructing a network model with inherent structural properties that sustain robustness.
(2) *Component strengthening*, which focuses on embedding specific substructures, including motifs, cliques, and communities, that have been empirically demonstrated to benefit the enhancement of robustness against failures and attacks.
(3) *Rewiring*, which modifies the network topology by introducing controlled randomness or strategic edge adjustments. Although effective in improving robustness, this approach often incurs significant computational overhead, particularly for large-scale networks [79].

Among the above three general strategies, model design and component strengthening are less universal because they rely on domain-specific knowledge and often have conflict with the intrinsic characteristics and constraints of real networks. For example, geographic limitations prevent a highway network from being redesigned to include multiple large fully-connected subnetworks. Component strengthening typically requires an additional budget, which can be practical in many engineering scenarios since the cost of edge addition is often more efficient than rewiring. However, this approach lacks clear criteria for efficiency, as limited budgets may be poorly allocated, potentially resulting in resource waste. Consequently, local structural edge rewiring emerged as the most widely adopted approach for improving robustness.

Using rewiring as the core mechanism, Figure 4.3 illustrates a typical paradigm in which iterative metaheuristic optimization modifies network structures to enhance performance. Table 4.3 summarizes 29 representative methods for optimizing network functionality and robustness for illustration and comparison.

Rewiring offers substantial flexibility, serving as a preventive measure prior to malicious attacks and also as a remedial solution after attacks occurred [198]. Among rewiring techniques, preserving the degree of each node during edge adjustments is in common practice, which has broad applicability across diverse network types. In certain scenarios, however, adding edges may provide a more cost-effective alternative [199, 200]. Based on these considerations, this chapter adopts a degree-preserving rewiring strategy to enhance the controllability robustness of general complex networks.

A major challenge in rewiring-based controllability robustness enhancement, however, lies in its high computational cost, which primarily stems from iterative robustness evaluations during attack simulations rather than from the optimization algorithm itself, as the rewiring operations are computationally negligible. Machine learning-based surrogate models can partially mitigate this burden by bypassing a portion of evaluations [79, 80]. Nevertheless, these models require large volumes of reliable training data, and the reduction in computational overhead remains limited.

Since rewiring-based controllability robustness enhancement is practical, which is widely adopted yet inherently costly, this chapter introduces a method to improve its efficiency. Under a given set of constraints, such as a fixed degree sequence or a limited budget, numerous network instances can be generated, each exhibiting different levels of controllability robustness. Denote the set of all such instances by

$$\mathcal{G}^c = \{\mathcal{G}_1^c, \mathcal{G}_2^c, \dots\},$$

with corresponding performance values

$$R^c = \{R_1^c, R_2^c, \dots\}.$$

Then, define the complete ordered set of R^c values, ranging from the lowest to the highest, as the *spectrum of performance*, and the corresponding set of network instances $\mathcal{G}^c$ as the *spectrum of network configurations*. These spectra should not be confused with the spectral metrics commonly used in network analysis. Quantifying this spectrum and positioning a given network within it, based on structural characteristics and functional capabilities, is critical for informed decision-making. Optimization should be pursued only when it is demonstrably *promising* and necessary; otherwise, alternative strategies such as redesign may offer greater efficiency than costly rewiring-based enhancement of controllability robustness.

This chapter addresses the critical challenge of anticipating the potential return on investment in network optimization, ensuring that structural enhancement is no longer a blind endeavor. Although evolutionary computation has been widely employed to improve network robustness, existing approaches lack prior knowledge of optimizability, leaving expectation management and termination criteria uncertain. To overcome this limitation, a framework is established for visualizing and assessing robustness potential under node degree-preserving rewiring. This framework enables efficient structural robustness optimization for general networks, which can be extended to other forms of robustness analysis and optimization.

In this chapter, first the robustness potential explorer (RPE) is designed, providing a framework for visualizing the robustness enhancement process and predicting the enhancement potential, thereby offering expectation and termination guidance prior to performing costly optimization. RPE comprises three integrated components: RPE-F, RPE-V, and RPE-P. Specifically, RPE-F extracts network features that capture the robustness potential; RPE-V visualizes network instances before and after enhancement-based on RPE-F; RPE-P leverages the extracted features together with machine learning techniques to predict the robustness potential. Finally, through extensive experiments, it is demonstrated that RPE-P significantly outperforms two state-of-the-art CNN- and GNN-based schemes in predicting robustness potential.

6.2 Network Features Associated with Controllability Robustness

In Section 4.1, a series of network representations were introduced, many of which are constructed from or learned using topological and spectral features. The discussions there suggest that widely-used network features may exhibit partial empirical associations with the robustness performance in terms of controllability, connectivity, or other functionalities, in specific scenarios. However, there is no clear evidence that any individual feature or fixed set of features consistently correlate with robustness performance across particular functionalities, nor do such patterns follow universal rules. In contrast, empirical studies indicate that a combination of features often demonstrates stronger associations with robustness than individual features, although these correlations remain non-universal and highly dependent on attack strategies [42].

Specifically, controllability robustness lacks a universal theoretical indicator despite extensive studies on structural features such as centrality, spectral metrics [77], assortativity [106], and natural connectivity [107]. These attributes exhibit correlations with robustness under certain conditions, yet their effectiveness varies significantly across attack strategies and evaluation metrics. Node importance, captured by measures such as degree, betweenness [52], and control centrality [76], also influences network robustness, while motifs including rings and chains provide additional structural support to the robustness [57–59].

Robustness against random failures or targeted attacks is usually assessed through driver-node requirements and connectivity preservation [57,71]. Optimization approaches encompass edge rewiring, spectral tuning, and multi-objective schemes [77,116,122]. Networks with onion-like structures demonstrate strong robustness [71,124], although connectedness and controllability robustness remain distinct properties that require separate evaluation.

6.2.1 *Representative Features*

In this subsection, twenty representative network features are reviewed, including five centrality metrics, nine structural properties, and six spectral metrics, each of which exhibits some degree of correlation with robustness. These features are selected for their ability to capture local, global and spectral characteristics, which are essential for robustness assessment and widely adopted in practice. Because definitions may vary across sources, all features are clearly and consistently defined below to ensure uniform interpretation.

The five centrality metrics are: betweenness (BET), clustering coefficient (CLU), closeness (CLO), eigenvector centrality (EIG), and Katz centrality (KAT). Since these metrics primarily describe individual nodes or edges, their global values are computed by averaging across all nodes or edges, providing a network-level representation.

6.2.1.1 *Betweenness Centrality*

Betweenness centrality measures the structural importance of a node or an edge by quantifying its involvement in shortest paths between other node pairs that pass through the concerned node or edge. For node v, its betweenness is defined as

$$\mathrm{BET}(v) = \sum_{s \neq v \neq t} \frac{\sigma_{st}(v)}{\sigma_{st}}, \tag{6.2}$$

where σ_{st} denotes the total number of shortest paths between nodes s and t, and $\sigma_{st}(v)$ represents the number of those paths that pass through v.

Although betweenness centrality is considered a global measure, each value $\mathrm{BET}(v)$ is computed for an individual node v. To obtain a network-level indicator, the average betweenness across all nodes is calculated and adopted. A higher average value indicates that network flow is concentrated through a small subset of nodes that are critical intermediaries in shortest-path routing. Such concentration increases vulnerability because a targeted removal of these nodes can severely damage the network connectivity and controllability.

6.2.1.2 *Clustering Coefficient*

The clustering coefficient quantifies the local cohesiveness of a network and reflects the tendency of nodes to form tightly interconnected neighborhoods. It serves as an indicator of localized structural patterns that can enhance robustness and facilitate efficient information propagation. A larger clustering coefficient suggests the presence of denser clusters, which often correspond to functional modules or communities within the network. The global clustering coefficient is obtained by averaging the node-wise coefficients across all nodes, where each node-wise coefficient is defined as

$$\mathrm{CLU}(v) = \frac{2m_v}{k_v(k_v - 1)}, \tag{6.3}$$

where m_v denotes the number of existing edges among the k_v neighbors of node v, and k_v represents the degree of node v, in which $2k_v(k_v - 1)$ is actually the total number of possible edges within the neighborhood of node v.

This metric ranges from 0 to 1, where 0 indicates no interconnections among neighbors and 1 represents a fully-connected neighborhood. Dense clustering generally improves robustness against random edge failures and edge-removal attacks by providing redundant local paths, but it may also create vulnerability under targeted attacks. Moreover, excessive clustering can reduce global data-transmission efficiency by increasing path redundancy without improving long-range connectivity.

6.2.1.3 *Eigenvector Centrality*

Eigenvector centrality measures the influence of a node within the network by considering not only its direct connections but also the importance of the nodes to which it is connected. This metric is based on the principle that edges linking to highly influential nodes contribute more to the node's score than edges linking to less influential ones. A high eigenvector score indicates that the node is embedded in a well-connected and influential neighborhood, which often corresponds to structurally critical regions.

Formally, eigenvector centrality for node v is defined as

$$\mathrm{EIG}(v) = \frac{1}{\lambda_{\max}} \sum_{u \in \mathcal{N}_v} A_{vu}\, \mathrm{EIG}(u)\,, \tag{6.4}$$

where A_{vu} denotes the (v, u) entry of the adjacency matrix, $\mathcal{N}_v$ represents the set of neighbors of node v, and $\lambda_{\max}$ is the largest eigenvalue of the adjacency matrix.

Eigenvector centrality is strongly correlated with global connectivity and robustness in networks. Nodes with high eigenvector scores often act as hubs or connectors within influential clusters, making them critical for maintaining controllability. However, this metric can be sensitive to network size and density, and its effectiveness in predicting robustness varies under different attack strategies.

6.2.1.4 *Katz Centrality*

Katz centrality [201] extends the concept of eigenvector centrality by accounting for the influence of both immediate and distant neighbors, while attenuating the contribution of longer paths. This attenuation ensures that direct connections exert a stronger impact on the centrality score than indirect ones, thereby capturing a more nuanced notion of influence propagation.

Unlike eigenvector centrality, which may assign zero scores to nodes in disconnected components, Katz centrality guarantees positive values for all nodes by including a constant term in its definition. Formally, Katz centrality for node v is defined as

$$\mathrm{KAT}(v) = \alpha \sum_{u \in \mathcal{N}_v} A_{uv}\, \mathrm{KAT}(u) + \beta\,, \tag{6.5}$$

where α is a damping factor satisfying $0 < \alpha < \frac{1}{\lambda_{\max}}$, β is a constant representing the initial centrality contribution, A_{uv} denotes the (u, v) entry of the adjacency matrix, and $\mathcal{N}_v$ is the set of neighbors of node v.

Katz centrality is particularly useful in networks where indirect influence matters, such as social and communication networks. A higher Katz score indicates that a node is better-positioned to propagate influence through both short and long paths. However, its computation requires solving a linear system of equations, which can be computationally expensive for large-scale networks. Additionally, the choice of α and β significantly affects the metric's sensitivity and interpretability.

The nine structural properties discussed below are transitivity (TRA), PageRank (PGR), average path length (APL), efficiency (EFF), network diameter (DIA), modularity (MOD), largest cycle (LGC), number of cycles (NOC), and assortativity (AST). These properties capture key aspects of network topology, including local clustering, global connectivity, hierarchical organization, and structural balance. Each reflects a distinct dimension of the network robustness subject to failures or attacks.

6.2.1.5 *Transitivity*

Transitivity quantifies the global clustering tendency of a network by measuring the probability that two neighbors of a node are also connected. It serves as a global counterpart to the local clustering coefficient and is defined by

$$\mathrm{TRA} = \frac{3n_{\Delta}}{n_{\gamma}}, \tag{6.6}$$

where n_{Δ} denotes the number of triangles in the network and n_{γ} represents the number of connected triplets, in which a *triangle* refers to three mutually connected nodes, whereas a *connected triplet* consists of three nodes with at least two edges among them.

High transitivity indicates strong global cohesion with a pronounced community structure. Networks with high transitivity often exhibit localized redundancy, which can improve robustness against random failures and random attacks by providing alternative paths within clusters. However, excessive clustering may also create vulnerability under targeted attacks, as highly cohesive regions can become critical points of destruction.

6.2.1.6 *PageRank*

PageRank, originally introduced for ranking web pages, is based on the principle that a node is considered important if it is linked to other important nodes. This measure incorporates both the quantity and quality of connections and is defined recursively by

$$\mathrm{PGR}(v) = \frac{1-\alpha}{n} + \alpha \sum_{u \in \mathcal{N}_v} \frac{\mathrm{PGR}(u)}{\mathrm{L}(u)}, \tag{6.7}$$

where α is the damping factor, typically set to 0.85 [202], $\mathrm{L}(u)$ denotes the number of outbound links from node u, and $\mathcal{N}_v$ represents the set of neighbors of node v. For undirected networks, each edge is treated as bidirectional.

PageRank captures both direct and indirect influences, making it suitable for identifying globally significant nodes that remarkably contribute to the network connectivity and controllability. Nodes with high PageRank scores often act as structural anchors, whose removal can disproportionately affect the overall network connectivity. However, its effectiveness in robustness analysis depends on the network density and attack patterns, and evaluating PageRank for a large-scale network can be computationally demanding.

6.2.1.7 *Average Path Length*

Average path length (APL) represents the mean of all shortest-path distances among node pairs and serves as a global indicator of how efficiently data information can traverse the network. Networks with smaller APL values typically exhibit higher connectivity and faster communication.

Formally, APL is defined as

$$\mathrm{APL} = \frac{1}{n(n-1)} \sum_{\substack{s,t \in \mathcal{V} \\ s \neq t}} d_{st}\,, \tag{6.8}$$

where d_{st} denotes the shortest-path distance between nodes s and t, and n is the total number of nodes in the network.

Lower APL values generally indicate efficient global connectivity, which can enhance controllability by reducing the number of steps required for signal propagation. However, networks optimized for minimal APL often exhibit hub-dominated structures, which may increase vulnerability under targeted attacks.

6.2.1.8 *Efficiency*

Efficiency (EFF) complements APL by evaluating the mean of the inverse shortest-path distances between all node pairs, emphasizing accessibility even in large or sparse networks. Higher EFF values indicate that nodes can reach each other with minimal effort, which is critical for maintaining effective communication and structural functionality.

Formally, EFF is defined as

$$\mathrm{EFF} = \frac{1}{n(n-1)} \sum_{\substack{s,t \in \mathcal{V} \\ s \neq t}} \frac{1}{d_{st}}\,, \tag{6.9}$$

where d_{st} denotes the shortest-path distance between nodes s and t, and n is the total number of nodes.

Unlike APL, which averages shortest-path lengths, EFF averages their reciprocals. Consequently, EFF is more sensitive to disconnected or distant node pairs, making it a valuable complement to APL for assessing global connectivity and robustness under structural variations or disturbances.

6.2.1.9 *Network Diameter*

Network diameter (DIA) represents the greatest shortest-path distance between any pair of nodes in the network, serving as a measure of its maximum extent. This metric reflects the worst-case communication delay and provides insight into the overall reachability.

Formally, DIA is defined as

$$\mathrm{DIA} = \max_{s,t \in \mathcal{V}} d_{st} , \tag{6.10}$$

where d_{st} denotes the shortest-path distance between nodes s and t.

Networks with large diameters tend to exhibit slower information transmission and reduced efficiency compared to those with smaller diameters. While a smaller diameter generally indicates better connectivity, minimizing diameter alone can lead to hub-dominated structures, which may increase vulnerability under targeted attacks.

6.2.1.10 *Modularity*

Modularity (MOD) evaluates the strength of a community structure within a network by comparing the observed density of intra-community edges to that expected in a random network with the same degree distribution. Higher MOD values indicate better-defined communities, which often correspond to functional or organizational modules.

Formally, MOD is defined as

$$\mathrm{MOD} = \frac{1}{2m} \sum_{u,v} \left(A_{uv} - \frac{k_u k_v}{2m} \right) \delta_{uv} , \tag{6.11}$$

where A_{uv} denotes the (u, v) entry of the adjacency matrix, k_u and k_v represent the degrees of nodes u and v, m is the total number of edges in the network, and $\delta_{uv} = 1$ if nodes u and v belong to the same community, and 0 otherwise.

Modularity is widely used in community detection and robustness analysis because networks with strong modularity typically exhibit localized fault tolerance. However, excessive modularity can reduce global connectivity and controllability, as inter-community links become sparse and critical for maintaining the overall network functionality.

6.2.1.11 *Largest Cycle*

Empirical studies suggest that cycle-related features exhibit a stronger correlation with network robustness than the degree-based assortativity [198]. Identifying the largest cycle in a graph is computationally challenging due to the combinatorial nature of cycle detection. A common approach employs depth-first search to enumerate cycles while tracking the largest one encountered.

6.2.1.12 *Number of Cycles*

Another metric under consideration is the number of cycles (NOC). The total number of cycles in a network provides insight into its structural redundancy and robustness. Counting these cycles can be performed concurrently with the search for the largest cycle by leveraging similar traversal strategies, such as the depth-first search or backtracking algorithm.

6.2.1.13 *Assortativity*

Assortativity measures the tendency of nodes to connect with other nodes that share similar structural attributes. A widely used similarity index is based on node degrees, capturing degree–degree correlations across edges.

Formally, AST is defined as

$$\text{AST} = \frac{\sum_i u_i v_i - \frac{1}{m}\sum_i u_i \sum_i v_i}{\sqrt{\left(\sum_i u_i^2 - \frac{1}{m}\left(\sum_i u_i\right)^2\right)\left(\sum_i v_i^2 - \frac{1}{m}\left(\sum_i v_i\right)^2\right)}}, \tag{6.12}$$

where u_i and v_i denote the degrees of the endpoints of the i-th edge, and m is the total number of edges. The value of AST ranges from -1 to 1, where AST > 0 indicates assortative mixing (nodes with similar degrees tend to connect to each other), and AST < 0 indicates disassortative mixing (nodes with dissimilar degrees are more likely to connect to each other).

Assortativity influences robustness by shaping connectivity patterns: assortative networks often exhibit strong local cohesion but may concentrate vulnerability within high-degree clusters, whereas disassortative networks distribute connectivity more evenly, reducing hub dependency but potentially increasing path lengths.

The spectral metrics commonly considered include spectral radius (RAD), spectral gap (GAP), natural connectivity (NCO), algebraic connectivity (ACO), effective resistance (EFR), and the number of spanning trees (NST) [77,107]. It is important to emphasize that, although both spectral metrics and eigenvector centrality (EIG) rely on eigen-decomposition of adjacency or Laplacian matrices, their scopes differ fundamentally: EIG is a node-level centrality measure that evaluates the relative influence of individual nodes, whereas spectral metrics characterize global structural properties of the entire network, providing insights into connectivity and robustness. Although both primarily reflect connectivity rather than controllability, they are included in the consideration because controllability is also implicitly and partially related to connectivity.

6.2.1.14 *Spectral Radius*

Spectral radius (RAD) represents the largest absolute eigenvalue of the adjacency matrix and serves as an indicator of overall connectivity strength. A larger spectral radius typically corresponds to denser connectivity and greater potential for a dynamic process such as diffusion or synchronization, but it may also concentrate vulnerability into a hub-dominated region, making the structure more susceptible to targeted attacks.

Formally, RAD is defined as

$$\mathrm{RAD} = \max\{|\lambda| : \lambda \text{ is an eigenvalue of } \mathbf{A}\}\,, \tag{6.13}$$

where $\mathbf{A}$ denotes the adjacency matrix.

6.2.1.15 *Spectral Gap*

Spectral gap (GAP) quantifies the difference between the largest and the second-largest eigenvalues of the adjacency matrix, offering insight into expansion properties and structural robustness against perturbations. A larger spectral gap generally indicates stronger connectivity and faster convergence of a dynamic process such as diffusion.

Let $\lambda_1 \geq \lambda_2 \geq \cdots \geq \lambda_N$ denote the eigenvalues of the adjacency matrix. Then,

$$\mathrm{GAP} = \lambda_1 - \lambda_2\,. \tag{6.14}$$

6.2.1.16 *Natural Connectivity*

Natural connectivity (NCO) measures the structural robustness by considering the redundancy of alternative paths. It is computed as the logarithm of the average exponential of the adjacency eigenvalues, which accounts for all possible walks in the network, as follows:

$$\text{NCO} = \ln\left(\frac{1}{n}\sum_{i=1}^{n} e^{\lambda_i}\right), \tag{6.15}$$

where λ_i denotes the i-th eigenvalue of the adjacency matrix and n is the number of nodes.

Larger NCO values indicate greater structural redundancy, which generally improves robustness against random failures and perturbations by providing multiple alternative paths for connectivity.

6.2.1.17 *Algebraic Connectivity*

Algebraic connectivity (ACO) is defined as the second-smallest eigenvalue of the Laplacian matrix, which reflects overall structural connectivity and tolerance to fragmentation. A larger ACO indicates stronger connectivity and higher resistance to node or edge removal.

Let $\mu_1 \leq \mu_2 \leq \cdots \leq \mu_n$ denote the Laplacian eigenvalues. Then,

$$\text{ACO} = \mu_2\,. \tag{6.16}$$

6.2.1.18 *Effective Resistance*

Effective resistance (EFR) evaluates the ease of flow across the network by considering all paths between nodes. It is expressed in terms of Laplacian eigenvalues, which is closely related to network reliability and electrical analogies, as follows:

$$\text{EFR} = n\sum_{i=2}^{n}\frac{1}{\mu_i}, \tag{6.17}$$

where μ_i denotes the i-th Laplacian eigenvalue and n is the number of nodes.

Smaller EFR values correspond to structures with better overall connectivity and multiple redundant paths, which reduce vulnerability to node- or edge-removal attacks.

6.2.1.19 *Number of Spanning Trees*

The number of spanning trees (NST) measures structural redundancy. A spanning tree is a cycle-free subgraph that connects all nodes. According to Kirchhoff's matrix-tree theorem, NST equals any cofactor of the Laplacian matrix:

$$\text{NST} = \det(\mathbf{L}^*)\,, \tag{6.18}$$

where **L**$*$ is the Laplacian matrix with any one row and its corresponding column removed.

A larger NST value indicates greater structural robustness and connectivity, as more spanning trees imply multiple alternative ways to maintain full connectivity to resist edge failures.

6.2.2 *Correlation Between Controllability Robustness and Structural Features*

Table 6.1: Pearson correlation coefficients between controllability robustness and twenty network features under maximum node-degree-based attack. A "$*$" symbol indicates statistical significance, without which means insignificant.

	ER	EH	SF	BA	QS	RT
BET	0.53*	0.50*	0.33*	0.27*	0.30*	0.35*
CLU	0.18*	0.02	−0.10*	0.03	0.32*	0.03
CLO	0.01	−0.09*	−0.19*	−0.24*	0.42*	−0.29*
EIG	0.34*	0.31*	0.41*	0.05	0.49*	0.09*
KAT	0.44*	0.37*	0.25*	0.12*	0.47*	0.26*
TRA	0.24*	0.02	0.08*	0.07	0.34*	0.11*
PRG	0.44*	0.36*	0.45*	0.14*	0.47*	0.23*
APL	−0.04	0.03	−0.45*	0.16*	−0.42*	0.10*
EFF	0.07	−0.03	−0.17*	−0.20*	0.45*	−0.25*
DIA	0.03	0.17*	−0.37*	0.22*	−0.40*	0.23*
MOD	0.16*	0.25*	0.14*	0.32*	−0.29*	0.41*
LGC	−0.40*	−0.30*	−0.18*	−0.21*	−0.40*	−0.30*
NOC	−0.46*	−0.40*	−0.44*	−0.25*	−0.33*	−0.37*
AST	0.22*	0.14*	0.03	0.00	−0.14*	−0.07
RAD	−0.28*	−0.38*	−0.53*	−0.30*	0.14*	−0.48*
GAP	−0.08*	−0.34*	−0.52*	−0.22*	0.25*	−0.18*
NCO	−0.22*	−0.37*	−0.53*	−0.32*	0.20*	−0.43*
ACO	−0.14*	−0.37*	−0.15*	−0.42*	0.32*	−0.53*
EFR	−0.20*	−0.27*	−0.13*	−0.10*	−0.33*	−0.23*
NST	−0.31*	−0.39*	−0.30*	−0.44*	0.16*	−0.57*

Table 6.1 presents Pearson correlation coefficients between controllability robustness and twenty structural features under maximum node-degree-

based attacks. The results reveal substantial variability across network types. For instance, features such as clustering coefficient (CLU), transitivity (TRA), spectral radius (RAD), spectral gap (GAP), and natural connectivity (NCO) exhibit strong positive correlations for controllability robustness of ER networks, suggesting their relevance in that topology. However, these relationships are not consistent across other network models, where both the magnitude and the sign of correlation coefficients vary significantly. In some cases, a feature shows positive correlation for one topology but negative correlation for another, indicating that no single metric can serve as a universal predictor of robustness.

If a single feature or a small set of features could consistently indicate network robustness under concentrated scenarios, for example, controllability robustness under maximum node-degree-based attacks, these features would serve as reliable indicators instead of the time-consuming attack simulations and data-driven approaches. This is because, in general, feature-based evaluation is significantly less costly than attack simulations or data-driven approaches. However, as shown in Table 6.1, even under the restricted setting of maximum node-degree-based attacks, no feature or fixed subset of features demonstrates consistent reliability. Both the magnitude and the sign of the correlation coefficient varies across network types, indicating that robustness cannot be captured by any single metric. This variability underscores the need for an ensemble approach that integrates multiple features for more reliable assessment.

6.3 Robustness Potential Exploration Framework

To facilitate the investigation of structural robustness under attacks and failures, a framework named robustness potential explorer (RPE) was introduced [26]. While the original work focused primarily on connectivity robustness, this book applies RPE to controllability robustness analysis. As a data-driven approach, RPE imposes no restrictions on metrics, attack strategies, or network types, making it broadly applicable.

RPE consists of three functional components: RPE-F, which represents networks through extracted structural and spectral features; RPE-V, which provides visualization for comparative analysis of controllability robustness enhancement; RPE-P, which predicts the potential for robustness improvement. Although RPE-P can also perform direct robustness evaluation, the emphasis here is on its capability to identify improvement potential but not for a static assessment.

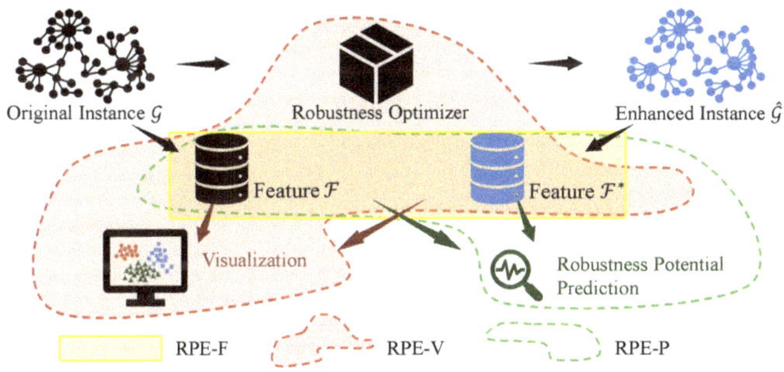

Fig. 6.1: Framework of the robustness potential explorer (RPE), illustrating its three components: RPE-F for feature extraction, RPE-V for visualization, and RPE-P for robustness potential prediction. The process begins with an original network instance $\mathcal{G}$, applies a robustness optimizer, and outputs an enhanced instance $\mathcal{G}^*$.

Figure 6.1 illustrates the framework of RPE. The robustness optimizer modifies the network topology to improve robustness, where any practical robustness metric expressed in a form similar to Equation (3.1) can be applied. Importantly, robustness enhancement is not the sole objective of RPE. In addition to optimization, the original network $\mathcal{G}$ is used to extract a feature set $\mathcal{F}$ comprising structural and spectral attributes. The same feature extraction process is applied to the enhanced instance $\mathcal{G}'$, yielding a corresponding set $\mathcal{F}'$. These feature sets support visualization and prediction of robustness potential.

Note that, although raw network data have been successfully used for robustness performance prediction [101], they are unsuitable for visualization and comparative analysis before and after enhancement. Moreover, the objective here is to uncover correlations between extracted features and robustness performance. Therefore, machine learning algorithms are employed to process feature sets rather than raw structural data, enabling more accurate prediction and improved interpretability.

6.3.1 *Visualization of Controllability Robustness Enhancement*

The twenty network features introduced in Subsection 6.2.1 form the RPE-F module, a core component of the RPE framework. However, extending RPE-F with additional features or assigning different weights is beyond the scope of this study.

The visualization module RPE-V illustrates controllability robustness enhancement from two perspectives: (1) the enhancement process and (2) the comparison of network instances before and after enhancement. Rather than relying on single robustness metric values, which are unreliable due to indeterminacy caused by ties in node selection and due to the impracticality of repeated attack simulations, RPE-V adopts a topological perspective. Direct visualization of network structures is challenging because adjacency matrices or simple plots fail to reveal meaningful differences. Therefore, feature-based visualization is employed.

For this purpose, feature sets before and after enhancement are projected into a two-dimensional space using dimensionality reduction techniques. Methods such as t-distributed stochastic neighbor embedding (t-SNE) [203], self-organizing maps (SOM) [204], and uniform manifold approximation and projection (UMAP) [205] are suitable. In the case study here, t-SNE is chosen for its popularity and ability to preserve local structure in higher-dimensional data. Unlike linear methods, such as principal component analysis (PCA), t-SNE captures complex patterns by minimizing divergence between feature distributions, making it effective for exploratory analysis. Other dimensionality reduction techniques can also be integrated into RPE-V, if needed.

6.3.2 *Predicting the Robustness Potential*

The robustness optimizer modifies network topology under practical constraints to search for structures with improved controllability robustness. However, robustness enhancement itself is not the primary focus of RPE.

In this study, a surrogate-assisted evolutionary algorithm [79] is employed, which integrates two key components: (1) mutation and crossover operators that introduce structural perturbations, and (2) a surrogate-assisted evaluation system, where machine-learning-based models approximate robustness metrics, which significantly reduce computational cost by partially bypassing attack-simulation-based evaluations.

RPE-P employs a robustness optimizer but focuses primarily on predicting the enhancement potential of controllability robustness rather than estimating static robustness performance, as in previous studies [22, 79, 97]. This distinction enables informed decisions on whether further optimization should be pursued.

Figure 6.2 illustrates the variability of controllability robustness among rewired variants of an original network $\mathcal{G}$. Even under strict constraints

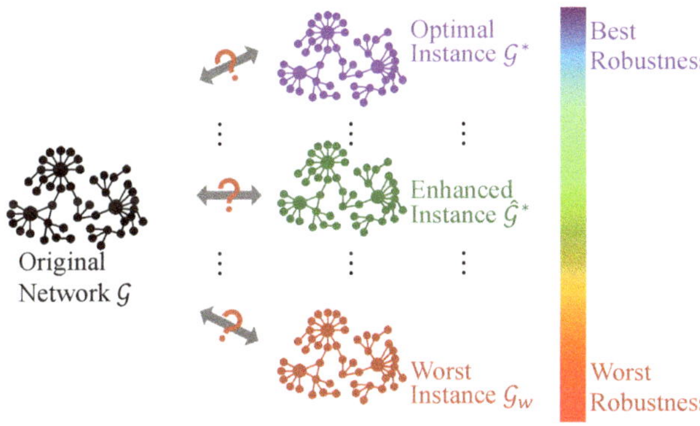

Fig. 6.2: Positioning a network within the spectrum of performance. The color bar represents robustness levels from worst (red) to best (purple). RPE evaluates a given network $\mathcal{G}$ within this spectrum based on its configuration and predicts the best achievable robustness ($\mathcal{G}^*$) through RPE-P.

such as degree preservation, numerous rewired configurations exist, spanning a wide spectrum of robustness from the worst-performing instance $\mathcal{G}_w$ to the optimal instance $\mathcal{G}^*$. The enhanced instance $\mathcal{G}'$, produced by a robustness optimizer, represents one possible improvement but not necessarily the best achievable configuration. Rather than mapping each structure to its exact position in the spectrum, which is unnecessary and indeed computationally infeasible, RPE-P aims to estimate an upper bound of robustness performance attainable by any rewired variant of $\mathcal{G}$.

To achieve this, RPE-P connects a set of rewired variants to the unique optimal robustness performance using extracted structural and spectral features instead of raw network data. This choice not only improves interpretability but also facilitates visualization in RPE-V, where dimensionality reduction techniques such as t-SNE are employed to compare feature distributions before and after enhancement.

6.4 Experimental Validation of the Robustness Potential Explorer

This section demonstrates the implementation of the robustness potential explorer (RPE) shown in Figure 6.1. The feature extraction module, RPE-F, utilizes the twenty structural and spectral features introduced in Subsection 6.2.1. For visualization, RPE-V employs t-distributed stochastic neighbor embedding (t-SNE) [203] to project higher-dimensional feature sets into a two-dimensional space, enabling comparative analysis before and after robustness enhancement. Finally, the prediction module, RPE-P, is implemented using three machine-learning models: random forest (RF) [171], K-nearest neighbors (KNN) [169], and ulti-layer perceptron (MLP) [172], which collectively estimate the controllability robustness enhancement potential of a given network.

A comprehensive robustness evaluation is performed on a total of six synthetic models with undirected networks, two small-world models, namely the Watts–Strogatz (WS) [55] model, the Newman–Watts (NW) [56] model are excluded from the eight network types introduced in Subsection 2.2.1. Thus, the six network types includes the Erdős–Rényi (ER) random-graph [49], extreme homogeneous (EH) [50], generic scale-free (SF) [53], Barabási–Albert (BA) scale-free [206], q-snapback (QS) [58, 59], and random triangle (RT) [62] networks. Details are shown in Subsection 2.2.1.

For different experimental purposes and considering the time consumption of optimization, the number of nodes is set differently in different experiments, uniformly generally within $n \in [100, 1000]$. The average degree of each network is uniformly randomly drawn from $\langle k \rangle \in [6, 12]$.

Here, the controllability robustness metric in Equation (3.1) is considered under maximum node-degree-based attacks, while the RPE framework is inherently invariant to any attack strategies, nor controllability robustness or any other robustness metrics. RPE is compared to two state-of-the-art methods: a CNN-based approach, spatial pyramid pooling (SPP) [180], and a GNN-based approach, graph isomorphism network (GIN) [101].

6.4.1 *Robustness Enhancement*

The robustness enhancement process is implemented using the surrogate-assisted evolutionary algorithm [79] in the following setting: population size of 15, maximum iterations of 200, network size $n = 1000$, mutation and crossover rates of 0.5, and rewiring of 10 edge pairs per mutation.

Figure 6.3 illustrates the optimization dynamics for controllability robustness, where each subplot presents the optimization trajectory of a single network instance. Because a smaller proportion of the required driver nodes indicates stronger controllability robustness, the enhancement task is formulated as a minimization problem. The blue dashed line shows the best robustness value achieved within the population at each iteration, whereas the red dashed line denotes the robustness of the original network instance. The light-blue shaded region reflects the variation in robustness values among

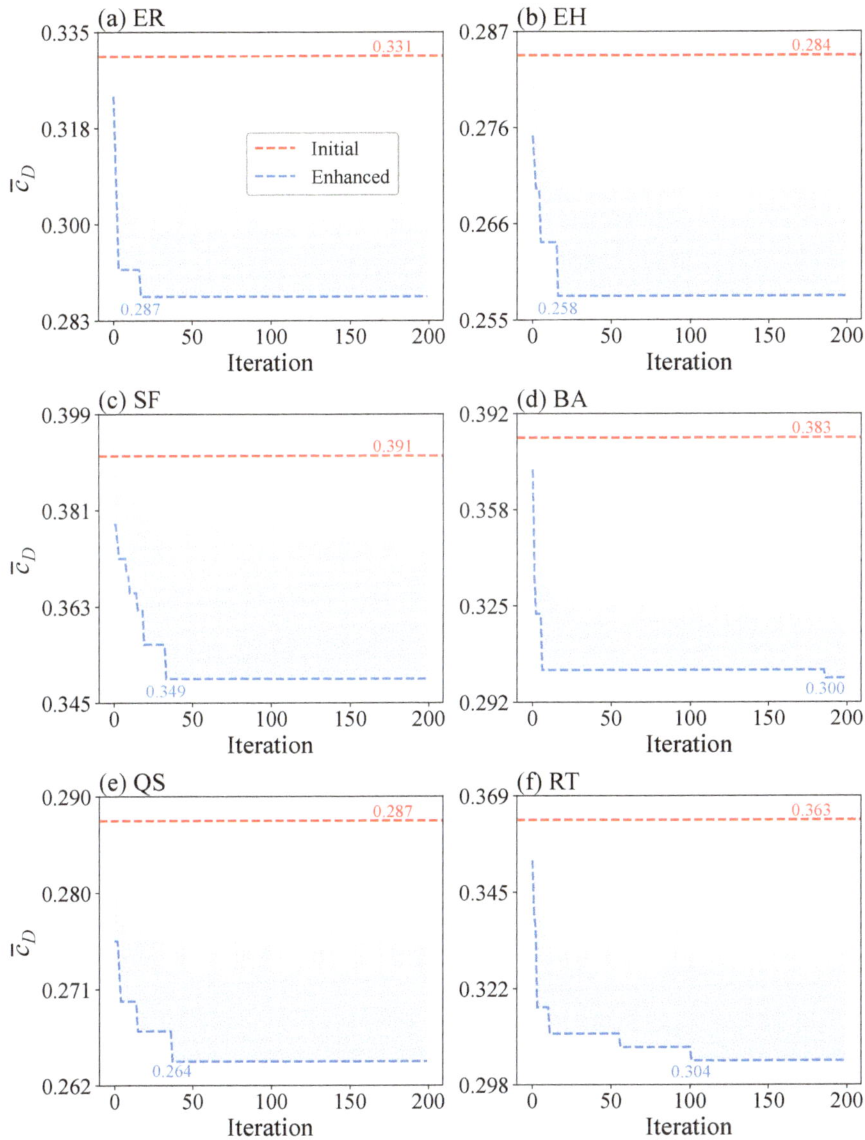

Fig. 6.3: Robustness enhancement trajectories for ER, EH, SF, BA, QS, and RT networks, where each subplot presents the optimization trajectory of a single network instance. The red dashed line denotes the initial controllability robustness, while the blue dashed line represents the best robustness obtained during optimization. Shaded regions illustrate variations across the population throughout iterations.

intermediate solutions. Across all network types, robustness improves progressively through iterative optimization; however, both the magnitude of improvement and the variation among intermediate instances differ substantially in topology. Considering the computational cost of robustness evaluation and the large number of candidate networks, the iteration limit is conservatively set to 200 for networks with 1000 nodes. The convergence patterns in Figure 6.3 demonstrate that this setting achieves a reasonable balance between optimization quality and computational feasibility.

Table 6.2: Average controllability robustness values ($\pm$ standard deviation) before and after enhancement. $\Delta_{R_{PT}}$ denotes the improvement in controllability robustness following sufficient enhancement. Results are averaged over 1000 instances for each network type.

	Initial Robustness	After Enhancement	$\Delta_{R_{PT}}$
ER	0.328 ± 0.064	0.307 ± 0.060	0.021 ± 0.009
EH	0.300 ± 0.060	0.288 ± 0.057	0.012 ± 0.006
SF	0.402 ± 0.077	0.382 ± 0.075	0.019 ± 0.011
BA	0.384 ± 0.076	0.315 ± 0.061	0.069 ± 0.019
QS	0.309 ± 0.061	0.299 ± 0.058	0.010 ± 0.006
RT	0.363 ± 0.074	0.323 ± 0.064	0.039 ± 0.016

Table 6.2 reports the average controllability robustness values computed using Equation (3.1) before and after enhancement, along with their differences. Results are averaged over 1000 instances for each network type. Although the percolation-theory-based robustness metric is employed here, the proposed framework is applicable to any robustness metric.

The overall results summarized in Table 6.2 are consistent with the single-instance optimization trajectories shown in Figure 6.3. Enhancement potential varies considerably across network types. Notably, EH networks, which are known to exhibit strong controllability robustness [50], start with the best initial robustness (smallest proportion of required driver nodes) among all six types but demonstrate relatively limited improvement potential. QS, a model specifically designed for enhanced controllability robustness, also shows strong initial robustness and similarly modest improvement potential.

In contrast, SF and BA networks exhibit weaker initial controllability robustness. However, their enhancement potential differs substantially: BA achieves the most significant improvement, whereas SF shows only minor gains. These findings suggest that networks with or without inherently strong controllability robustness can benefit from structural optimization. Predicting enhancement potential accurately is therefore critical for guiding further investigation.

The variation observed from Table 6.2 stems from three sources of randomness: (1) the initial robustness of randomly generated instances, which determines their positions within the robustness spectrum; (2) the stochastic nature of the evolutionary optimization process; (3) the robustness evaluation procedure based on attack simulations. To mitigate these diverse effects, 1000 random instances are generated for each network type, and their average robustness values along with standard deviations are reported in Table 6.2. These aggregated results provide a reliable estimate of enhancement potential and highlight the topology-dependent nature of controllability robustness optimization.

Rather than presenting only robustness metrics, RPE-V provides a visualization of feature sets before and after enhancement in a two-dimensional space using t-SNE. Figure 6.4 shows the visualization for each network type, where asterisks ($*$) denote robustness-enhanced instances. For the twenty selected features, clear separation between the original and the enhanced instances is evident for ER, SF, BA, and RT networks, indicating that robustness enhancement induces substantial structural changes in these topologies. However, EH and QS networks exhibit overlapping clusters, suggesting that enhancement modifies their feature distributions less significantly. These two types of networks also correspond to the lowest overall enhancement potential.

The above observation reveals that the impact of rewiring on structural properties is topology-dependent: networks with strong hierarchical organization (e.g., SF, BA, and RT) and higher enhancement potential tend to exhibit more pronounced feature shifts, whereas homogeneous or random-like networks with modest potential (e.g., EH and QS) show limited differentiation after enhancement. Notably, the degree of separation observed from Figure 6.4 appears proportional to the robustness enhancement potential reported in Table 6.2.

Together with Figure 6.3, the subplots in Figure 6.4 demonstrate the effectiveness of the selected feature set. When the original and the robustness-enhanced instances are clearly distinguishable, the features exhibit a strong correlation with controllability robustness, and the visualization conveys this relationship more intuitively than the numerical correlations shown in

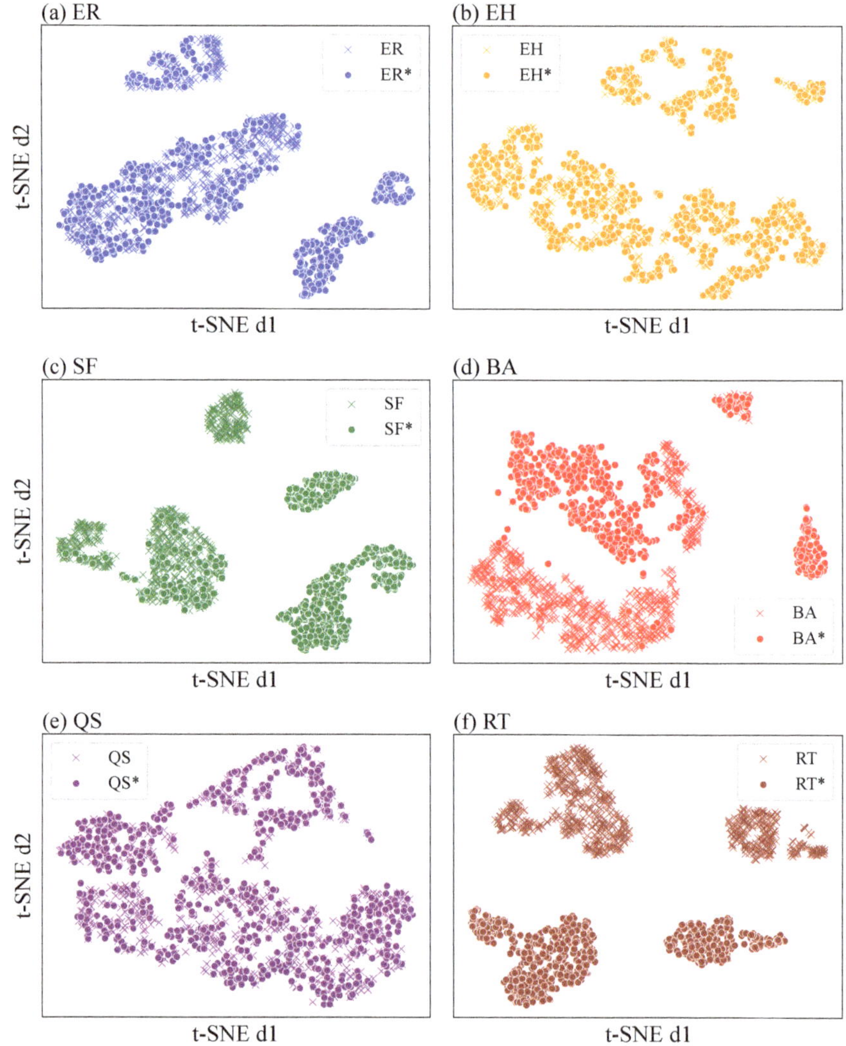

Fig. 6.4: RPE-V visualization of feature sets (RPE-F) before and after robustness enhancement for ER, EH, SF, BA, QS, and RT networks using t-SNE. Colors indicate different network types, and markers distinguish original instances from enhanced ones ($*$). Each panel illustrates structural changes induced by enhancement in a two-dimensional feature space.

Table 6.1. Conversely, overlapping clusters suggest that the chosen features are insufficient for capturing robustness enhancement. Thus, RPE-V not only visualizes the representation of network instances through RPE-F but also serves as an implicit diagnostic tool for assessing the adequacy of the selected features, motivating further exploration of more informative robustness-related attributes.

Figure 6.5 presents a t-SNE visualization that combines all six network types into a unified two-dimensional feature space, including both original and robustness-enhanced instances. Compared to the visualizations in [26], where RPE-V was applied to connectivity robustness, the clusters in Figures 6.4 and 6.5 are less distinguishable. This observation suggests that the widely-used twenty features capture connectivity robustness more effectively than controllability robustness, underscoring the need for designing more informative features specifically tailored to controllability robustness. Nevertheless, the integrated view reveals cross-topology relationships while retaining patterns observed from individual networks. Enhanced instances generally shift away from their original positions, indicating structural changes induced by optimization. In this figure, SF, BA, and RT form distinct clusters, whereas ER, EH, and QS exhibit overlapping regions, suggesting similar feature distributions after enhancement. These patterns align with Figure 6.4. Moreover, the separation between BA and SF, despite the fact that both are scale-free, further demonstrates that degree distribution alone does not determine the controllability robustness.

6.4.2 *Robustness Potential Prediction*

Different from RPE-V, which focuses on visualization and assessing the adequacy of RPE-F, RPE-P provides a practical measure of the controllability robustness potential of complex networks. As illustrated by Figure 6.2, RPE-P estimates the best achievable robustness for any given network instance by positioning it into the spectrum of performance based on its structural configuration in the optimization space.

The training dataset for RPE-P consists of 1000 randomly generated instances for each network type of ER, EH, SF, BA, QS, and RT, paired with their corresponding optimized robustness values obtained through degree-preserving rewiring. In total, 6000 instances are used for training and 600 for testing, with 100 test instances per network type. To implement RPE-P, three classical regression models are employed: RF [171], KNN [169], and MLP [172]. Instead of employing more expressive and powerful deep neural

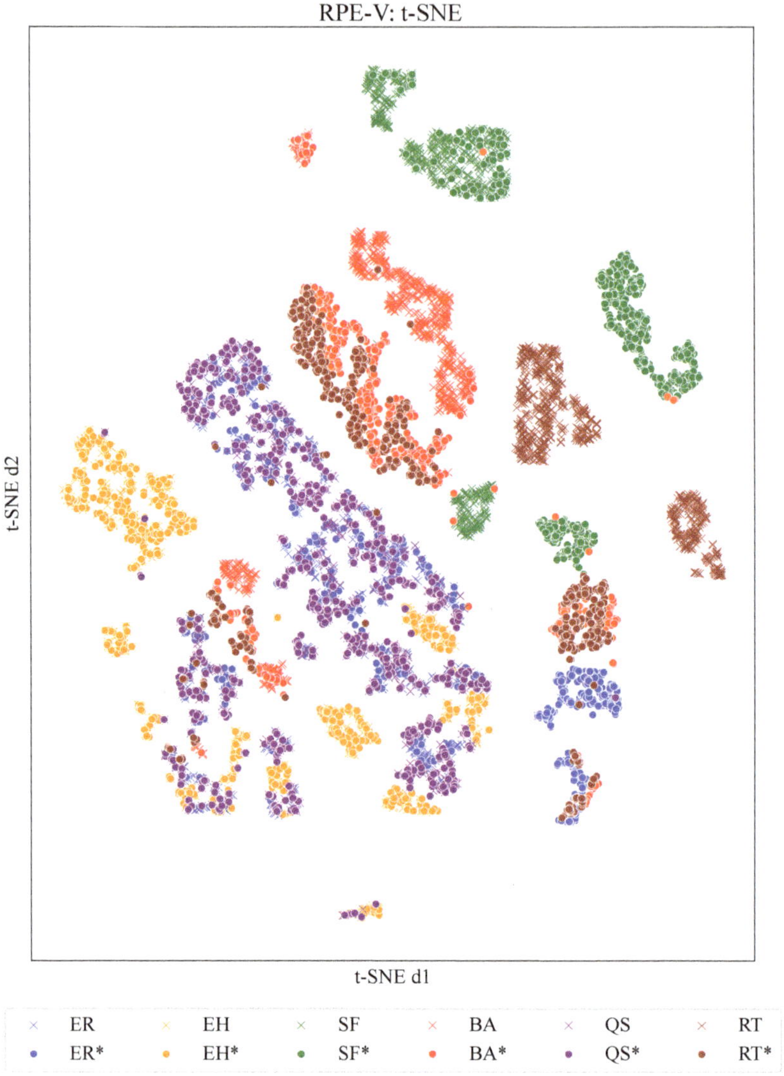

Fig. 6.5: RPE-V visualization of feature sets (RPE-F) before and after robustness enhancement for ER, EH, SF, BA, QS, and RT networks using t-SNE, combined into a single plot. Colors distinguish network types, and markers indicate original (∗) and enhanced instances.

network models, shallow machine learning methods are used because the approach relies on a diverse set of extracted features. Deep neural networks are generally more suitable for processing raw network structures or learned tensors rather than abstracted feature sets. Although RPE-P already offers complementary strengths in handling nonlinear relationships and feature interactions, more advanced and expressive models may be incorporated in future implementations for further improvement.

As discussed in Subsection 6.3.1, the feature set in RPE-F is comprehensive but may include redundant or less-informative attributes, thereby reducing efficiency. To address this issue, recursive feature elimination with cross-validation (RFECV) [207] is applied for feature selection. RFECV iteratively removes the least important features based on model performance, retrains the model on the remaining features, and uses cross-validation to validate predictive accuracy and prevent overfitting. This process ensures that only the most relevant features are retained, improving computational efficiency and enhancing the reliability of subsequent predictions.

The RPE-F feature selection process begins with the twenty features and iteratively applies RFECV until an optimal subset of eight is identified. Because randomness may occur during selection, a representative subset generated from multiple runs is adopted for experimental comparisons: {BET, TRA, LGC, NOC, AST, RAD, GAP, NST}. These features were chosen for their strong predictive relevance and reduced redundancy, ensuring improved computational efficiency and model performance.

Table 6.3 presents the prediction errors under maximum node-degree-based attacks, with all values scaled by 10^{-3}. RPE-P is compared with SPP [180] and GIN [101] for two evaluation tasks: (I) predicting robustness enhancement potential, computed as the difference between robustness before and after enhancement, and (II) predicting robustness after enhancement. Prediction error, defined in Equation (5.12), measures the absolute difference between predicted and true robustness values. These criteria follow from the methodology presented in Subsection 5.5.2, which ensure consistency across experiments. True values for both metrics are obtained from attack simulations. The top four methods are highlighted in color: red for first place, blue for second, green for third, and yellow for fourth. Remaining results are shown in black.

Two main observations arise. First, the reduced set of eight features selected via RFECV, namely, {BET, TRA, LGC, NOC, AST, RAD, GAP, NST}, achieves accuracy comparable to or somewhat better than using all twenty features, particularly for task (II) predicting robustness after

Table 6.3: Prediction errors for controllability robustness enhancement potential (Part I) and for controllability robustness after enhancement (Part II) under node-degree-based attacks. "All" uses all twenty features as RPE-F; "Selected Features" uses eight features {BET, TRA, LGC, NOC, AST, RAD, GAP, NST}; "Raw" uses the adjacency matrix as input. Error values are scaled by 10^{-3}. Color coding: red indicates first place, blue indicates second place, green indicates third place, and yellow indicates fourth place.

Predicting Controllability Robustness Enhancement Potential (I)								
$\times 10^{-3}$	All			Selected Features			Raw	
	RF	MLP	KNN	RF	MLP	KNN	SPP	GIN
ER	6.65	8.05	5.72	6.30	8.03	6.12	9.60	9.11
EH	4.38	10.43	4.47	4.36	6.46	4.61	7.97	13.27
SF	7.77	14.21	8.24	7.82	14.13	7.87	10.23	15.60
BA	11.24	14.33	11.35	11.15	13.36	11.74	11.51	16.21
QS	4.24	9.12	4.65	4.38	8.23	4.45	6.97	7.23
RT	7.58	12.59	8.17	7.67	9.83	8.24	12.08	17.47
Avg	6.98	11.46	7.10	6.95	10.01	7.17	9.73	13.15
Predicting Controllability Robustness *after* Enhancement (II)								
$\times 10^{-3}$	All			Selected Features			Raw	
	RF	MLP	KNN	RF	MLP	KNN	SPP	GIN
ER	42.60	49.44	46.55	23.37	51.66	29.35	44.77	47.13
EH	47.03	50.75	49.95	25.06	57.80	34.99	55.69	51.62
SF	72.33	65.31	70.08	54.58	65.29	70.93	58.90	53.40
BA	42.48	46.17	44.20	20.29	51.48	41.50	42.77	37.50
QS	48.95	60.22	57.27	19.67	58.80	27.57	54.93	57.83
RT	52.99	56.88	50.57	23.48	45.49	33.27	46.76	42.82
Avg	51.06	54.80	53.10	27.74	55.09	39.60	50.64	48.38

enhancement. This confirms that feature selection effectively removes redundancy without degrading performance and can even improve accuracy.

Second, RPE-P consistently delivers lower or comparable prediction errors compared to state-of-the-art CNN- and GNN-based approaches, demonstrating its superior accuracy and efficiency for large-scale network analysis. Figure 6.2 illustrates that identifying the robustness of a given network within the performance spectrum is unnecessary, as robustness potential can be predicted directly without inferring topological configuration. Table 6.3 demonstrates the effectiveness of the present framework.

Note that SPP and GIN rely on raw adjacency matrices, which perform well for static evaluations but struggling when predicting robustness after structural modifications. RPE-P leverages curate structural and spectral features, providing an interpretable and computationally efficient representation that enhances the predictive performance.

These findings are consistent with the results obtained under edge-betweenness-based attacks reported in [26], where RPE also excels in predicting connectivity robustness. Overall, Table 6.3 confirms the capability of the present framework to accurately forecast robustness potential and post-enhancement robustness.

6.4.3 *Runtime Comparison*

Table 6.4: Runtime comparison under maximum node-degree-based attacks for two tasks: (I) predicting robustness enhancement potential and (II) predicting robustness *after* enhancement. All values are reported in milliseconds (ms).

	RF	MLP	KNN	SPP	GIN
(I)	62.91	5.88	14.77	67.87	1.69
(II)	57.00	5.95	14.95	66.74	1.74

Table 6.4 compares the runtime of different prediction methods under maximum node-degree-based attacks, with execution time reported in milliseconds (ms). Each value represents the average over 100 independent runs. The results show that SPP incurs the highest computational cost, followed by RF and KNN, whereas GIN achieves the fastest execution among all tested models.

In contrast, robustness enhancement using the surrogate-assisted evolutionary algorithm [79] requires several tens of seconds for networks of similar sizes, and this cost increases rapidly with network scaling. This substantial difference underscores the advantage of machine-learning-based prediction approaches, which do not scale at the same order as the optimization-based methods [101]. Therefore, RPE-P provides a practical solution for large-scale scenarios by significantly reducing computational overhead while maintaining high predictive accuracy.

6.4.4 *Discussions on Robustness Potential Explorer*

6.4.4.1 *Features*

Twenty widely-used features empirically associated with robustness, introduced in Subsection 6.2.1, were initially selected for RPE-F. However, Table 6.1 shows that no single feature reliably captures overall robustness performance, and Table 6.3 indicates that using all twenty features may introduce redundancy.

Figures 6.4 and 6.5 further demonstrate that even the complete set of twenty features is insufficient to consistently distinguish the original and the enhanced networks across all considered topologies.

This contradictory observation highlights two issues: the absence of highly effective features and the redundancy among existing ones. More informative features should be explored, while feature selection remains essential for improving efficiency and predictive accuracy in RPE-P, as confirmed by Table 6.3, where reducing the feature set may not degrade performance and may even enhance performance.

For different attack strategies, such as node-degree-based and edge-betweenness-based attacks, RPE-F may generate different subsets of selected features through the feature selection process, as reported in [26]. Different feature selection algorithms also produce varying subsets of features. This suggests that, in the absence of prior knowledge, incorporating as many empirically relevant features as possible is a safe initial strategy. At the same time, it strongly motivates the development of more effective feature sets, as no single feature can fully capture the changes in robustness performance.

RPE-V and RPE-P serve for distinct purposes, although both rely on features extracted by RPE-F. RPE-V focuses on visualizing higher-dimensional feature vectors in a two-dimensional space, where the separation between the original and the robustness-enhanced instances reflects structural changes induced by optimization. In contrast, RPE-P trains machine learning models to predict robustness enhancement potential based on these features, providing actionable insights for guiding optimization decisions.

The results summarized in Table 6.3 confirm that the selected features effectively capture robustness enhancement potential. Nevertheless, if more discriminative features can be constructed to improve visualization in RPE-V, these features may also enhance predictive performance in RPE-P. However, distinguishability in RPE-V is not a prerequisite for accurate prediction in RPE-P. For example, Table 6.3 shows that prediction accuracy for RT and RH is not significantly better despite their clear visual separation before and after enhancement. While RPE-P primarily targets robustness potential estimation, exploring feature sets that improve both visualization and prediction remains an interesting direction for future research.

6.4.4.2 *Robustness Measure of a Random Instance*

From the performance spectrum shown in Figure 6.2, a natural question arises: what is the distribution of network instances within this performance spectrum, and where would a random instance be located within the spectrum?

The true distribution is unknown, as exploring the upper and lower bounds of performance can be computationally prohibitive for many large-scale networks, let alone estimating distribution or density. The following discussion provides intuitive empirical insights and serves as a small starting point for future exploration of the above question.

A substantial number of synthetic networks are generated using respective models and then tested. For each random network instance, several unbiased rewiring operations are performed, whereas random edges are rewired while preserving node degrees. In the results shown in Table 6.5, $(0.01m)$ is used, where m denotes the total number of edges in the network. If controllability robustness improves after rewiring, the change is recorded as an increase (Inc); otherwise, it is recorded as a decrease (Dec). The ratio of (Inc) to (Dec) serves as an indicator of the relative position of the instance within the robustness performance spectrum.

Thousands of random instances are generated, subject to uniformly random rewiring, with results summarized in Table 6.5. For ER networks, the ratios of (Inc) and (Dec) are close to 0.5, suggesting that random instances are approximately evenly distributed across the robustness performance spectrum. Although the exact distribution shape remains unknown, this observation provides a rough indication that the spectrum for ER may be relatively balanced.

For other network types, including EH, SF, BA, QS, and RT, larger values of (Inc) than (Dec) are observed, indicating that most random instances generated by these models are positioned near low-robustness regions in the performance spectrum. Consequently, random structural disturbances tend to enhance performance, implying a certain potential for improvement.

As indicated by the results shown in Table 6.2, ER ranks third among the six network types in terms of robustness enhancement potential, with random structural disturbances leading to an increase or decrease in robustness with approximately equal probability of (0.5). In contrast, QS exhibits half the enhancement potential of ER, yet random disturbances increase robustness with a probability of 0.83. BA demonstrates the greatest enhancement potential, with random disturbances increasing robustness with a probability of 0.91.

Overall, the findings indicate that the magnitude of robustness enhancement potential is independent of the probability of robustness improvement under random disturbances. A high probability of improvement suggests that the generation mechanisms of synthetic models introduce structural biases that position instances into near low-robustness regions of the performance spectrum. This observation further emphasizes the practical importance of enhancing network robustness. For networks other than ER, no clear evidence is observed regarding whether the corresponding spectra are biased or balanced.

Table 6.5: Rates of robustness increase (*Inc*) and decrease (*Dec*) under random rewiring for different synthetic network models.

	ER	EH	SF	BA	QS	RT
Inc	0.49	0.86	0.74	0.91	0.83	0.86
Dec	0.51	0.14	0.26	0.09	0.17	0.15

Although RPE-P can effectively evaluate robustness enhancement potential without considering the information given in Table 6.5, incorporating this information provides additional insights into the behavior of random instances generated by different synthetic models.

6.4.4.3 *Comparison of Different Pathways*

Figure 6.6 summarizes four pathways for evaluating robustness $\mathcal{R}(\mathcal{G})$, robustness enhancement potential $\mathcal{R}^*(\mathcal{G})$, and optimization performance.

Pathway 1 illustrates deep neural network (DNN)-based approaches for robustness evaluation and robustness potential prediction. These methods process raw network data in a single step, directly predicting $\mathcal{R}$ or $\mathcal{R}^*$ from $\mathcal{G}$ without generating an optimized structure $\mathcal{G}^*$. While computationally efficient, these approaches often lack interpretability and typically require large-scale training data to achieve high accuracy.

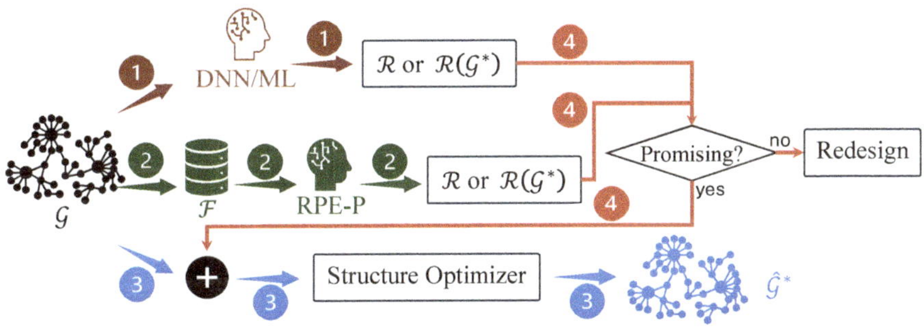

Fig. 6.6: Four pathways for robustness evaluation and optimization: (1) using deep neural networks (DNN) or machine learning for robustness prediction, (2) using feature-based machine learning for robustness potential prediction (RPE-F), (3) robustness enhancement without prior exploration of robustness potential, and (4) general pathway of RPE-P for robustness enhancement potential evaluation.

Pathway 2 adopts a feature-based approach through RPE-F. It first extracts structural and spectral features ($\mathcal{F}$), optionally refines them via feature selection ($\mathcal{F}'$), and then predicts robustness enhancement potential using machine learning models. Although this introduces an additional step compared to Pathway 1, it offers improved interpretability and flexibility, as feature sets can be tailored to different attack strategies or network types.

Pathway 3 shows direct optimization of network structures without prior exploration of robustness enhancement potential. This approach may require substantial computational effort while achieving only marginal improvements in robustness.

Pathway 4 represents a general pathway of RPE-P, where either raw data or abstracted features are used to explore robustness enhancement potential.

A recommended strategy for network structure optimization is to apply Pathway 4 first to assess robustness potential. Only if the potential is promising should the instance proceed to Pathway 3, which involves conventional structure modification, typically using metaheuristics through rewiring and iterative robustness evaluation. Unlike other pathways, this method must generate an optimized instance $\mathcal{G}^*$ before computing $\mathcal{R}^*$, making it computationally intensive. The most demanding operation is robustness evaluation, which may require hundreds to tens of thousands of iterations. Surrogate models can partially alleviate this burden by approximating robustness metrics, but they still depend on a substantial number of real evaluations and may introduce risks of performance degradation during optimization. Since Pathway 3 is computationally expensive, performing Pathway 4 before Pathway 3 is effective and cost-efficient.

6.5 Summary

This chapter introduces the concept of robustness enhancement potential for controllability in complex networks and presents the robustness potential explorer (RPE) as a practical evaluation framework. Unlike conventional optimization approaches that rely on iterative rewiring and extensive robustness simulations, RPE provides a feature-driven, machine-learning-based alternative to estimate whether further optimization is worthwhile, thereby making the process more efficient and effective.

The chapter begins by motivating the need for robustness potential assessment and reviewing twenty structural and spectral features commonly linked to controllability robustness. It then details the RPE framework, which comprises three components: RPE-F for feature extraction and selection, RPE-V for visualizing feature changes before and after enhancement, and RPE-P for predicting robustness enhancement potential using regression models.

Comprehensive experiments verify and demonstrate the effectiveness of RPE. Results indicate that RPE-P achieves higher predictive accuracy with substantially lower computational cost compared to optimization-based methods, while RPE-V enhances interpretability and provides diagnostic insights into feature adequacy. Feature selection using RFECV further improves the efficiency without sacrificing the accuracy. Comparative analyses under maximum node-degree-based attacks confirm the scalability and robustness of this promising approach.

The chapter concludes by discussing limitations of current feature sets, the independence between visualization and prediction tasks, and future research directions, including the development of more discriminative features and advanced learning paradigms, to improve both interpretability and predictive performance.

Chapter 7

Discussions, Feature Directions, and Conclusions

This chapter presents recent advances, existing challenges, and future directions in the study of network controllability robustness, offering a comprehensive discussion of analytical foundations, simulation frameworks, and enhancement strategies, while highlighting unresolved issues and emerging opportunities.

The chapter is organized as follows. Section 7.1 reviews recent developments in network controllability robustness research, including metrics, modeling techniques and enhancement approaches. Section 7.2 analyzes currently existing issues and limitations, focusing on gaps in metrics, scalability, uncertainty handling, and integration of data-driven methods. Section 7.3 outlines promising research directions, emphasizing unified metrics, scalable algorithms, uncertainty-aware frameworks, and emerging technologies.

7.1 Recent Developments in Network Controllability Robustness Research

7.1.1 *Metrics and Attack Strategies*

Based on the recently established theoretical foundation for network controllability and controllability robustness [1–5, 9, 10], progress has been made in defining robustness-oriented metrics that go beyond traditional controllability measures. The unification, normalization and extension of controllability and controllability robustness metrics have provided a basis for systematic evaluation of their properties and performances. These developments enable more precise quantification of the controllability robustness under adversarial attacks and structural perturbations, promoting further development of the recent research on analytical, simulational, computational, and data-driven approaches to controllability robustness analysis, evaluation, and optimization [5, 26]. The existing frameworks incorporate multiple tasks and objectives [101], considering scalability, computational efficiency, and functionality robustness simultaneously.

In parallel, attack strategies have evolved from simple structural-based approaches to sophisticated computational intelligence and data-driven methods. These strategies allow for realistic simulation of adversarial scenarios and provide insights into understanding various network vulnerabilities.

Despite the notable progress in defining robustness-oriented metrics, several critical challenges persist. Current metrics often lack universality across diverse network classes and fail to capture multi-objective trade-offs involving adaptability and resilience under dynamic conditions, as well as integration with functional performance. Many formulations rely on unrealistic assumptions, such as static topologies or homogeneous attack models, which limit their applicability to real-world heterogeneous environments.

Although normalization and unification efforts have improved comparability, inconsistencies remain when integrating controllability and robustness measures under varying structural and operational conditions. Furthermore, attack strategies have advanced toward computational intelligence and data-driven paradigms, but their increasing complexity introduces challenges in reproducibility, interpretability, and transparency. The absence of standardized benchmarks and evaluation protocols for adversarial scenarios further constrains systematic assessment and cross-framework comparison, hindering the progress toward universally accepted robustness evaluation standards.

7.1.2 *Analytical Modeling and Simulation*

Advances in controllability robustness emphasize analytical modeling techniques designed to reduce reliance on explicit attack simulations. These approaches assume complete structural knowledge and require mathematically well-defined attack models, such as random edge-removal [92, 102]. By leveraging the adjacency matrix, controllability configurations and critical edges can be identified, enabling the approximation of controllability curves under random edge-attacks through uniformly random removal of critical edges [92]. This framework accommodates both percolation-based metrics [92] and reachability-based metrics [83].

Analytical models frequently apply the statistical equivalence principle to represent attack dynamics. For example, random edge-removal on random graphs can be modeled by generating synthetic random graphs under specific constraints. Networks are further classified as dense, median or sparse, where hybrid approximation strategies incorporating prior knowledge estimate the controllability performance under attacks. These approximations closely match simulation results for random edge-removal attacks but remain limited to this particular scenario [103].

In parallel, the integration of advanced learning tools in artificial intelligence (AI) has accelerated the development of simulation frameworks [21, 79, 80]. Analytical models for controllability degeneration, including critical edge-based approximations and hybrid modeling approaches, have emerged as key techniques for predicting deterioration under targeted attacks. Coupled with practical stopping criteria and simulation environments, these models bridge theoretical analysis and empirical validation.

Despite the above-mentioned advances, analytical modeling techniques remain constrained by assumptions of complete structural knowledge and predefined attack models. Existing approximations, such as critical edge-based and hybrid strategies, are effective for random edge-removal attacks but exhibit limited generalizability to targeted or adaptive attacks. Statistical equivalence-based models simplify attack dynamics but often oversimplify heterogeneity in real-world scenarios. Simulation frameworks incorporating AI tools have improved the scalability; however, they demand substantial computational resources and lack adaptive mechanisms for evolving network conditions. Bridging theoretical models and empirical validation continues remains a challenge, particularly for large-scale and complex dynamic networks.

7.1.3 *Controllability Robustness Enhancement*

Recent advancements in controllability robustness enhancement converge onto three primary directions. First, design-oriented strategies emphasize structural optimization and edge reinforcement guided by controllability metrics to strengthen resilience against targeted disruptions. Second, simulation-driven approaches integrate hybrid analysis-simulation frameworks with adaptive stopping criteria, enabling efficient evaluation of robustness under large-scale and complex attack scenarios. Third, data-driven methods exploit machine learning and AI to predict vulnerability patterns, optimize reinforcement policies, and implement proactive defense mechanisms using real-time network data. Collectively, these developments establish a foundation for dynamic, scalable and intelligent solutions to enhance controllability robustness in complex dynamical networks.

The concept of robustness potential introduces predictive capabilities into enhancement strategies. Recent progress includes visualization tools and predictive models that estimate achievable improvements through structural modifications, supporting informed design decisions. Experimental validation confirms the effectiveness of these frameworks in guiding robustness-oriented interventions. Furthermore, emerging technologies such as large language models and digital twins are being integrated into simulation and data-driven pipelines, enabling automated hypothesis generation and real-time optimization. These advancements extend analytical and simulation-based approaches toward adaptive and intelligent robustness enhancement.

Despite these promising directions, unresolved challenges remain. Design-oriented approaches often rely on static structural optimization, limiting adaptability to evolving network topologies. Simulation-driven methods, although powerful, are computationally intensive and sensitive to parameter tuning. Data-driven techniques depend on large-scale, high-quality datasets that are usually unavailable in practice. Additionally, the integration of predictive frameworks and emerging technologies requires standardized protocols and interoperability to ensure practical deployment. Addressing these gaps is essential for achieving robust, adaptive and scalable solutions in future research.

7.2 Current Issues in Network Controllability Robustness Research

Despite the limitations in measurement, analysis, and optimization illustrated above, several ubiquitous issues persist in network controllability robustness research.

7.2.1 *Lack of Unified Robustness Metrics*

A fundamental challenge in this study is the absence of standardized and universally accepted metrics for evaluating controllability robustness. Existing measures often emphasize on structural properties or energy cost, yet fail to capture multi-dimensional aspects such as adaptability to dynamic conditions, resilience against uncertainties, and trade-offs between performance and computational overhead. This lack of consensus not only complicates cross-framework comparisons but also hinders the creation of benchmark datasets and reproducible evaluation protocols, limiting the progress toward systematic and scalable solutions.

7.2.2 *Computational Complexity and Scalability*

Algorithms for robustness analysis and optimization frequently suffer from prohibitive computational complexity, particularly when applied to large-scale networks. Techniques based on maximum matching or computations of Gramian controllability matrices become infeasible for large-scale networks, e.g., with millions of nodes. While heuristic and approximation methods have been proposed, they often compromise accuracy and generalizability, creating a persistent gap between theoretical models and practical deployment of real-world systems such as power grids, transportation networks, and communication infrastructures.

7.2.3 *Limited Consideration of Uncertainty*

Most existing studies assume deterministic network structures and dynamics, neglecting uncertainties such as stochastic variation, fluctuating link weights, and evolving topologies. This oversimplification usually results in robustness evaluations that fail to reflect real-world conditions. Incorporating probabilistic models, uncertainty-aware frameworks, and robust optimization techniques remains an open research problem, requiring advanced mathematical tools and scalable algorithms capable of handling higher-dimensional uncertainty spaces.

7.2.4 *Insufficient Integration of Data-driven Approaches*

Although machine learning and graph neural networks have shown considerable potential in predicting controllability robustness and its optimization, their integration with traditional control-theoretic theory is still in its infancy stage. Current data-driven methods often lack interpretability and fail to provide theoretical guarantees, which reduces their reliability for critical infrastructure systems. Moreover, these approaches heavily depend on large, high-quality datasets, which limits their applicability and significantly increases implementation costs. Bridging this gap requires hybrid frameworks that combine the adaptability of learning-based techniques with rigorous analytical validation, ensuring scalability, interpretability, and robustness in practical deployments.

7.2.5 *Challenges in Multi-layer and Temporal Networks*

Modern systems are inherently multi-layered and time-varying, involving interdependent networks with dynamic interactions. Existing robustness frameworks primarily target static, single-layer networks, leaving multi-layer and temporal networks largely underexplored. Developing models that account for cross-layer dependencies, temporal evolution, and adaptive control strategies is essential for realistic robustness analysis and for addressing cascading failures in interconnected systems.

7.2.6 *Limited Use of Emerging Technologies*

Recent advances such as large language models, digital twins, and federated learning offer transformative opportunities for automated feature extraction, simulation-based robustness testing, and distributed optimization. However, their applications in controllability robustness research remains minimal. Leveraging these technologies could significantly accelerate hypothesis generation, scenario analysis, and real-time decision-making, paving the way for building intelligent and adaptive robustness enhancement frameworks.

7.3 Research Directions for Network Controllability Robustness

Considering both advantages and limitations of the network controllability robustness evaluation methodologies discussed above, several promising research directions can be suggested, as outlined below.

7.3.1 *Dynamic and Multi-objective Robustness Metrics*

Recent research emphasizes the need for robustness metrics that go beyond static evaluations. Promising directions include defining metrics that account for dynamic network evolution and adaptive controllability under changing conditions. Multi-objective optimization frameworks are essential to balance among control energy, network resilience and implementation cost. The tasks of robustness evaluation should also be extended to multi-task scenarios, covering diverse failure modes and adversarial strategies. Furthermore, integrating controllability Gramian properties for time-varying networks [208] and network spectral characteristics in robustness indices can provide deeper insights into structural vulnerabilities and control performance.

7.3.2 *Feature-driven and Learning-based Key Node Identification*

Identifying key nodes for controllability remains a critical task in robustness evaluation and analysis, with significant implications for both attack and defense strategies. Recent approaches leverage structural features to locate nodes whose removal disrupts control loops or chains, potentially causing significant local damages without necessarily inducing global failure. Beyond structural heuristics, advanced learning-based techniques have emerged. Graph neural networks enable data-driven ranking by capturing higher-order dependencies that traditional metrics have overlooked. Sensitivity analysis further evaluates driver node redundancy, ensuring robustness against structural perturbations. Hybrid frameworks that combine theoretical measures with machine learning models attract increasing attention, since they can offer both interpretability and adaptability for large-scale and dynamic networks.

7.3.3 *Uncertainty-aware and Learning-based Robustness Features*

Robustness analysis increasingly incorporates probabilistic and adaptive perspectives to address real-world complexity. Stochastic modeling of node and edge failures enables evaluation under random disruptions, while uncertainty-aware frameworks consider variations of edge weights and network dynamics. Bayesian and probabilistic approaches provide predictive capabilities for controllability under uncertain conditions. In parallel, reinforcement learning and other adaptive learning techniques are emerging as powerful tools for designing robust control strategies that evolve with network dynamics. These developments collectively advance robustness evaluation beyond static assumptions toward intelligent and resilient solutions.

7.3.4 *Controllability in Advanced Network Structures*

Modern networks often exhibit complex structures beyond simple graphs, introducing new challenges for controllability analysis. Higher-order interactions captured by hypergraph-based models provide a richer representation of group dynamics, requiring extended controllability measures. Multi-layer and interdependent networks demand robustness evaluation across coupled layers, where failures can propagate through cross-layer dependencies. Temporal networks add further complexity, as evolving structures necessitate adaptive driver nodes allocation and dynamic control strategies. Heterogeneity in node centrality, edge types, and their interaction patterns further complicates modeling and control, making traditional single-layer assumptions inadequate and insufficient. Recent studies also emphasize the role of coupling strength in failure propagation, highlighting the need for integrated models that combine structural, temporal and functional dimensions for realistic robustness assessment.

7.3.5 *Emerging AI Technologies for Controllability Robustness Evaluation*

Advances in AI and distributed computing are reshaping strategies for controllability robustness. Large language models (LLMs) enable automated feature extraction and hypothesis generation, accelerating the search for robustness-oriented solutions. When combined with graph neural networks, LLMs enhance predictive modeling by capturing both structural and semantic patterns in complex networks. However, LLMs also face notable drawbacks, including limited interpretability and extremely high computational costs, which restrict their practical deployment to large-scale complex systems. To address these limitations, emerging paradigms that integrate symbolic reasoning with connectionist models offer promising alternatives, which combine logical consistency with adaptive learning. Digital twin environments provide realistic simulation platforms for robustness evaluation under diverse scenarios, bridging theoretical models with practical validation.

Last but not least, quantum computing and other next-generation technologies are expected to significantly advance network structure analysis and graph learning, enabling breakthroughs in scalability and robustness optimization. Furthermore, synergy between edge AI and federated learning facilitates distributed control and real-time decision-making, which can ensure adaptability in large-scale heterogeneous dynamical systems, helping resolve challenging problems such as the evaluation of network controllability robustness discussed throughout this book.

Bibliography

[1] G. Chen, X. F. Wang and X. Li, *Fundamentals of Complex Networks: Models, Structures and Dynamics*, 2nd edn. John Wiley & Sons (2014).

[2] A.-L. Barabási, *Network Science*. Cambridge University Press (2016).

[3] M. E. Newman, *Networks*, 2nd edn. Oxford University Press (2018).

[4] L. Xiang, F. Chen, W. Ren and G. Chen, Advances in network controllability, *IEEE Circuits and Systems Magazine* **19**, 2, pp. 8–32 (2019).

[5] Y. Lou, L. Wang and G. Chen, Toward robust network controllability: Insights and future directions, *Europhysics Letters* **149**, 4, p. 41003 (2025).

[6] G. Chen, Pinning control and synchronization on complex dynamical networks, *International Journal of Control, Automation and Systems* **12**, 2, pp. 221–230 (2014).

[7] E. D. Sontag, Kalman's controllability rank condition: From linear to nonlinear, in *Mathematical System Theory*. Springer, pp. 453–462 (1991).

[8] C.-T. Chen, *Linear System Theory and Design*, 3rd edn. Oxford University Press (1998).

[9] Z. Z. Yuan, C. Zhao, Z. R. Di, W.-X. Wang and Y.-C. Lai, Exact controllability of complex networks, *Nature Communications* **4**, p. 2447 (2013).

[10] Y.-Y. Liu, J.-J. Slotine and A.-L. Barabási, Controllability of complex networks, *Nature* **473**, 7346, pp. 167–173 (2011).

[11] F. Pasqualetti, S. Zampieri and F. Bullo, Controllability metrics, limitations and algorithms for complex networks, *IEEE Transactions on Control of Network Systems* **1**, 1, pp. 40–52 (2014).

[12] C. W. Wu, Synchronization and convergence of linear dynamics in random directed networks, *IEEE Transactions on Automatic Control* **51**, 7, pp. 1207–1210 (2006).

[13] X. F. Wang, X. Li and J. Lu, Control and flocking of networked systems via pinning, *IEEE Circuits and Systems Magazine* **10**, 3, pp. 83–91 (2010).

[14] G. Chen, Pinning control and controllability of complex dynamical networks, *International Journal of Automation and Computing* **14**, pp. 1–9 (2017).

[15] J. Jiang and Y.-C. Lai, Irrelevance of linear controllability to nonlinear dynamical networks, *Nature Communications* **10**, 1, p. 3961 (2019).

[16] L. C. G. Lebon, F. L. Iudice and C. Altafini, On controllability of temporal networks, *European Journal of Control* **80** (2024).
[17] Y. Zhang, A. Garas and I. Scholtes, Higher-order models capture changes in controllability of temporal networks, *Journal of Physics: Complexity* **2**, 1, p. 015007 (2021).
[18] C. Hou, Energy-efficient control of multiple smart sensors with uncertain controllability, *IEEE Transactions on Automation Science and Engineering* (2024).
[19] J. Gao, Y.-Y. Liu, R. M. D'souza and A.-L. Barabási, Target control of complex networks, *Nature Communications* **5**, 1, pp. 1–8 (2014).
[20] L. Wang, Z. Li, L. Cao, G. Guo and Z. Kong, Controllability of multi-relational networks with heterogeneous dynamical nodes, *IEEE/CAA Journal of Automatica Sinica* **11**, 12, pp. 2476–2486 (2024).
[21] C. Fan, L. Zeng, Y. Sun and Y.-Y. Liu, Finding key players in complex networks through deep reinforcement learning, *Nature Machine Intelligence* **2**, pp. 317–324 (2020).
[22] Y. Lou, Y. He, L. Wang and G. Chen, Predicting network controllability robustness: A convolutional neural network approach, *IEEE Transactions on Cybernetics* **52**, 5, pp. 4052–4063 (2022).
[23] A. Said, O. U. Ahmad, W. Abbas, M. Shabbir and X. Koutsoukos, Network controllability perspectives on graph representation, *IEEE Transactions on Knowledge and Data Engineering* **36**, 8, pp. 4116–4127 (2024).
[24] Y. Zhang, J. Li, J. Ding and X. Li, A graph transformer-driven approach for network robustness learning, *IEEE Transactions on Circuits and Systems I: Regular Papers* **71**, 5, pp. 1992–2005 (2024a).
[25] Y. Zhang, J. Ding and X. Li, Network controllability robustness learning via spatial graph neural networks, *IEEE Transactions on Network Science and Engineering* **11**, 5, pp. 4045–4058 (2024b).
[26] Y. Lou, C. Wu, L. Chen, W. Huang, L. Zhou, L. Wang and G. Chen, Exploring the potential for enhancing structural robustness of complex networks, *IEEE Computational Intelligence Magazine* **20**, 4 (2025).
[27] S. Gu, F. Pasqualetti, M. Cieslak, Q. K. Telesford, A. B. Yu, A. E. Kahn, J. D. Medaglia, J. M. Vettel, M. B. Miller, S. T. Grafton and D. S. Bassett, Controllability of structural brain networks, *Nature Communications* **6**, p. 8414 (2015).
[28] Z. Chen, X. Zhou, Z. Liu, R. Zeng, X. Gong, X. Wu and F. Tang, Impedance network model based modal observability and controllability analysis for renewable integrated power systems, *IEEE Transactions on Power Systems* **35**, 3, pp. 1853–1865 (2020).
[29] M. Rinaldi, Controllability of transportation networks, *Transportation Research Part B: Methodological* **118**, pp. 381–406 (2018).
[30] M. Pósfai, J. Gao, S. P. Cornelius, A.-L. Barabási and R. M. D'Souza, Controllability of multiplex, multi-time-scale networks, *Physical Review E* **94**, 3, p. 032316 (2016).
[31] R. Zhang, X. Wang, M. Cheng and T. Jia, The evolution of network controllability in growing networks, *Physica A: Statistical Mechanics and Its Applications* **520**, pp. 257–266 (2019).

[32] L. Wang, X. F. Wang, G. Chen and W. K. S. Tang, Controllability of networked MIMO systems, *Automatica* **69**, pp. 405–409 (2016).
[33] M. R. Rahmati and G. Flores, On brunovsky numbers and observability and controllability indices in nonlinear mimo systems, *SIAM Journal on Control and Optimization* **63**, 2, pp. 1485–1513 (2025).
[34] Z. Xie, Y. Su, G. Liu, Y. Yang and P. Arebi, Dynamical repair strategy of data network controllability processes against DoS attack on complex temporal networks, *Peer-to-Peer Networking and Applications* **18**, pp. 1–15 (2025).
[35] E. Ortiz-Ospina and M. Roser, Corruption, https://ourworldindata.org/corruption (2024), accessed: 2024-01-03.
[36] B. Gu, D. Li, H. Ding, G. Wang and C. Tellambura, Breaking the interference and fading gridlock in backscatter communications: State-of-the-art, design challenges, and future directions, *IEEE Communications Surveys & Tutorials* (2024), doi:10.1109/COMST.2024.3436082.
[37] E.-C. Chen, P.-Y. Chen, I.-H. Chung and C.-R. Lee, Overload: Latency attacks on object detection for edge devices, in *Proceedings of the IEEE/CVF Conference on Computer Vision and Pattern Recognition*, pp. 24716–24725 (2024).
[38] N. M. Sami and M. Naeini, Machine learning applications in cascading failure analysis in power systems: A review, *Electric Power Systems Research* **210**, p. 108024 (2024).
[39] U.S. Government Accountability Office, Securing the u.s. electricity grid from cyberattacks, https://www.gao.gov/blog/securing-u.s.-electricity-grid-cyberattacks (2022), accessed: 2025-08-26.
[40] K. Ayano, Cybersecurity in critical infrastructure: Protecting power grids and smart grids, (2024), https://www.cyberdefensemagazine.com/cybersecurity-in-critical-infrastructure-protecting-power-grids-and-smart-grids, accessed: 2025-08-26.
[41] T. Krause, R. Ernst, B. Klaer, I. Hacker and M. Henze, Cybersecurity in power grids: Challenges and opportunities, *Sensors* **21**, 18, p. 6225 (2021).
[42] Y. Lou, L. Wang and G. Chen, Structural robustness of complex networks: A survey of *a posteriori* measures, *IEEE Circuits and Systems Magazine* **23**, 1, pp. 12–35 (2023).
[43] R. E. Kalman, Mathematical description of linear dynamical systems, *Journal of the Society for Industrial and Applied Mathematics, Series A: Control* **1**, 2, pp. 152–192 (1963).
[44] C. K. Chui and G. Chen, *Linear Systems and Optimal Control.* Springer-Verlag Berlin Heidelberg (1989).
[45] N. Jacobson, *Lie Algebras.* Courier Corporation (2013).
[46] M. L. J. Hautus, Controllability and observability conditions of linear autonomous systems, in *Indagationes Mathematicae (Proceedings)*, Vol. 72, pp. 443–448 (1969).
[47] C.-T. Lin, Structural controllability, *IEEE Transactions on Automatic Control* **19**, 3, pp. 201–208 (1974).

[48] A. Y. Yazıcıoğlu, W. Abbas and M. Egerstedt, Graph distances and controllability of networks, *IEEE Transactions on Automatic Control* **61**, 12, pp. 4125–4130 (2016).

[49] P. Erdös and A. Rényi, On the strength of connectedness of a random graph, *Acta Mathematica Hungarica* **12**, 1-2, pp. 261–267 (1964).

[50] Y. Lou, L. Wang, K.-F. Tsang and G. Chen, Towards optimal robustness of network controllability: An empirical necessary condition, *IEEE Transactions on Circuits and Systems I: Regular Papers* **67**, 9, pp. 3163–3174 (2020).

[51] A.-L. Barabási and R. Albert, Emergence of scaling in random networks, *Science* **286**, 5439, pp. 509–512 (1999).

[52] C.-L. Pu, W.-J. Pei and A. Michaelson, Robustness analysis of network controllability, *Physica A: Statistical Mechanics and its Applications* **391**, 18, pp. 4420–4425 (2012).

[53] K.-I. Goh, B. Kahng and D. Kim, Universal behavior of load distribution in scale-free networks, *Physical Review Letters* **87**, 27, p. 278701 (2001).

[54] F. Sorrentino, Effects of the network structural properties on its controllability, *Chaos: An Interdisciplinary Journal of Nonlinear Science* **17**, 3, p. 033101 (2007).

[55] D. J. Watts and S. H. Strogatz, Collective dynamics of 'small-world' networks, *Nature* **393**, 6684, pp. 440–442 (1998).

[56] M. E. Newman and D. J. Watts, Renormalization group analysis of the small-world network model, *Physics Letters A* **263**, 4-6, pp. 341–346 (1999).

[57] G. Chen, Y. Lou and L. Wang, A comparative study on controllability robustness of complex networks, *IEEE Transactions on Circuits and Systems II: Express Briefs* **66**, 5, pp. 828–832 (2019).

[58] Y. Lou, L. Wang and G. Chen, Toward stronger robustness of network controllability: A snapback network model, *IEEE Transactions on Circuits and Systems I: Regular Papers* **65**, 9, pp. 2983–2991 (2018).

[59] Y. Lou, L. Wang and G. Chen, Enhancing controllability robustness of q-snapback networks through redirecting edges, *Research* **2019**, 7857534 (2019).

[60] J. Leskovec, L. Backstrom, R. Kumar and A. Tomkins, Microscopic evolution of social networks, in *International Conference on Knowledge Discovery and Data Mining*, pp. 462–470 (2008).

[61] J. Ugander, B. Karrer, L. Backstrom and C. Marlow, The anatomy of the facebook social graph, *arXiv preprint arXiv:1111.4503* (2011).

[62] Y. Lou, D. Yang, L. Wang, C. Tang and G. Chen, Controllability robustness of henneberg-growth complex networks, *IEEE Access* **10**, pp. 5103–5114 (2022).

[63] B. Rozemberczki, O. Kiss and R. Sarkar, Karate club: an api oriented open-source python framework for unsupervised learning on graphs, in *ACM International Conference on Information and Knowledge Management*, pp. 3125–3132 (2020).

[64] K. M. Borgwardt, C. S. Ong, S. Schönauer, S. Vishwanathan, A. J. Smola and H.-P. Kriegel, Protein function prediction via graph kernels, *Bioinformatics* **21**, suppl_1, pp. i47–i56 (2005).

[65] P. D. Dobson and A. J. Doig, Distinguishing enzyme structures from non-enzymes without alignments, *Journal of Molecular Biology* **330**, 4, pp. 771–783 (2003).
[66] P. Yanardag and S. Vishwanathan, Deep graph kernels, in *Proceedings of the ACM SIGKDD International Conference on Knowledge Discovery and Data Mining*, pp. 1365–1374 (2015).
[67] G. Menichetti, L. Dall'Asta and G. Bianconi, Network controllability is determined by the density of low in-degree and out-degree nodes, *Physical Review Letters* **113**, 7, p. 078701 (2014).
[68] X.-Y. Yan, W.-X. Wang, G. Chen and D. Shi, Multiplex congruence network of natural numbers, *Scientific Reports* **6**, p. 23714 (2016).
[69] T. Österlund, S. Bordel and J. Nielsen, Controllability analysis of transcriptional regulatory networks reveals circular control patterns among transcription factors, *Integrative Biology* **7**, 5, pp. 560–568 (2015).
[70] J. Li, L. Dueñas-Osorio, C. Chen, B. Berryhill and A. Yazdani, Characterizing the topological and controllability features of US power transmission networks, *Physica A: Statistical Mechanics and Its Applications* **453**, pp. 84–98 (2016).
[71] C. M. Schneider, A. A. Moreira, J. S. Andrade, S. Havlin and H. J. Herrmann, Mitigation of malicious attacks on networks, *Proceedings of the National Academy of Sciences* **108**, 10, pp. 3838–3841 (2011).
[72] Y. Lou, R. Wu, J. Li, L. Wang and G. Chen, A convolutional neural network approach to predicting network connectedness robustness, *IEEE Transactions on Network Science and Engineering* **8**, 4, pp. 3209–3219 (2021).
[73] M. Cremonini and F. Casamassima, Controllability of social networks and the strategic use of random information, *Computational Social Networks* **4**, pp. 1–22 (2017).
[74] Q. Miao, Z. Rong, Y. Tang and J. Fang, Effects of degree correlation on the controllability of networks, *Physica A: Statistical Mechanics and Its Applications* **387**, 24, pp. 6225–6230 (2008).
[75] H. J. Herrmann, C. M. Schneider, A. A. Moreira, J. S. Andrade Jr and S. Havlin, Onion-like network topology enhances robustness against malicious attacks, *Journal of Statistical Mechanics: Theory and Experiment* **2011**, 01, p. P01027 (2011).
[76] Y.-Y. Liu, J.-J. Slotine and A.-L. Barabási, Control centrality and hierarchical structure in complex networks, *PLoS One* **7**, 9, p. e44459 (2012).
[77] H. Chan and L. Akoglu, Optimizing network robustness by edge rewiring: A general framework, *Data Mining and Knowledge Discovery* **30**, 5, pp. 1395–1425 (2016).
[78] S. Freitas, D. Yang, S. Kumar, H. Tong and D. H. Chau, Graph vulnerability and robustness: A survey, *IEEE Transactions on Knowledge and Data Engineering* **35**, 6, pp. 5915–5934 (2023).
[79] S. Wang, J. Liu and Y. Jin, Surrogate-assisted robust optimization of large-scale networks based on graph embedding, *IEEE Transactions on Evolutionary Computation* **24**, 4, pp. 735–749 (2020).

[80] S. Wang, J. Liu and Y. Jin, A computationally efficient evolutionary algorithm for multiobjective network robustness optimization, *IEEE Transactions on Evolutionary Computation* **25**, 3, pp. 419–432 (2021).

[81] U. Usman, A. Mahmood and L. Wang, Robust control centrality, *2019 Chinese Control Conference* , pp. 5486–5491 (2019).

[82] D. Parekh, D. Ruths and J. Ruths, Reachability-based robustness of network controllability under node and edge attacks, in *International Conference on Signal-Image Technology and Internet-Based Systems*. IEEE, pp. 424–431 (2014).

[83] P. Sun, R. E. Kooij and P. Van Mieghem, Reachability-based robustness of controllability in sparse communication networks, *IEEE Transactions on Network and Service Management* (2021).

[84] B. R. da Cunha, J. C. Gonzalez-Avella and S. Goncalves, Fast fragmentation of networks using module-based attacks, *PLoS One* **10**, 11 (2015).

[85] S. Shai, D. Y. Kenett, Y. N. Kenett, M. Faust, S. Dobson and S. Havlin, Critical tipping point distinguishing two types of transitions in modular network structures, *Physical Review E* **92**, 6, p. 062805 (2015).

[86] X.-L. Ren, N. Gleinig, D. Helbing and N. Antulov-Fantulin, Generalized network dismantling, *Proceedings of the National Academy of Sciences* **116**, 14, pp. 6554–6559 (2019).

[87] M. Engsig, A. Tejedor, Y. Moreno, E. Foufoula-Georgiou and C. Kasmi, Domirank centrality reveals structural fragility of complex networks via node dominance, *Nature Communications* **15**, 1, p. 56 (2024).

[88] T. Nie, Z. Guo, K. Zhao and Z.-M. Lu, New attack strategies for complex networks, *Physica A: Statistical Mechanics and Its Applications* **424**, pp. 248–253 (2015).

[89] Z.-M. Lu and X.-F. Li, Attack vulnerability of network controllability, *PLoS One* **11**, 9 (2016).

[90] H. Wang, J. Huang, X. Xu and Y. Xiao, Damage attack on complex networks, *Physica A: Statistical Mechanics and Its Applications* **408**, pp. 134–148 (2014).

[91] Y. Lou, L. Wang and G. Chen, A framework of hierarchical attacks to network controllability, *Communications in Nonlinear Science and Numerical Simulation* **98**, p. 105780 (2021).

[92] P. Sun, R. E. Kooij, Z. He and P. Van Mieghem, Quantifying the robustness of network controllability, in *International Conference on System Reliability and Safety*. IEEE, pp. 66–76 (2019).

[93] A. Braunstein, L. Dall'Asta, G. Semerjian and L. Zdeborová, Network dismantling, *Proceedings of the National Academy of Sciences* **113**, 44, pp. 12368–12373 (2016).

[94] A. E. Eiben and J. E. Smith, From evolutionary computation to the evolution of things, *Nature* **521**, pp. 476–482 (2015).

[95] D. H. Wolpert and W. G. Macready, No free lunch theorems for optimization, *IEEE Transactions on Evolutionary Computation* **1**, 1, pp. 67–82 (1997).

[96] M. Grassia, M. De Domenico and G. Mangioni, Machine learning dismantling and early-warning signals of disintegration in complex systems, *Nature Communications* **12**, 5190 (2021).
[97] A. Dhiman, P. Sun and R. Kooij, Using machine learning to quantify the robustness of network controllability, in *International Conference on Machine Learning for Networking*. Springer, pp. 19–39 (2021).
[98] Y. Lou, Y. He, L. Wang, K. F. Tsang and G. Chen, Knowledge-based prediction of network controllability robustness, *IEEE Transactions on Neural Networks and Learning Systems* **33**, 10, pp. 5739–5750 (2022).
[99] J. Yan, H. He, X. Zhong and Y. Tang, Q-learning-based vulnerability analysis of smart grid against sequential topology attacks, *IEEE Transactions on Information Forensics and Security* **12**, 1, pp. 200–210 (2016).
[100] O. Lordan and M. Albareda-Sambola, Exact calculation of network robustness, *Reliability Engineering & System Safety* **183**, pp. 276–280 (2019).
[101] C. Wu, Y. Lou, J. Li, L. Wang, S. Xie and G. Chen, A multitask network robustness analysis system based on the graph isomorphism network, *IEEE Transactions on Cybernetics* **54**, 11, pp. 6630–6642 (2024).
[102] Q. Cai, S. Alam, M. Pratama and J. Liu, Robustness evaluation of multipartite complex networks based on percolation theory, *IEEE Transactions on Systems, Man, and Cybernetics: Systems* **51**, 10, pp. 6244–6257 (2021).
[103] Y. Lou, L. Wang, S. Xie and G. Chen, Approximating the controllability robustness of directed random-graph networks against random edge-removal attacks, *International Journal of Control, Automation and Systems* **21**, 2, pp. 376–388 (2023).
[104] E. N. Gilbert, Random graphs, *The Annals of Mathematical Statistics* **30**, 4, pp. 1141–1144 (1959).
[105] P. Erdös and A. Rényi, On the evolution of random graphs, *Mathematical Institute of the Hungarian Academy of Sciences* **5**, pp. 17–61 (1960).
[106] D. Shizuka and D. R. Farine, Measuring the robustness of network community structure using assortativity, *Animal Behaviour* **112**, pp. 237–246 (2016).
[107] J. Wu, M. Barahona, Y.-J. Tan and H.-Z. Deng, Spectral measure of structural robustness in complex networks, *IEEE Transactions on Systems, Man, and Cybernetics-Part A: Systems and Humans* **41**, 6, pp. 1244–1252 (2011).
[108] M. Pósfai, Y.-Y. Liu, J.-J. Slotine and A.-L. Barabási, Effect of correlations on network controllability, *Scientific Reports* **3**, p. 1067 (2013).
[109] E. Wu-Yan, R. F. Betzel, E. Tang, S. Gu, F. Pasqualetti and D. S. Bassett, Benchmarking measures of network controllability on canonical graph models, *Journal of Nonlinear Science* , pp. 1–39 (2018).
[110] Y. Hao, Z. Duan and G. Chen, Further on the controllability of networked MIMO LTI systems, *International Journal of Robust and Nonlinear Control* **28**, 5, pp. 1778–1788 (2018).
[111] P. Holme, B. J. Kim, C. N. Yoon and S. K. Han, Attack vulnerability of complex networks, *Physical Review E* **65**, 5, p. 056109 (2002).

[112] B. Shargel, H. Sayama, I. R. Epstein and Y. Bar-Yam, Optimization of robustness and connectivity in complex networks, *Physical Review Letters* **90**, 6, p. 068701 (2003).
[113] A. Bashan, Y. Berezin, S. Buldyrev and S. Havlin, The extreme vulnerability of interdependent spatially embedded networks, *Nature Physics* **9**, pp. 667–672 (2013).
[114] Y.-D. Xiao, S.-Y. Lao, L.-L. Hou and L. Bai, Optimization of robustness of network controllability against malicious attacks, *Chinese Physics B* **23**, 11, p. 118902 (2014).
[115] S. Wang and J. Liu, A multi-objective evolutionary algorithm for promoting the emergence of cooperation and controllable robustness on directed networks, *IEEE Transactions on Network Science and Engineering* **5**, 2, pp. 92–100 (2018).
[116] L. Bai, Y.-D. Xiao, L.-L. Hou and S.-Y. Lao, Smart rewiring: Improving network robustness faster, *Chinese Physics Letters* **32**, 7, p. 078901 (2015).
[117] K. Yamashita, Y. Yasuda, R. Nakamura and H. Ohsaki, On the predictability of network robustness from spectral measures, in *2019 IEEE 43rd Annual Computer Software and Applications Conference*, Vol. 2. IEEE, pp. 24–29 (2019).
[118] L. Hou, S. Lao, B. Jiang and L. Bai, Enhancing complex network controllability by rewiring links, in *International Conference on Intelligent System Design and Engineering Applications*. IEEE, pp. 709–711 (2013).
[119] J. Xu, J. Wang, H. Zhao and S. Jia, Improving controllability of complex networks by rewiring links regularly, in *Chinese Control and Decision Conference*, pp. 642–645 (2014).
[120] J. Liu, H. A. Abbass and K. C. Tan, Evolving robust networks using evolutionary algorithms, in *Evolutionary Computation and Complex Networks*. Springer, pp. 117–140 (2019).
[121] S. Wang and J. Liu, Designing comprehensively robust networks against intentional attacks and cascading failures, *Information Sciences* **478**, pp. 125–140 (2019).
[122] R. C. Gunasekara, C. K. Mohan and K. Mehrotra, Multi-objective optimization to improve robustness in networks, in *Multi-Objective Optimization*. Springer, pp. 115–139 (2018).
[123] A. Zeng and W. Liu, Enhancing network robustness against malicious attacks, *Physical Review E* **85**, 6, p. 066130 (2012).
[124] Z.-X. Wu and P. Holme, Onion structure and network robustness, *Physical Review E* **84**, 2, p. 026106 (2011).
[125] T. Tanizawa, S. Havlin and H. E. Stanley, Robustness of onionlike correlated networks against targeted attacks, *Physical Review E* **85**, 4, p. 046109 (2012).
[126] Y. Hayashi and N. Uchiyama, Onion-like networks are both robust and resilient, *Scientific Reports* **8** (2018).
[127] L. Ma, J. Liu and B. Duan, Evolution of network robustness under continuous topological changes, *Physica A: Statistical Mechanics and Its Applications* **451**, pp. 623–631 (2016).

[128] D. Yang, M. Liu, Y. Zhang, D. Lin, Z. Fan and G. Chen, Henneberg growth of social networks: Modeling the facebook, *IEEE Transactions on Network Science and Engineering* **7**, 2, pp. 701–712 (2018).
[129] P. Buesser, F. Daolio and M. Tomassini, Optimizing the robustness of scale-free networks with simulated annealing, in *International Conference on Adaptive and Natural Computing Algorithms*. Springer, pp. 167–176 (2011).
[130] T. P. Peixoto and S. Bornholdt, Evolution of robust network topologies: Emergence of central backbones, *Physical Review Letters* **109**, 11, p. 118703 (2012).
[131] R. Fletcher, *Practical Methods of Optimization*. John Wiley & Sons (2013).
[132] X.-B. Cao, C. Hong, W.-B. Du and J. Zhang, Improving the network robustness against cascading failures by adding links, *Chaos, Solitons & Fractals* **57**, pp. 35–40 (2013).
[133] M. Zhou and J. Liu, A memetic algorithm for enhancing the robustness of scale-free networks against malicious attacks, *Physica A: Statistical Mechanics and Its Applications* **410**, pp. 131–143 (2014).
[134] L. Bai, Y.-D. Xiao, L.-L. Hou and S.-Y. Lao, Smart rewiring: Improving network robustness faster, *Chinese Physics Letters* **32**, 7, p. 078901 (2015).
[135] Y. Yang, Z. Li, Y. Chen, X. Zhang and S. Wang, Improving the robustness of complex networks with preserving community structure, *PLoS One* **10**, 2, p. e0116551 (2015).
[136] X. Tang, J. Liu and M. Zhou, Enhancing network robustness against targeted and random attacks using a memetic algorithm, *EPL (Europhysics Letters)* **111**, 3, p. 38005 (2015).
[137] S.-w. Sun, Y.-l. Ma, R.-q. Li, L. Wang and C.-y. Xia, Tabu search enhances network robustness under targeted attacks, *Physica A: Statistical Mechanics and Its Applications* **446**, pp. 82–91 (2016).
[138] X. Tang, J. Liu and X. Hao, Mitigate cascading failures on networks using a memetic algorithm, *Scientific Reports* **6**, 1, pp. 1–12 (2016).
[139] J. Park and S. G. Hahn, Bypass rewiring and robustness of complex networks, *Physical Review E* **94**, 2, p. 022310 (2016).
[140] L.-Z. Wang, Y.-Z. Chen, W.-X. Wang and Y.-C. Lai, Physical controllability of complex networks, *Scientific Reports* **7**, p. 40198 (2017).
[141] S. Wang and J. Liu, A multi-agent genetic algorithm for improving the robustness of communities in complex networks against attacks, in *2017 IEEE Congress on Evolutionary Computation*. IEEE, pp. 17–22 (2017).
[142] L. Ma, M. Gong, Q. Cai and L. Jiao, Enhancing community integrity of networks against multilevel targeted attacks, *Physical Review E* **88**, 2, p. 022810 (2013).
[143] S. Wang, J. Liu and X. Wang, Mitigation of attacks and errors on community structure in complex networks, *Journal of Statistical Mechanics: Theory and Experiment* **2017**, 4, p. 043405 (2017).
[144] L. Rong and J. Liu, A heuristic algorithm for enhancing the robustness of scale-free networks based on edge classification, *Physica A: Statistical Mechanics and Its Applications* **503**, pp. 503–515 (2018).

[145] Y. Liu, X. Wang and J. Kurths, Framework of evolutionary algorithm for investigation of influential nodes in complex networks, *IEEE Transactions on Evolutionary Computation* **23**, 6, pp. 1049–1063 (2019).
[146] T. Qiu, J. Liu, W. Si and D. O. Wu, Robustness optimization scheme with multi-population co-evolution for scale-free wireless sensor networks, *IEEE/ACM Transactions on Networking* **27**, 3, pp. 1028–1042 (2019).
[147] Q. Cai, S. Alam, H. Ang and V. Duong, A braess's paradox inspired method for enhancing the robustness of air traffic networks, in *2020 IEEE Symposium Series on Computational Intelligence*. IEEE, pp. 798–805 (2020).
[148] Y. Lou, S. Xie and G. Chen, Searching better rewiring strategies and objective functions for stronger controllability robustness, *IEEE Transactions on Circuits and Systems II: Express Briefs* **68**, 6, pp. 2112–2116 (2021).
[149] J. Liu, M. Zhou, S. Wang and P. Liu, A comparative study of network robustness measures, *Frontiers of Computer Science* **11**, 4, pp. 568–584 (2017).
[150] B. Mburano, W. Si and W. X. Zheng, A comparative study on the variants of r metric for network robustness, in *International Symposium on Networks, Computers and Communications*. IEEE, pp. 1–6 (2021).
[151] D. Shi, G. Chen, W. W. K. Thong and X. Yan, Searching for optimal network topology with best possible synchronizability, *IEEE Circuits and Systems Magazine* **13**, 1, pp. 66–75 (2013).
[152] J. Leskovec and A. Krevl, SNAP Datasets: Stanford large network dataset collection, http://snap.stanford.edu (2014).
[153] K. Wu, P. Watters and M. Magdon-Ismail, Network classification using adjacency matrix embeddings and deep learning, in *IEEE/ACM International Conference on Advances in Social Networks Analysis and Mining*. IEEE, pp. 299–306 (2016).
[154] K. Hegde, M. Magdon-Ismail, R. Ramanathan and B. Thapa, Network signatures from image representation of adjacency matrices: Deep/transfer learning for subgraph classification, in *International Workshop on Mining and Learning with Graphs*. London, UK, pp. 1–8 (2018).
[155] Y.-S. Kim, M. K. Kim, N. Fu, J. Liu, J. Wang and J. Srebric, Investigating the impact of data normalization methods on predicting electricity consumption in a building using different artificial neural network models, *Sustainable Cities and Society* **118**, p. 105570 (2025).
[156] H. Cai, V. W. Zheng and K. C.-C. Chang, A comprehensive survey of graph embedding: Problems, techniques, and applications, *IEEE Transactions on Knowledge and Data Engineering* **30**, 9, pp. 1616–1637 (2018).
[157] M. Niepert, M. Ahmed and K. Kutzkov, Learning convolutional neural networks for graphs, in *International Conference on Machine Learning*, pp. 2014–2023 (2016).
[158] Y. Lou, R. Wu, J. Li, L. Wang, X. Li and G. Chen, A learning convolutional neural network approach for network robustness prediction, *IEEE Transactions on Cybernetics* **53**, 7, pp. 4531–4544 (2023).
[159] B. Perozzi, R. Al-Rfou and S. Skiena, Deepwalk: Online learning of social representations, in *Proceedings of the 20th ACM SIGKDD Interna-*

tional Conference on Knowledge Discovery and Data Mining, pp. 701–710 (2014).

[160] T. Mikolov, K. Chen, G. Corrado and J. Dean, Efficient estimation of word representations in vector space, in *Proceedings of the International Conference on Learning Representations* (2013a).

[161] T. Mikolov, I. Sutskever, K. Chen, G. S. Corrado and J. Dean, Distributed representations of words and phrases and their compositionality, in *Proceedings of the Neural Information Processing Systems*, Vol. 26 (2013b).

[162] J. Tang, M. Qu, M. Wang, M. Zhang, J. Yan and Q. Mei, Line: Large-scale information network embedding, in *Proceedings of the 24th International Conference on World Wide Web*, pp. 1067–1077 (2015).

[163] A. Grover and J. Leskovec, node2vec: Scalable feature learning for networks, in *Proceedings of the ACM SIGKDD International Conference on Knowledge Discovery and Data Mining*, pp. 855–864 (2016).

[164] D. Wang, P. Cui and W. Zhu, Structural deep network embedding, in *Proceedings of the ACM SIGKDD International Conference on Knowledge Discovery and Data Mining*, pp. 1225–1234 (2016).

[165] L. F. Ribeiro, P. H. Saverese and D. R. Figueiredo, struc2vec: Learning node representations from structural identity, in *Proceedings of the ACM SIGKDD International Conference on Knowledge Discovery and Data Mining*, pp. 385–394 (2017).

[166] C. Cai and Y. Wang, A simple yet effective baseline for non-attributed graph classification, in *Proceedings of the International Conference on Learning Representations* (2019).

[167] S. Abu-El-Haija, B. Perozzi, R. Al-Rfou and A. Alemi, Watch your step: Learning node embeddings via graph attention, in *Advances in Neural Information Processing Systems*, pp. 4575–4584 (2018).

[168] Y. Xie, Y. Ma, Z. Xu, Y. Wang, X. H. Li, Y. Wang and S. Ji, Task-agnostic graph explanations (tage), in *Advances in Neural Information Processing Systems* (2022).

[169] A. Mucherino, P. J. Papajorgji, P. M. Pardalos, A. Mucherino, P. J. Papajorgji and P. M. Pardalos, k-nearest neighbor classification, *Data Mining in Agriculture* , pp. 83–106 (2009).

[170] G. James, D. Witten, T. Hastie, R. Tibshirani *et al.*, *An Introduction to Statistical Learning*, Vol. 112. Springer (2013).

[171] J. R. Quinlan, Induction of decision trees, *Machine Learning* **1**, pp. 81–106 (1986).

[172] D. E. Rumelhart, G. E. Hinton and R. J. Williams, Learning representations by back-propagating errors, *Nature* **323**, pp. 533–536 (1986).

[173] S. Wang, J. Liu and Y. Jin, Robust structural balance in signed networks using a multiobjective evolutionary algorithm, *IEEE Computational Intelligence Magazine* **15**, 2, pp. 24–35 (2020).

[174] W. L. Hamilton, R. Ying and J. Leskovec, Inductive representation learning on large graphs, in *International Conference on Neural Information Processing Systems*, pp. 1025–1035 (2017).

[175] W. L. Hamilton, Graph representation learning, *Synthesis Lectures on Artifical Intelligence and Machine Learning* **14**, 3, pp. 1–159 (2020).
[176] M. Raissi, P. Perdikaris and G. E. Karniadakis, Physics-informed neural networks: A deep learning framework for solving forward and inverse problems involving nonlinear partial differential equations, *Journal of Computational Physics* **378**, pp. 686–707 (2019).
[177] K. He, X. Zhang, S. Ren and J. Sun, Spatial pyramid pooling in deep convolutional networks for visual recognition, *IEEE Transactions on Pattern Analysis and Machine Intelligence* **37**, 9, pp. 1904–1916 (2015).
[178] K. Grauman and T. Darrell, The pyramid match kernel: Discriminative classification with sets of image features, in *IEEE International Conference on Computer Vision*, Vol. 2. IEEE, pp. 1458–1465 (2005).
[179] S. Lazebnik, C. Schmid and J. Ponce, Beyond bags of features: Spatial pyramid matching for recognizing natural scene categories, in *IEEE Conference on Computer Vision and Pattern Recognition*, Vol. 2. IEEE, pp. 2169–2178 (2006).
[180] C. Wu, Y. Lou, L. Wang, J. Li, X. Li and G. Chen, SPP-CNN: An efficient framework for network robustness prediction, *IEEE Transactions on Circuits and Systems I: Regular Papers* **70**, 10, pp. 4067–4079 (2023).
[181] Y. Lou, R. Wu, J. Li, L. Wang, C.-B. Tang and G. Chen, Classification-based prediction of network connectivity robustness, *Neural Networks* **157**, pp. 136–146 (2023).
[182] J. Sun, W. Zheng, Q. Zhang and Z. Xu, Graph neural network encoding for community detection in attribute networks, *IEEE Transactions on Cybernetics* **52**, 8, pp. 7791–7804 (2022).
[183] Z. Wu, S. Pan, F. Chen, G. Long, C. Zhang and S. Y. Philip, A comprehensive survey on graph neural networks, *IEEE Transactions on Neural Networks and Learning Systems* **32**, 1, pp. 4–24 (2021).
[184] J. Li, Y. Ji, Y. Zhang, J. Ding, C. Li and X. Li, Graph neural networks for network science: A mini review, *Europhysics Letters* (2025).
[185] P. Veličković, Everything is connected: Graph neural networks, *Current Opinion in Structural Biology* **79**, p. 102538 (2023).
[186] J. Gilmer, S. S. Schoenholz, P. F. Riley, O. Vinyals and G. E. Dahl, Neural message passing for quantum chemistry, in *International Conference on Machine Learning*. PMLR, pp. 1263–1272 (2017).
[187] T. N. Kipf and M. Welling, Semi-supervised classification with graph convolutional networks, in *International Conference on Learning Representations* (2017).
[188] P. Veličković, G. Cucurull, A. Casanova, A. Romero, P. Lio and Y. Bengio, Graph attention networks, (2018).
[189] M. Zhang, Z. Cui, M. Neumann and Y. Chen, An end-to-end deep learning architecture for graph classification, in *AAAI Conference on Artificial Intelligence*, Vol. 32 (2018).
[190] K. Xu, C. Li, Y. Tian, T. Sonobe, K.-i. Kawarabayashi and S. Jegelka, Representation learning on graphs with jumping knowledge networks, in *International Conference on Machine Learning*. PMLR, pp. 5453–5462 (2018).

[191] K. Xu, W. Hu, J. Leskovec and S. Jegelka, How powerful are graph neural networks? in *International Conference on Machine Learning* (2019).

[192] Y. Zhang, J. Li, J. Ding and X. Li, A graph transformer-driven approach for network robustness learning, *IEEE Transactions on Circuits and Systems I: Regular Papers* **71**, 5, pp. 1992–2005 (2024).

[193] A. Kendall, Y. Gal and R. Cipolla, Multi-task learning using uncertainty to weigh losses for scene geometry and semantics, in *IEEE Conference on Computer Vision and Pattern Recognition*, pp. 7482–7491 (2018).

[194] R. Rossi and N. Ahmed, The network data repository with interactive graph analytics and visualization, in *Proceedings of the AAAI Conference on Artificial Intelligence*, Vol. 29 (2015).

[195] J. Zhang, E. Modiano and D. Hay, Enhancing network robustness via shielding, *IEEE/ACM Transactions on Networking* **25**, 4, pp. 2209–2222 (2017).

[196] S. Wang, W. Lv, J. Zhang, S. Luan, C. Chen and X. Gu, Method of power network critical nodes identification and robustness enhancement based on a cooperative framework, *Reliability Engineering & System Safety* **207**, p. 107313 (2021).

[197] L. Ma, X. Zhang, J. Li, Q. Lin, M. Gong, C. A. C. Coello and A. K. Nandi, Enhancing robustness and resilience of multiplex networks against node-community cascading failures, *IEEE Transactions on Systems, Man, and Cybernetics: Systems* **52**, 6, pp. 3808–3821 (2021).

[198] M. Chujyo and F. Toriumi, Link-limited bypass rewiring for enhancing the robustness of complex networks, *Applied Network Science* **9**, 1, pp. 1–17 (2024).

[199] A. Beygelzimer, G. Grinstein, R. Linsker and I. Rish, Improving network robustness by edge modification, *Physica A: Statistical Mechanics and Its Applications* **357**, 3-4, pp. 593–612 (2005).

[200] M. Tomassini, Rewiring or adding links: A real-world case study of network vulnerability, *Physica A: Statistical Mechanics and its Applications* **630**, p. 129241 (2023).

[201] L. Katz, A new status index derived from sociometric analysis, *Psychometrika* **18**, pp. 39–43 (1953).

[202] S. Brin and L. Page, The anatomy of a large-scale hypertextual web search engine, *Computer Networks and ISDN Systems* **30**, 1-7, pp. 107–117 (1998).

[203] L. v. d. Maaten and G. Hinton, Visualizing data using t-SNE, *Journal of Machine Learning Research* **9**, 11, pp. 2579–2605 (2008).

[204] T. Kohonen, The self-organizing map, *Proceedings of the IEEE* **78**, 9, pp. 1464–1480 (1990).

[205] L. McInnes, J. Healy and J. Melville, UMAP: Uniform manifold approximation and projection for dimension reduction, *arXiv preprint arXiv:1802.03426* (2018).

[206] A.-L. Barabási, Scale-free networks: A decade and beyond, *Science* **325**, 5939, pp. 412–413 (2009).

[207] P. Misra and A. S. Yadav, Improving the classification accuracy using recursive feature elimination with cross-validation, *International Journal on Emerging Technologies* **11**, 3, pp. 659–665 (2020).
[208] S. Zhao and F. Pasqualetti, Networks with diagonal controllability gramian: Analysis, graphical conditions, and design algorithms, *Automatica* **102**, pp. 10–18 (2019).

Appendix A

Lists of Symbols, Notation, Acronyms, Abbreviations

List of Symbols and Notation

- $A_{i,j}$: Entry of adjacency matrix
- $\bar{\xi}$: Mean prediction error
- $\mathbf{A}$: System matrix
- $\mathbf{A}^{(k)}$: High-order adjacency matrix
- $\mathbf{B}$: Input/Incidence matrix
- $\mathbf{C}$: Controllability matrix
- $\mathbf{D}$: Degree matrix
- $\mathbf{H}$: Modularity matrix
- $\mathbf{L}$: Laplacian matrix
- $\mathbf{L}^*$: Laplacian matrix with one row and column removed
- $\mathbf{W}^{(\ell)}$: Weight matrix at layer ℓ
- γ: Power-law exponent
- $\lambda_{\max}$: Largest eigenvalue
- $\langle k \rangle$: Average degree
- $\langle m \rangle$: Average number of edges
- $\langle n \rangle$: Average number of nodes
- n_D: Number of driver nodes
- $\mathbb{R}$: Real number field
- $\mathcal{E}^*$: Maximum matching set
- $|\mathcal{E}^*|$: Number of edges in maximum matching
- $\mathcal{F}$: Feature/Importance metric
- $\mathcal{G}^*$: Optimal network instance
- $\hat{\mathcal{G}}^*$: Approximate optimal network
- $\mathcal{L}$: Loss function
- σ: Proportion of nodes/edges been attacked

- $\sigma(\cdot)$: Activation function
- $\xi(i)$: Error at step i
- d_{st}: Shortest-path distance between nodes s, t
- $h_v^{(\ell)}$: Node representation at layer ℓ
- $h_{\mathcal{N}_v}^{(\ell+1)}$: Aggregated neighborhood representation
- $H_{\mathcal{G}}$: Graph-level representation
- k_i: Degree of node i
- k_i^{in}: In-degree of node i
- k_i^{out}: Out-degree of node i
- L: Total number of layers
- m: Number of edges
- m_c: Number of critical edges
- n: Number of nodes
- c_D: Ratio and minimum number of driver nodes
- n_D: Minimum number of driver nodes
- $n_{\mathcal{N}}$: Number of nearest neighbors
- p_c: Connection or rewiring probability
- q: Snapback probability
- q_{QS}: Snapback probability in QS model
- r_{QS}: Layer index in QS model

List of Acronyms and Abbreviations

- ACO: Algebraic Connectivity
- APL: Average Path Length
- AST: Assortativity
- BDC: Betweenness-Clustering-Degree Embedding
- CNN: Convolutional Neural Network
- DeepWalk: Random Walk-Based Embedding Method
- DIA: Network Diameter
- DT: Decision Tree
- EFF: Efficiency
- EFR: Effective Resistance
- GAP: Spectral Gap
- GAT: Graph Attention Network
- GCN: Graph Convolutional Network
- GIN: Graph Isomorphism Network
- GNN: Graph Neural Network
- KNN: K-Nearest Neighbors

- LDP: Local Degree Profile
- LFR: Learning Feature Representation
- LINE: Large-Scale Information Network Embedding
- LR: Linear Regression
- LGC: Largest Circle
- MLP: Multi-Layer Perceptron
- MOD: Modularity
- mCNN-RP: Multi-Expert CNN Robustness Predictor
- NCO: Natural Connectivity
- NOC: Number of Circles
- NST: Number of Spanning Trees
- PATCHY-SAN: CNN-Based Graph Representation Method
- PCA: Principal Component Analysis
- PGR: PageRank
- RAD: Spectral Radius
- RF: Random Forest
- RPE: Robustness Potential Explorer
- RPE-F: Feature Extraction Module in RPE
- RPE-P: Prediction Module in RPE
- RPE-V: Visualization Module in RPE
- SDNE: Structural Deep Network Embedding
- SOM: Self-Organizing Map
- SPP: Spatial Pyramid Pooling
- struc2vec: Structural Role-Based Embedding Method
- t-SNE: t-Distributed Stochastic Neighbor Embedding
- TRA: Transitivity
- UMAP: Uniform Manifold Approximation and Projection

Appendix B

Lists of Figures and Tables

List of Figures

List of Tables

Index

www.ingramcontent.com/pod-product-compliance
Ingram Content Group UK Ltd.
Pitfield, Milton Keynes, MK11 3LW, UK
UKHW061933100926
8556IPUK00007B/900

9 789819 833580